AB58

Reading for Life

Reading for Life

Beauty, Pluralism, and Responsibility

Margaret R. Miles

CONTINUUM · NEW YORK

1997

The Continuum Publishing Company
370 Lexington Avenue, New York, NY 10017

Printed in the United States of America

Library of Congress Cataloging-in-Publication Data
Miles, Margaret Ruth.
    Reading for life : beauty, pluralism, and responsibility /
Margaret R. Miles.
        p. cm.
    Includes bibliographical references and index.
    ISBN 0-8264-1009-X (alk. paper)
    1. Books and reading. 2. Literature – History and criticism.
I. Title.
PN511.M42   1997
028′.8 – dc21   96-40925

For Susan
daughter and friend

Contents

———— • ————

PREFACE

———— • ————

All we need is some light to read by.
— MARY CATHERINE RICHARDS,
Centering in Pottery, Poetry, and the Person

A T THE END of a long day of labor, my mother read far into
the night. Tethered to home, children, and the obligations of a
Protestant minister's wife by choice as well as by others' demands,
she used reading as a window onto experiences she would never
have, onto a big world of excitement and happening she would
never inhabit. She liked biography best; in biographies she entered, in
imagination, adventurous, daring lives. Lives outside the home. She
read desperately, and reading made her happy. That happiness was,
to her, well worth the precious hours of sleep she lost.

I read, as a child, for information, for excitement, and to learn
about the adult world. I recall two books with special clarity — one
that I was urged to read and one that was placed on a top shelf in
hopes I would not read it. *The Pilgrim's Progress* was placed on my
bedside table, and I read it occasionally when nothing more interesting was available, but I found its characters, flattened to a single
trait — Madame Bubble, Mr. Worldly Wiseman, Evangelist, and Mr.
Talkative — disconcerting. I quickly caught on that Christian's trip
to the Celestial City was, in fact, a journey toward death, so I did
not find the goal attractive.

What John Bunyan's chaste description of Vanity Fair withheld
from me, however, *Foxe's Book of Martyrs* amply provided. I do not
remember how I discovered the book on the top shelf of my father's
study, but once I did, it held an endless fascination for me. It became
the pornography of my childhood. I risked life and limb to sneak
it down from the shelf and pore over illustrations of burning martyrs, women and men thrust through with swords or hanging limply
while crowds jeered. My first anatomy lessons came from *Foxe's
Book of Martyrs*; I saw a baby leaping from the stomach walls of

a woman burned at the stake, a man with a huge codpiece whipping a man with bared buttocks, and other titillating horrors. Not until much later did I grasp the relationship of those violent stories and illustrations to the book's English Protestant anti-Catholicism.

Later, as a young adult, I read for other reasons. I read to construct a lively, beautiful, and generous world not always offered by my immediate surroundings. I read to find my life, to "add to the stock of available reality."[1] Eventually, psychotherapy was also available to me, and I was able to make good use of it because I had already understood, from reading, its potential and its limitations.

My daughter read as a small child, to escape adult conversations and to make her own world. She would sit reading in the midst of adult company until an interesting word or phrase caught her ear. Then she would emerge briefly to absorb the conversation, retreating to her book the minute it became dull again. Now a mother and businesswoman, she still reads every day. Her daughter, my granddaughter, reads, begging each night for just a few more minutes before the light is turned off. Each of us reads happily *and* desperately, for information, for nourishment, and for the images that help us imagine our lives.

None of us would describe our reading in words that emphasize commitment or moral seriousness. Reading is simply something we need to do. By reading we escape the constrictions of the ordinary, sometimes by reading books everyone labels "escape" reading, sometimes by reading books that provide tools by which we can reimagine the ordinary, seeing its miraculous beauty. In *The Notebooks of Malte Laurids Brigge,* the poet Rainer Maria Rilke wrote concerning the fairy tales he and his mother sometimes read together: "We had a different idea of the marvelous; we thought if everything happened naturally that would always be the most marvelous."[2] How to describe the playful seriousness, or serious playfulness, of the kind of reading that prompts us to look up from the book and to see the room we sit in and the world outside the window as utterly, magically, beautiful?

Reading for life is desperate, but it is also pleasurable. Pleasure is the medium that carries the morally serious meanings of books. For reading books is a serious activity; books shape the life of their reader for better or worse — frivolous, sentimental, or gratuitously violent books as well as books that exemplify courage and gracefulness. They may do this by their content or by what they take for granted or what they ignore. The reader shares, of course, in this shaping. Her eye, mind, and psyche select according to her readiness to hear. Pleasure is not only compatible with seriousness; it is by pleasure that we notice, retain, and recall a book's offerings.

Authors, however, are human, and the word "human" itself carries a curious ambiguity. Sometimes we use it to refer to a condition we must aspire to and work at throughout life, slowly becoming "fully human." Sometimes we mean by it the lowest common denominator, a flawed, voraciously lustful, even vicious condition to which even the most intentionally virtuous might sink, as in "human, all too human." I use the word here to refer to both its honorific and its pejorative meanings. Books have "human" authors who, from their particular perspective, can offer profoundly generous ways of seeing and being in the world, but who, simultaneously, can be expected to exhibit no less fundamental limitations of vision. The one who reads for life must develop an eye that discerns both.

This book illustrates the potentially life-orienting seriousness of reading. In it, I retrace my own journey through books that have changed and energized me, identifying both the riveting ideas they offered and their seductions, their gifts, and their failures of generosity. Together, these chapters describe and illustrate a committed practice of desperate and highly pleasurable reading, reading for life.

Acknowledgments

I owe an obvious debt to Martha Nussbaum's *Love's Knowledge* and, to a lesser extent, to her *Poetic Justice*. Her thoughtful and inspiring discussions about relationships between literature and life suggested to me the feasibility of this project, and one of Nussbaum's chapter titles in *Love's Knowledge* provided the title of this book.

An earlier version of chapter 4 appeared as " '*Jesus patibilis*': Augustine's Debate with the Manichaeans," in *Faithful Imagining: Essays in Honor of Richard R. Niebuhr,* edited by Sang Lee and Wayne Proudfoot (Atlanta: Scholars Press, 1995).

I am also indebted to a Henry Luce III Fellowship that gave me the time to begin writing this book; to Justus George Lawler of Continuum, a gentle editor; and to Susan Worst for suggestions about chapter 1.

Part I

Chapter 1

HOW SHOULD WE LIVE?

———— • ————

When I think of it, the picture always rises in my mind, of a summer evening, the boys at play in the churchyard, and I sitting on my bed, reading as if for life.
— Charles Dickens, *David Copperfield*

PLATO'S *Symposium* describes a training in the perception of beauty that energizes and leads a person to the richest possible human life, a life characterized by accurate orientation within the universe, wisdom both profound and flexible, and participation in divine beauty. Plato remarks that a life whose most salient attribute is the ability to perceive beauty is as close as mortals can come to immortality (*Symp.* 210–12). It is not, however, a life focused on seeking and enjoying beautiful objects of art or nature. The person is initially alerted to beauty by recognizing one beautiful object; she feels excitement and longing, but this is just the beginning. Plato describes an incremental process by which a person develops skill in perceiving beauty in thoughts, institutions, laws, and fields of learning. Arriving through practice at an ability to recognize beauty itself, the student has nevertheless not reached the ultimate goal until she "brings forth" or augments beauty by "true virtue," or generous responsibility. Ultimately, a developed perception of beauty has moral effects. With Plato, I believe that perceptions of beauty fund a generosity of spirit that is essential to moral responsibility.

The capacity for perceiving beauty is not an inborn gift; it can, Plato insisted, be exercised and developed. Even though the experience of beauty often seems to occur gratuitously, one can, on later reflection, usually detect both a process of preparation and a learned quality of attention that contributed to the experience. For example, many years ago, while engaged in a long and painful psychotherapy,

I suddenly, with strong emotion, beheld my psyche as a mass of congested and twisted vines, apparently hopelessly embrangled, but precisely because they sought light with such energy and intransigence. Similarly, we sometimes see a face that is not conventionally beautiful with a comparable strong feeling because we notice that the whole life of the person is perfectly revealed in her face. Or we may suddenly see an ordinary and familiar room as beautiful, ordered to the lives it cradles. Books too may strike us as beautiful when they describe with precision a world we recognize and long for but have not known how to define.

Such experiences of beauty do not rely on beautiful sensible objects. Nor, though filled with feeling, do they emerge from sentimentality. Sentimentality is triggered by the appearance of objects or events to which we are socialized to respond emotionally. A sentimental feeling has little intellectual content or particularity and is quickly forgotten. But unsentimental experiences of beauty have profound effects. They produce, in the first place, a relaxation of our habitual anxious interests. Augustine described one such experience: "I relaxed a little from myself."[1] It is only when I "relax a little" from my habitual anxious interests that I notice the interconnection of my own life with those of other living beings. Curiously, attentiveness is achieved not by teeth-gritting effort but by the kind of relaxation produced by perceiving beauty.

As the early chapters of this book will suggest, generosity of spirit has often been in short supply, even — perhaps especially — among people with a mission. But interest in the common good that begins with concern with the economically, politically, and socially disenfranchised seems to be increasingly rare in late twentieth-century American public discourse. "Safety nets" against indigence and its multiple sufferings grow ever more slack as welfare support, food programs, and medical provisions for the poor, for children and the elderly, and for those with physical and mental disabilities are cut. The ancient question Who is my neighbor? becomes more and more pressing. How far should a society's generosity extend? For whom must I as an individual, and we as a society, feel responsibility? A society that answers these questions only in terms of certain class, race, and gender loyalties lacks generosity.

The religiously, ethnically, and racially pluralistic society in which late twentieth-century Americans live gives urgency to issues of responsibility. If perceptions of beauty really do produce spontaneous

generosity, which, in turn, augments responsibility, it is crucial to
know how these effects might be generated and stimulated.

Can we, as a society, recognize the diverse beauty of the differing
ethnic and cultural resources within American society? Can we reach
across the particular manifestations of beauty we recognize in order
to perceive the beauty of cultures other than our own? Can we do
so despite the fact that every culture naturalizes by attention and
repetition the particular beauty it identifies, and ignores others?

There is, however, more commonality than may immediately meet
the eye in experiences of beauty. While agreement on the beauty
of particular objects is culturally specific, perceptions of beauty are
not. Moreover, the ability to perceive beauty is contagious; one person can catch it from another. Our diverse experiences of beauty
could become a basis for mutual understanding, for a central aspect
of knowing other groups or individuals is the ability to see beauty
through their eyes.

The primary project of this book is to give a coherent account
of how the perception of beauty and moral responsibility can be
reconciled in the context of an individual life, a life whose most
salient characteristic is sociality or interconnection with other human
beings and with the natural world. I will also address indirectly
contemporary issues surrounding beauty and social responsibility, especially in the fields of art history and theology. On one side are
modernist contentions that beauty transcends both the social and political conditions of its origin and any consideration of its political,
institutional, and social loyalties. On the other side are the urgent
postmodern voices of people who have been marginalized within
Western societies. These voices describe the ways by which beauty
has often masked injustice and oppression. Beauty is not innocent.

There is, I believe, an effective method for practicing integration
of perceptions of beauty and critical scrutiny of beauty's social effects. It is the practice of reading for life. My model is that of the
desperate reader, the one who reads to discover and grasp the vision
necessary for changing his life. And we are all, at a profound level,
and whether we recognize it or not, desperate readers. Whatever our
circumstances, we each have a short, pressured, and dazzling life in
which to learn how to fully inhabit and enjoy that life. I will shortly
describe my own process of coming to understand the importance of
the demanding reading that plunders books for the provisions they
offer as well as to detect their seductions.

The ability to perceive beauty is not enough for a rich human life if it is perceived as an end in itself rather than as a moment in the circulation of the universe's generosity. Some of the strongest proponents of beauty advocate an aesthetic enjoyment that may personally enrich its subject but does not lead either to increased self-knowledge or to engagement with others' sufferings. For example, one who sees suffering and poverty but thinks of it as part of a larger picture of perfection and beauty dismisses any need to alter oppressive conditions. Among the authors I discuss, Plotinus and Rilke voiced this attitude to suffering. In late twentieth-century media, news photography often shows beauty in squalor, in the ravaged faces and bodies of refugees, and in inner-city bleakness and despair, implicitly encouraging the viewer to conclude that because those scenes contain beauty, there is no immediate urgency to alleviate this suffering. But this is to make an egregious and self-serving error of judgment.

Those who urge that beauty is an end in itself sometimes appeal to the statement Dostoyevsky places in the mouth of his protagonist in *The Idiot,* "Beauty will save the world." Others, however, claim that it is not beauty but political action that will go the furthest toward saving the world. Does beauty transcend political concerns? Or, as many critical thinkers claim, is beauty all too likely to encourage people to ignore injustice, even if they suffer from it?

Clearly, it is tempting to understand the experience of beauty as a goal or reward in itself, a temporary respite from a real world of trouble and sorrow. There is no doubt that beauty can rationalize injustice or distract from moral responsibility rather than inform and energize it. Several of the authors I discuss allowed beauty to blind them to the oppressive effects of the beauty they created. Beauty alone is not enough.

However, critical thinkers may also overlook beauty's capacity to prompt and energize change in individuals and in society. Their acute awareness of the inevitable political entailments of human-made beauty — whether art, literature, institutions, or liturgies — makes them rightly suspicious of the seductive power of beauty. So critical theologians, postmodern philosophers, and cultural critics who have detected beauty's capacity to blind people to injustice often focus exclusively on exposing the gender, social-location, race, and institutional loyalties embedded in traditional social arrangements. Righteously angry at oppressive political, social, and sexual relationships, they rip away the beauty that masked them to reveal the concealed injustice.

But just as experiences of beauty cannot be ends in themselves, moral responsibility is similarly not enough to create and sustain a richly sensitive and generous human life. Moral responsibility, if it is not to consist merely of teeth-gritting determination, requires the incentive of beauty and the enjoyment it affords, accompanied by feelings of gratitude that lead to a flexible, relational, and respectful practice of responsibility. Perceptions of beauty and responsibility are both central to a life that is simultaneously enjoyable and generous. Yet it is not easy to integrate them; each seems to require a different quality and focus of attention.

The problem of integrating beauty and social responsibility also emerges vividly in the halls and classrooms of the academic institutions where I spend my time. Most of the people — students and teachers — who engage in graduate education do so because at a particular time in our lives we were utterly moved and enchanted by a book. Our attraction to the book has led us to examine it closely and thus to learn the considerable pleasure of analyzing how the text achieves its remarkable effects. To paraphrase Plato's description in the *Symposium,* our attraction to one beautiful book leads us to recognize the existence of other beautiful books. Then comes the capacity to detect other kinds of beauty — actions, ways of life, and even qualities like generosity, justice, and love. By this time, we are deeply invested in the beauties we recognize. Their compelling and formative power in our lives encourages us to continue, or to return to, formal education in order to explore them more thoroughly and to learn how to communicate our fascination to others.

Once back in the classroom, we learn critical methods of reading. We learn, from colleagues with different perspectives and loyalties than our own, that the same book can communicate vastly different things to different people. If we listen respectfully to our colleagues' interpretations, we often come to recognize that the book we had thought so unambiguously delightful and profound in fact incorporates strong allegiances and blinders. It may assume a certain class experience as normative. It may, from the perspective of a Native American, an African-American, a Hispanic, or an Asian-American, exude the unexamined privileged whiteness of American public society. We learn to conceal our disappointment in our dawning awareness that, in fact, we loved the book not in spite of but *because* it so ably reflected and reinforced our own perspective. Thus, the passion that brought us to graduate education often vanishes as we hear our colleagues describe a text's unmarked seductions while ignoring its transformative potential.

At this point, we may respond in one of two ways: we may resist or refuse to entertain the critical questions that reveal a book's social and institutional loyalties, or we may convert wholeheartedly to deconstructive critical reading, scorning our own former naive reading. Either of these responses, however, fails to incorporate some pivotal insights. The first response fails most fundamentally in generosity. It refuses to see the text as a cultural product that actively participates in the cultural assumptions, privileges, and myopia of its author's social location. It declines, in short, to see the loved book through another person's eyes. To do so, it must marginalize or trivialize the other's perspective, gained, like one's own, through multiple and varied experiences. The first response focuses on discerning the author's intentions as they can be discovered either within his writing or in the historical circumstances that frame his work.

The second response, the enthusiastic embrace of deconstructive approaches to books, also fails in generosity, but differently. It ignores the power and beauty of the book in order to exhibit its questionable assumptions and limitations. The pleasure of a narrowly deconstructive reading lies in exposing the book's political horrors. In contrast to a reading that attends only to the author's intentions, a deconstructive reading attends primarily, if not solely, to the work's effects within its society of origin as well as its subsequent use. Lecturers often deconstruct a book's political loyalties in such a way that the audience is left wondering why the speaker even bothered to discuss a work so blatantly flawed. Yet the importance of the critical reading relates directly to the work's power of seduction.

In short, any adequate interpretation requires an integration of both critical reading and passionate reading. Critical readings are as essential to reading for life as are passionate readings. And acknowledging and exploring the power of our naive readings is not only legitimate but also central to classroom discussion. *The Odyssey* offers a vivid metaphor for the expectation and demand that a text must be useful for life. In fact, it suggests that this expectation underlies the only kind of reading that adequately respects the work's original inspiration. In book 11, Odysseus visits the Underworld, hoping to get some crucial advice from the dead poet and seer, Tieresias. As Odysseus enters the gates, Tieresias approaches along with other shades, and Odysseus puts his dilemma to him. But the shades cannot communicate with him until he brings them a bowl of blood to drink. They can only speak when they are vivified by an infusion of that life-substance.[2] Similarly, only when the pressing life-interest of a living reader is brought to a text can it speak in its most vivid and powerful language.

When one begins to recognize the importance of readings that balance the energy and passion of a naive reading with a critical reading, a question arises: Is it possible to read a text *both* appreciatively and critically? This is a question that cannot be answered abstractly; it requires the demonstrations provided in this book. Some of my readings, I believe, are more successful than others. The success or failure of particular readings, however, is not as important as the project itself. If my readings begin to inspire readers to develop and refine their own readings of books they love, I am content.

The urgency of understanding both the beauty and the seductions of a text takes us out of classrooms, in which methods of reading and interpretation are discussed, and into life. I have claimed that the ability to perceive beauty is foundational to a rich enjoyment of life and to developing a generosity that permits us imaginatively and sympathetically to enter other people's perspectives as they are revealed to us. Yet reading is one of the activities in which alertness to beauty can be practiced and trained. The generosity we exercise and develop in reading can extend to our relationships, our political commitments, and our sense of our ecological and global responsibility.[3] Reading books "for life" trains the habits of attentive listening and critical evaluation we need in all dimensions of life, whether we are speaking with friends, reading newspapers, or deciding which actions are appropriate in particular situations.

To sum up the argument of the last several pages: reading for life entails two different but related interests. It is motivated by a committed search for the knowledge of self and world that one needs in order to live a life characterized by enjoyment and generosity, a life richly informed by the willingness imaginatively to enter perspectives other than those of one's own race, gender, age, ethnicity, and class. And it requires the reader to ask those critical questions that identify and challenge a text's commitment to particular readers, institutions, politics, or social arrangements.

Although increments of enjoyment and generosity can enrich and expand the lives of those who occupy the mainstream of American society, my primary concern is not for their increased horizons. It is rather to make a potentially shocking suggestion, namely, that women and minority people can fruitfully study and appropriate flawed cultural resources not in order to understand and forgive the privileged other but in order to appropriate critically the entitlement, support, and encouragement to be found in books. This suggestion comes from my experience with the books I discuss. For example, a text written explicitly to empower a "young [male] poet" nevertheless supplied me with energizing and motivating ideas at a crucial time in my life, ideas to which I had access nowhere else. My lack of critical tools at the time I encountered Rilke's *Duino Elegies,* however, ensured that I was also affected by the elegies' social assumptions in ways I will describe. My experience illustrates vividly the need for a reading for life that incorporates attention both to the text's transformational potential and to its seductions.

It would be naive to claim that a reading practice that seeks both the beauty and the dangers of a literary work can redistribute agency, values, and the power of self-definition in American society. For this, a complex redeployment of economic, educational, and institutional resources is necessary. Nevertheless, it can, I believe, provide a model for a more generous and lively redistribution of power, privilege, and social and cultural resources.

Too long ago to remember where or when, I read that everything one must know to lead a rich human life could be learned by an attentive reading of the right eight or ten books. Ever since then, I have kept an informal list of what I thought those books might be. In this book, I explore my current list.

The texts I discuss agree with one another about certain things, but each also provides a perspective or information not to be found in the others. Collectively, they represent an exciting debate over how to conceptualize a world and a universe in which human thought and actions *matter.* They construct a world that, as Rilke wrote, "seems to require us and strangely concerns us. Us the most fleeting of all."[4] All of these texts have frequently attracted, and sometimes beguiled, me across forty years of adult engagement with books.

Reading them "for life" has given me questions and complaints as well as nourishment and energy.

Each of my texts omits some crucial feature of life-knowledge. One confines its focus to its characters' past and present lives, neglecting to sketch a picture of time and space, the cosmos and history within which human lives perdure. Another does not show how its vision of an intimately connected universe might affect a particular life, a historical moment in time, a community or a society. I have found that in order to imagine a world in which human beings can feel part of a meaningful whole, I need the suggestions and the warnings offered by Plotinus and Augustine, Toni Morrison and Leni Riefenstahl, Rilke and Jung. Each provides something of irreducible importance; each also illustrates the need for critical reading. These authors also demonstrate interest in the relationship between perceptions of beauty and moral responsibility in various Western literary genres: philosophy, theology, autobiography, the novel, and poetry.

I suspect that most people, like myself, construct a livable world from reading and watching. Our social and institutional environments and our families and friends, even though profoundly formative, do not reveal the full range of human possibility. Moreover, American media culture seldom reaches beyond a relatively narrow range of interests. We also learn from our educational and institutional experiences, of course, but even our most direct experience is informed by the expectations we have developed from reading and watching. The picture of a rich human life I will cumulatively paint here, then, is a proposal — an interesting and responsible one, I hope, but one that I invite the reader to argue with, to adjust and adapt, or even to reject in favor of a more comprehensive, more generous, more energizing picture.

My training is that of a historian of late antiquity. Some of my academic interests appear in this book — especially in my discussions of Plotinus and Augustine. These chapters are likely to interest readers who share my interest in reconstructing the way things were in other times and places, while readers who prefer twentieth-century authors will no doubt be more interested in the chapters of part 2. Both kinds of readers should be forewarned that my primary agenda is not that of a historian who seeks to understand the past for its own sake. Rather, I believe that the technical skills and tools a historian develops can be placed in the service of a more adequate understanding of both past and present human lives. Hazardous as is the endeavor to learn from the past something of use for the present, immersion in historical perspectives vastly different from one's own is one of a very few ways to reveal the social and individual blind spots of the present. In these pages, then, I will be somewhat less interested in understanding the role of each of my texts in the complex cultural discourse of its time than in the present insight it can offer. I will try to say what the text teaches me, and I hope these lessons will also be useful to others.

My interpretations of texts and my ideas about humanness have, of course, been formed by my social location and personal history. I am a middle-aged, middle-class white woman. I have had a range of experiences common (and uncommon) to my age, class, geographical location, and gender. These experiences include an early marriage and children, a later education for which I had to struggle, divorce, the 1960s and 1970s in California, and the 1980s and half of the 1990s at Harvard University as a professor. In 1996 I returned to California to become dean of the Graduate Theological Union of Berkeley. Remembering my childhood as the daughter of immigrant, religiously fundamentalist parents, I often think: "You can't get here from there." I have experienced a sometimes bewildering blend of privilege and oppression: I have struggled, and I have been given opportunities I neither dreamed of nor sought.

Several of the works I will discuss began their usefulness within my life by providing aphorisms. "Staying is nowhere," I told myself firmly, setting out for college at the age of twenty-seven.[5] "A capacity is a need," I quoted, to explain why I went to college rather than seeking gainful employment as the impoverished divorced mother of two children.[6] For a long time I lived on words. Like a fourth-century desert ascetic demanding of a spiritual master, "Speak to me some word, some phrase," I garnered aphorisms from everything I read, putting them on bits of paper and sticking them to the refrigerator or on a corkboard above my desk, carrying them in memory and in notebooks. I shaped my life around these words, holding on to them "for dear life." I ignored the experiences and the friends who said I couldn't do what the poems and quotations incited me to do. The words sustained and motivated me.

I must travel an unknown road and fight a strange battle.[7]

The dream was marvelous but the terror was great. We must treasure the dream whatever the terror.[8]

We only learn through death. Nothing else really impresses our memory. So we must die many times, until we know all we have to know to be of any use. And we must also learn to die in joy.[9]

In the great terror lies the great hope.[10]

It is impossible to overstate the force of these and other words in my life. As Plotinus wrote when describing encounters with beauty, I was "delighted and overwhelmed and excited," filled with "wonder and a shock of delight and longing and passion and a happy excitement."[11]

Aphorisms, uncritically but passionately appropriated for their power and energy, got me to the nearest junior college, then to the nearest university, then to the nearest graduate school, where I eventually learned more sophisticated ways of using words. But I have endeavored to acquire the skills of analysis without losing the passionate energy of reading for life. I still expect texts to offer me something, to challenge or criticize, to provide something that I, standing resolutely within my life, will be able to use.

My primary preoccupation here, I have said, is not literary-critical concerns such as the author's intended communication, the formal properties of a text, its place in a history of style, and the social discourse within which it originally made meaning. Nevertheless, I do not dismiss these interests. Indeed, the richer and more precise the interpretive tools, the more a text can be seen "in the life," that is, as a voice within a much more complex conversation than the text can reproduce, and in relation to the lives of its author and original readers. Academic readers tend to err on the side of extended demonstration of their interpretive tools, while those who read desperately often ignore these tools. Is it possible to attend to both reading projects — the careful reconstruction of text in context and the search for the present usefulness of the text?

It is, if not impossible, certainly difficult, as this book will, no doubt, demonstrate. I have brought to each of the texts my life(blood) as a medium through which they might speak. I have also, through concentrated study, learned what is involved in a thoroughly responsible understanding of an author. I have studied as fully as possible two of the authors I will discuss, Plotinus and Augustine, learning the languages they spoke and wrote, as well as about the societies and institutions within which they lived. I have tried, with expert help, to distinguish their intellectual debts from their innovative ideas. Having covered that ground, I am very respectful of the patient work of historical reconstruction, but I cannot deny the life-altering energy to be gained by seeking the text's communication to me, in my life. Another example may make this more vivid: in a dinner-table argument, a conversation partner of Martin Luther once urged a point by quoting a scripture verse. "Yes," Luther responded, "I know that is the Word of God, but is it the Word of God *for me?*"

Together, the texts I explore suggest that, in addition to a capacity for enjoyment and generosity, the way we see the world intimately affects our continuous process of adjustment, understanding, and response. My habitual responses will be affected by whether I see the world as grounded in a mechanistic operation observable to science, in a spiritual dynamic accessible to psychological or mental powers, or in a religious dynamic governed by a supernatural origin and goal. Moreover, our worldviews are saturated with values. Do I think people are fundamentally good, turning to meanness only when they are deprived and frustrated? Or do I hold some version of the "original sin" thesis, by which all people have evil urges that must be governed and restrained? We communicate our basic dispositions daily in myriad reactions, whether or not we formulate them explicitly. I learned my parents' belief when, as a child, I had a headache or was crabby, and my mother said, "This is your real self coming out." When my friend was in a similar mood, her mother remarked, "You're not yourself today, Dear."

Is a personal God's love the center and defining attribute of the universe, as Christians claim? Or, as Camus's stranger realized, is the world "benignly indifferent" to individuals' pain? Or, as Plotinus believed, does a providential generosity support and protect the *whole* whirling universe, rather than care in detail for each of its participants? Our attitudes, decisions, and actions emerge from our conceptual schemes. Whether articulated or implicit, however, a settled belief in the provident (though not necessarily personal) generosity of life and the universe is needed if one is both to enjoy one's life and to think and act generously.

Generations of thinkers from Plato forward have assumed or argued that a fruitful understanding of one's particular life must rely on a conceptual orientation to the cosmos and history. This recognition stands as a watershed between ancient and modern thinkers. For example, the first part of Augustine's *Confessions* often seems to twentieth-century readers very contemporary in his painstaking reconstruction of a personal history, but the last four books puzzle and bewilder us. Is he still writing his "confessions" when he sketches his understanding of creation, time, and memory? Yes, because the world he conceives himself as formed by and responsive to is an indispensable aspect of his idea of him*self*.

But the need for an articulated worldview is not self-evident any more. Many Americans reject the religious language of former descriptions, preferring not to articulate a broad conceptual scheme of the universe and history. Nevertheless, unexamined quasi-religious beliefs remain, implicit in our lifestyles, decisions, and actions. However, some twentieth-century people avoid an articulated worldview for another reason. We have learned that our pictures of the world are constructed and perspectival. We therefore think it more honest and realistic to live without imaginary pictures. Why not handle on an ad hoc basis whatever crosses one's path? Isn't a conceptual scheme — any conceptual scheme — more confining than helpful? Isn't it better to relinquish any merely plausible picture of one's location in the cosmos and in history, limiting oneself to a realistic set of social and personal expectations?

I reply to these questions with another question: Is it really possible to do without any conception of one's placement in the universe? It is certainly possible not to articulate one's conception, the assumptions on which it is based, and the expectations that follow from it. But I have not found it possible, much less helpful, to jettison all traces of a picture of my place in a universe of immense space and time. If indeed it is limiting, if not impossible, to forgo such orientation, the alternative is to articulate one's picture of the world so that it can be examined and compared with others' proposals. Constructive proposals are needed that stimulate us to imagine more generously and inclusively and to begin to devise practical methods for achieving a consistent orientation to the universe we imagine. And conceptual beauty is necessary if a proposed worldview is to have "strong power," in Michel Foucault's definition, the power of attraction.[12] Perhaps refusal to criticize our own deeply held beliefs lies at the root of many Americans' rejection of articulated worldviews.

Foucault once said that "everything is dangerous." Worldviews are among the most dangerous of cultural products; war, persecution, and oppression are their products as readily as are sympathy, generosity, and concern for the common good. In the absence of critical worldviews, unexamined systems of belief that may do untold damage can emerge. I believe there is something between tenaciously held but critically unexamined worldviews and refusal to acknowledge and articulate the beliefs by which one actually lives. Worldviews can be proposed, relentlessly and unflinchingly examined, endlessly revised, or overturned if their inadequacies are sufficiently significant.

The relationship of enjoyment of beauty to responsible morality has not always been evident to historical authors within the Western Christian tradition. Rather, Christian authors have addressed the religious role of beautiful objects, objects ranging from the visible beauty of "this-worldly" objects to God, the ultimately attracting beauty.[13] However, the tradition is not monolithic on this issue. Devotional manuals consistently cautioned their readers about visible beauty's potential to distract and seduce, while theologians described visible beauty as a reflection of the Creator. Augustine, Pseudo-Dionysius, Anselm, and Thomas Aquinas agreed that the strong beauties of God's creation reflected God's beauty and gave anyone with eyesight sufficient evidence of the existence and activity of a Creator. In short, Christian authors have exhibited an intractable ambivalence about beauty, seeing it either as seductive surface noise or as profoundly orienting; as misleading appearance or as trace or symbol of divine beauty.

Moreover, these two attitudes toward beauty have acquired gender affiliations. Both in art and in literature, virtue has been symbolized by virile (male) beauty. Surface beauty, or appearance, has been associated with women and labeled as "false" beauty. A long tradition in visual art associated the male nude with spiritual athleticism, while female nakedness signaled sex, sin, and death.[14] Moreover, men have been thought to produce spiritual and intellectual beauty, while women preside over physical beauty. Male and female beauty are consistently pictured as competing for attention and affection.

Like historical authors, but for different reasons, contemporary critics of diverse perspectives distrust beauty. Indeed, in American media culture, repetitiously reiterated identifications of beauty specify the people, social arrangements, and institutions considered beautiful in ways that consistently exclude minority people and their cultures. Yet beauty is not the problem; it is rather the media's narrow and repetitive identification of beauty that needs to be revised.

I will not pursue the question of what makes beautiful objects beautiful in this book. Rather, through readings of the texts I have chosen, I will endeavor to describe the components of the *perception* of beauty, an experience that simultaneously alerts and eases a person, opening her to a rich world beyond the practical concerns that ordinarily usurp attention. An example may help to illustrate the difference between thinking of beauty as a feature of objects of a certain sort and focusing on *perception of beauty* as an activity and skill. Recently, I understood the meaning of the old proverb that bluebirds bring happiness. Seeing a bluebird one day, I experienced an intense burst of sharp happiness. On later reflection, I realized that sighting a bluebird does not bring happiness in some magical way but that the experience of seeing a bluebird *is* itself happiness. The absolute blueness of the bird's graceful body roused and filled my eye and psyche, evoking without enumerating all former occasions of happiness.

Perception of beauty is not primarily a judgment about a beautiful object; it is an experience. The experience may later submit to analysis, but while we are experiencing it, it bathes and captivates consciousness, releasing anxieties and tensions and suspending even our most native fears. Such experiences fund a generosity formerly unknown to us.[15]

Although it is notoriously difficult to define beauty as a property of objects, it is possible to sketch some experiential characteristics of *perceptions* of beauty. The texts I discuss in the chapters of this book will further articulate and flesh out what I sketch here.

1. Order: organization and arrangement, rather than chaos, are sensed. Yet living order intimates not perfection and repose but that chaotic energies and unpredictable and uncontrollable events are barely contained and ordered.

2. Comprehensiveness: a feeling of expanded consciousness in which human life exists in its broadest setting, time and space, history and cosmos.[16]

3. Complexity: intricate and intimate relationships between parts and whole are intuited. Contradiction — irreducible, unresolvable contradiction — can also be part of complexity. Contradiction produces *movement,* oscillations of thought in which two very important but logically contradictory things must be said simultaneously

and in full strength. The "spin" generated by contradiction maintains energy, resisting the resolution for which every trained thinker longs. Contradiction as a component of the perception of beauty also signals that something profound, difficult, and fragile is at hand. At the end of his exploration of the nature of beauty in the *Greater Hippias,* Plato concludes with lively frustration, "The beautiful things are difficult."

4. Detail: a poignant recognition of the simultaneous dailiness and astonishing richness of human life in its many circumstances.

5. Vividness: a heightened sense of the colors, tones, and tastes of the world of human experience.

6. Value: a highly concentrated perception of the simultaneous fragility and consummate preciousness of the world, other living beings, and human life.[17]

7. Pleasure: The pleasure entailed in perception of beauty is not, as Aristotle said, that of "pleasures" added to one's life as one might put on a necklace but the deep intrinsic pleasure of seeing life itself as beautiful, in part and in whole.

Other components of the experience or perception of beauty might certainly be proposed, but these seem to me central and irreducible.

In short, this book begins with a topic, a method, and a thesis. Its topic is the relationship of beauty and responsibility in a pluralistic society. Its method is to gather from selected texts a *practical* understanding of the function of perceptions of beauty in a rich, unpredictable, and pressured human life. To the perennial question How should we live? I propose a deceptively simple answer: with enjoyment and generosity.

Chapter 2

"BEAUTY IS REALITY"
Plotinus's *Enneads*

———— • ————

If you expect the material world to be an icon of divine beauty you may be more easily satisfied with it as it is than if you expect it to be a place in which virtuous [people] prosper.

— A. H. ARMSTRONG, "Neoplatonic Valuations
of Nature, Body, and Intellect"

THE EXERCISE OF *thinking with* a mind in which there are no superfluities, no elisions or evasions, every idea examined and its relation to other ideas explored, is both humbling and exhilarating. It is also difficult, not least because it inevitably disorients one from comfortably familiar habits of thought. After reading a great philosopher for a long time, you can stand at a window looking out and see the world as that philosopher saw it.

Plotinus did precisely this exercise with Plato's philosophy.[1] He studied Plato intensively and passionately until he was able to see the world as Plato saw it. Then he tried to explain both what he saw and what helped him to see it. He did not attempt to explain away the points of tension and contradiction in Plato. He even increased the strain and the urgency of these points. Nor did he endeavor to clarify or render more precise Plato's vaguenesses. He defended obscurity on the grounds that what was important was not the idea itself but the struggle to understand (*Enn.* 4.8.1). Plotinus understood himself not as a constructive philosopher or a "Neoplatonist" but as a faithful interpreter of Plato.

What *is* a "faithful interpreter" of another author? It is not someone who reports what that author said. It is not even someone who demonstrates the integrity, complexity, and cohesion of that author's thought. To be the most faithful interpreter in this narrow sense would be simply to read aloud the author's words. Rather, a faithful interpreter is one who relates the earlier author's thought to the present in a way that makes that thought alive, vivid, and directly relevant. Thus, Plotinus tried to supply for his friends and students what he himself had needed in order to see the world as Plato saw it. Inevitably, necessarily, he altered Plato's philosophy in making it his own.

When I first read Plotinus, I was so overwhelmed with the gentle beauty of his universe that all I could do was to copy quotations:

No real being ever ceases to be. (*Enn.* 4.3.5)

The universe lies in safety. (*Enn.* 3.3.4)

All opposites are entwined together. (*Enn.* 3.3.6)

There will be a time when vision will be continuous. (*Enn.* 6.9.10)

What does "really exists" mean? That they exist as beauties. (*Enn.* 1.6.5)

Gradually I began to sort Plotinus's ideas, to sift foundational ideas from those he merely considered and from the views of others, which he sometimes pondered at length. I began to understand, and to delight in, Plotinus's interconnected universe and to explore the psychological and moral effects of thinking within his universe. What difference does it make, in a daily relationship with the world, if one believes, as Plotinus did, not that the world is made up of a hodge-podge collection of living beings but that all are intimately related by the same informing soul? What practical effects might it have to believe, as Plotinus did, that the source and energy of everything one sees is spiritual? These are not questions I have answered but questions I live with, exploring them every day.

The social and economic world of late twentieth-century America does not encourage or support investigation of these questions. Far from it: the media society in which I live urges me to ignore the complex fabric of life on which I am dependent. It incites me to use more than my share of the limited resources of the planet and to turn deaf ears to the cries of misery from the people and animals who suffer so that I may live carelessly. In Plotinus's universe I notice sharp joys and pains I had not noticed formerly, my own and those of other living beings. Curiously, though Plotinus lived in a social world profoundly different from my own, his conceptual universe provides me with a perspective from which I notice, enjoy, and take responsibility for the life that circulates through and animates living bodies.

Reading Plotinus for life, I encountered a problem. It was a problem not so much of Plotinus's thought or expression as of the adequacy of my own reading skills. Educated readers are trained to think that to understand a philosopher is to be able to detect, and to describe, the self-consistency of his ideas. But often, as in Plotinus's writings, the most interesting and revealing features of a philosophy are the points of tension or even contradiction within it. Those puzzling moments occur either when language fails or when the complexity of the world reflected in the philosophy makes necessary virtually opposite statements. Can anything that can be said, be said with clarity and precision? Plotinus didn't think so. In trying to describe the vision he considers essential to human well-being, Plotinus pleads that words must necessarily be used sloppily and that his reader should append "in a manner of speaking" to everything he says (*Enn.* 6.8.13). Moreover, imprecise language requires that the student strain to understand, bringing all his resources of experience and intelligence to making the understanding his own. At many points, language is strained and inadequate; opposites must be said and awkwardly and stubbornly *held* without modification or resolution. Eventually, one must be able to stand again at the window looking out and see that these points of awkwardness, of clumsy tension, must occur in the philosophy because they are in the world, and philosophy reflects the world. I will explore one of these areas of tension shortly.

In the first century of the Common Era, Platonic thought became popular, and, because it addressed itself to teaching people how to live, it became essentially religious. It was highly eclectic in response to the urgent perennial questions of human life: How should we live? Why are we unhappy *really*? What happens when we die? Plotinus's immediate predecessors, the so-called middle Platonists, were a group of thinkers from whom not a single philosophical work survives, only a few popular works. According to reports and fragments of their writings, middle Platonists like Numenius (the most influential thinker of the second century) gave dualistic answers to these questions, emphasizing the separateness of God and matter, mind

and body, spirit and flesh, teaching their followers to identify themselves with the mind/spirit side of the polarity. In order to avoid the
dogmatic dualism of his immediate predecessors, Plotinus reintro-
duced Plato's *ambivalence* about the relative value of body and soul,
matter and intellect, rather than choosing between Plato's conflicting
descriptions of the value of bodies.

Having read Plotinus with attention and affection for over twenty
years, I will try to explain the world I see when I look through the
window at the world (I think) Plotinus saw. I'll begin with his writing
style because *what* one manages to say always depends on *how* one
says it, especially when style is part of an examined commitment, as
it was with Plotinus.

Although the dialogue form of the Platonic writings has disap-
peared from Plotinus's prose, his treatises follow the spirit of Plato in
that they are explorations, investigations, discussions, and responses
to the actual questions he encouraged his students and friends to
ask. Porphyry, Plotinus's friend, disciple, and the author of Plotinus's
biography, tells of one occasion when a visitor to the school was ir-
ritated by Plotinus's patient and thorough responses to a student's
questions. A rare picture of a fourth-century philosophical school
and its lively discussion emerges from Porphyry's description. He
acknowledged that Plotinus's teaching style "lacked order," at least
partly because he encouraged these interruptions. There was, Porphyry admits, "a lot of pointless chatter" (Porphyry, *Life* 11). Yet
during these interruptions, as well as during conversations, Plotinus
was able to maintain his own train of thought, resuming his teaching or thinking at precisely the point at which it was broken off by a
question; he was able, Porphyry reported, "to be present at once to
himself and to others":

> Even if he was talking to someone, engaged in continuous
> conversation, he kept to his train of thought. He could take
> his necessary part in the conversation to the full, and at the
> same time keep his mind fixed without a break on what he
> was considering. When the person he had been talking to was
> gone,... he went straight on with what came next, keeping the
> connection, just as if there had been no interval of conversation
> between. In this way he was present at once to himself and to
> others, and he never relaxed his self-turned attention except in
> sleep. (*Life* 8)

Plotinus's treatises, then, like his teaching style, are not the equivalent of an Aristotelian essay. They do not argue a thesis from a starting point to a conclusion defined in advance. Rather, in his writing as in the classroom, he considered, as they occurred, questions and issues; or he examined proposals by his immediate interlocutors or by one or another of his philosophical or religious predecessors. Porphyry reports that Plotinus had problems with his eyes that prevented him from rereading and revising his writings; thus, they follow his disciplined train of thought.

Plotinus's Universe

Plotinus's universe is complex. I explore it here in some detail because I believe that it offers a vision that can be fruitfully, if critically, appropriated as a framework in which to imagine human life. His proposal for a universe in which human beings can achieve maximal enjoyment and generosity begins with a picture in which each entity has a place where it may stand in its own light. His interest lies in protecting each living being from being either flooded by undifferentiated chaos or marginalized by stronger realities. Plotinus's conceptual scheme has frequently been diagrammed as a ladder: matter lies at the bottom, supporting the ladder; body lies on the first rung; higher "up" are soul and intellect and finally the One, the source of the whole. This image, so deplored by twentieth-century people suspicious of hierarchies of all sorts, represents Plotinus's thought accurately only if one focuses on the uprights or sides of the ladder, rather than on the rungs.

Although he was not averse to saying that some entities are higher and some are lower, it was the interconnection of the whole that interested Plotinus. Each entity, informed to the full extent of its capacity by the being, goodness, and reality that emanates from the One, participates in a common life-force. The commonality, rather than the differentness of the various entities, is the basis for Plotinus's theory of the continuous circulation of being through all living beings. Each catches, absorbs, and is formed by reflecting the being above it. It's all done with mirrors. The One emanates its undifferentiated rays to Intellect effortlessly, spontaneously, and without diminishment. In Intellect, thoughts as well as the forms of everything that exists originate. Far from a realm of abstraction, Intellect localizes or "reduces" — as a cook reduces a sauce to its most potent flavors — the powerful but undefined energy of the One, making it into the world we see and experience. Plotinus describes intellect twice as "boiling with life" (*Enn.* 6.5.2; 6.7.12).

The One births Intellect spontaneously, effortlessly, without losing anything of itself. And Intellect contains thoughts, differentiations, movement and rest, qualities and quantities. Intellect, in turn, beams its myriad forms to the common Soul of all living creatures. At the level of Soul, a further differentiation occurs; Soul is responsible for transmogrifying the forms it receives from Intellect into bodies.[2] Bodies are created and supported in life by the continuous emanations circulating through the universe: "The One does not give, and pass, but gives on forever" (*Enn.* 6.9.9). Matter defines the limit of the One's emanations and supports the myriad forms of life. The life of living beings does not perish, even at death, but spins off to animate other forms. Like light, life depends on its source, not on the body illuminated or animated by it: "When the body perishes — for nothing can exist without a share of soul — . . . how could the life still remain? Well, then, has this life perished? No, certainly not, for this too is the image of a radiance; it is simply no longer *there*" (*Enn.* 4.5.7; see also 1.91).[3]

In Plato's and Plotinus's universe, the order of discovery is opposite to the order of value. To discover reality, one starts with the body — with one beautiful body, as Plato said in the *Symposium*. The psychic adrenaline that results from *seeing*, from the perception of beauty, is the jolt that springs a person from her chair, breathlessly following an ever-intensifying saturation of beauty, reality, and value. Plotinus suggests that an alternative route is possible, that one can, if she chooses, start at the level of Intellect. It is not, however, possible to start "at the top," for nothing can be said about the One. The One is beyond being; it has no thoughts or activities; it plans nothing; it has no movement or rest (*Enn.* 6.9.3). It does not love, since it has no activity of any kind. But there is a sense in which the One *is* love: it gives and sustains life and intelligence and beauty in everything that whirls out from it.

All the forms of life contained by intellect must also exist in the world perceived by the senses (*Enn.* 4.8.1). Plotinus insists on this in some detail: "Does the world there have everything that is here? Yes, everything that is made by forming principle and according to form." The condition of existence "here" is presence "there." He enumerates:

> Certainly the sky there must be a living being, and so a sky not bare of stars.... But obviously there is earth there too, not barren, but much more full of life, and all animals are in it ... and, obviously, plants, ... and sea is there, and all water in abiding flow and life, and all the living beings in water ... and air, and aerial living things. (*Enn.* 6.7.11)

Plotinus's vision of the universal life permeating everything is expansively inclusive; even rocks partake of the universal life: "The growth, then, and shaping of stones and the inner patterning of mountains as they grow one must certainly suppose to take place because an ensouled forming principle is working within them and giving them form" (*Enn.* 6.7.11).[4] Plotinus's universe is the arena of life, in which "these things here below are carried along with those things in heaven, and those in heaven with these on earth, and both together contribute to the consistency and everlastingness of the universe" (*Enn.* 3.3.6).

Because the universe would not be complete without the sensible world, intellect beams its thoughts and forms into Soul, and Soul uses its acquired energies to create and animate living beings. However, in addition to the creation of bodies, a further differentiation occurs within Soul: part "remains above," contemplating intellect, while part maintains the integrity of physical life. The person is a composite of soul and body, but intellect contains the form of each individual as well as the higher Soul common to all.

The individual soul, then, has the alternative of either leaning, by its directed attention and affection, toward Intellect, the source of its existence, or running over into body, identifying itself with body and grasping at — seeking to possess — the bodies and objects that cross its path. Plotinus's universe, like that of Origen (a Christian), is a mobile, volatile universe in which human beings, if not always in motion, are poised at any moment to move in one direction or another. It is simultaneously an intimate and a cosmic dynamism, at once happening in a person's most secret interiority and in cosmic space. If one seeks to identify the strongest locations of reality, the position of body on the lowest rung is ambiguous. Body is simultaneously starting point or first step — and lowest in value. But Plotinus has much more to say about body.

What was his assessment of the "lower" entities? Here is a frequently noticed point of tension in his philosophy. Porphyry says that Plotinus was "ashamed of being in a body" (*Life* 1). But Porphyry's interpretation of Plotinus may reveal more about Porphyry than about Plotinus. As is inevitable, the facts he gives are selected, and his interpretations are open to question, even when he claims to be quoting Plotinus. Was Plotinus really "ashamed of being in a body"? This statement by Porphyry has been quoted by generations of historians of ideas who believe that "dualistic" aspects within Christianity can be traced to the influence of Neoplatonism. Yet Plotinus himself said that "the parts of our bodies with their powers are...traces of the parts and powers of the universe" (*Enn.* 4.4.36). And: "[T]he whole body is sense organ of the soul" (*Enn.* 4.3.23); and: "[I]t is beautiful to abide here" (*Enn.* 3.8.11). Moreover, bodies are not excluded from Plotinus's vision of beauty: "[T]he beauty of beautiful bodies is by participation in the Great Beauty" (*Enn.* 3.1.15). Nor is body responsible for evil, which must ultimately be referred to the composite human being (*Enn.* 3.3.5).

Apart from his occasional statements about the beauty and worth of body, moreover, Plotinus has a more systematic argument for the value of body and the visible world. In a late Roman intellectual world replete with polemics, his only polemical treatise is *Ennead* 2.9, titled by Porphyry "Against the Gnostics," written during the middle period of his authorship, a time when, Porphyry claims, his writings were of the "highest perfection" (*Life* 6).[5] Like many other polemical treatises in late antiquity, the treatise was written to be read not primarily by the Gnostics Plotinus seeks to refute but by "our own intimate pupils." His argument gives a strong sense of his regard for the lower entities. Plotinus criticizes Gnostics for believing that the world of bodies and material substances was created by an evil Creator. Although he acknowledges that some of the Gnostics' ideas may have come from certain Platonic suggestions, he accuses them of ignoring and misunderstanding Plato on some crucial points (*Enn.* 2.9.6). The logical conclusion of the Gnostics' negative evaluation of the visible world, he writes, is to desire to be put to death so that the life of the mind can be enjoyed without the distraction and encumbrance of a body (*Enn.* 2.9.17). He tells a parable:

> Two people inhabit the same stately house; one of them declaims against its plan and its architect, but none the less

maintains his residence in it; the other makes no complaint, asserts the entire competency of the architect and waits cheerfully for the day when he may leave it, having no further need of a house: the malcontent imagines himself to be the wiser and to be the readier to leave because he has learned to repeat that the walls are of soulless stone and timber and that the place falls far short of a true home. (*Enn.* 2.9.17)

Plotinus suggests somewhat snidely that Gnostics' complaints assume, and serve to mask, a "secret admiration" for the very bodies they disdain. He concludes, "As long as we have bodies we must inhabit the dwellings prepared for us by our good sister the Soul in her vast power of laborless creation" (*Enn.* 2.9.17). Because the Gnostics carried Plato's low esteem for body and the material world to its most extreme statement, ignoring his more positive statements, Plotinus was able to see that such views needed to be corrected. He set out to do this. Paraphrasing Plato's *Symposium* discussion of beauty as key to understanding the human world, Plotinus comments:

But perhaps [Gnostics] may say that they are not moved, and do not look any differently at ugly or beautiful bodies; but if this is so, they do not look any differently at ugly or beautiful ways of life, or beautiful subjects of study; they have no contemplation, then, and hence, no God. For the beauties here exist because of the first beauties. If, then, these here do not exist, neither do those.... But one should notice that they would not give themselves airs if they despised something ugly; they do so because they despise something they begin by calling beautiful: and what sort of a way of managing is that?

The more adequate attitude, he says is to acknowledge that

there are such beauties in things perceived by the senses that one admires their Maker and believes that they come from a higher world, and *judging from them,* says that the beauty there is overwhelming; one does not cling to them, but goes on from them to the beauties of the higher world, but without insulting these beauties here. (*Enn.* 2.9.17; emphasis added)

In this statement, Plotinus insists that the key to understanding the universe is recognizing its intimate interconnection. To grasp its interconnectedness is to see its beauty. I will return to this point.

Yet Plotinus also had some complaints about body and the sensible world. He accuses body of hindering thought by filling the soul with desires, pleasures, and griefs (*Enn.* 4.8.2). Bodies also separate human beings from one another, from other living beings, and from effortless participation in the universal circulation. There is certainly a sense in which Plotinus thought that the condition of embodiment needs to be overcome: "But now, since a part of us is held by the body, as if someone had his feet in water, but the rest of his body was above it, we lift ourselves up by the part which is not submerged in the body and by this join ourselves at our own centers to something like the center of all things" (*Enn.* 6.9.8). Plotinus, I think, maintains, rather than endeavors to resolve, Plato's contradictory statements about the body. He preserved Plato's ambiguity because he found ambiguity in the world. Like Plato, he found it necessary in different rhetorical contexts to speak of body differently. Body and the visible world oscillate in value according to the subject at hand.[6] His disparaging statements about body occur in the context of exhortations to identify with and develop the mind, the mind being less strongly differentiated from other minds than the body is from other bodies.

The decisive clue to understanding Plotinus's attitude to body, however, is to recognize that body is not "matter." This single point is the most frequently misunderstood principle of Plotinus's thought. Matter, Plotinus wrote, "is incorporeal, [is nothing more than] a tendency toward substantial existence. Even if you look closely, you cannot see it" (*Enn.* 3.6.7). Body is matter already informed — given form — by the rational principle, soul. Nevertheless, Plotinus says that body is "opposed" to soul (*Enn.* 3.6.6). The context of his discussion, however, indicates that the mutual opposition of body and soul is more analogous to that of the opposable thumb to the rest of the hand than to the opposition of an enemy. The opposable thumb is the original tool, making possible a range of delicate hand motions. Body is as necessary to soul — as its sense organ — as the thumb is to the hand (*Enn.* 4.3.23).

In fact, a dynamic unity is composed by the coordination of opposites: "For all things sprung from a unity come together into a unity by natural necessity, so that, though they grow out different and come into being as opposites they are, all the same, drawn together into a single common order by the fact that they come from a unity" (*Enn.* 3.3.1). Thus, "all opposites are entwined together" (*Enn.* 3.3.6).[7]

On the level of the individual, body and soul oppose and define each other; on the cosmic level, Intellect and Matter oppose each other in the same collegial way. Matter can be clothed by form, but it cannot be substantially changed; matter remains as residue or inertial passivity in bodies. "Anything that is affected is body, not matter" (*Enn.* 3.16.13). Yet matter is absolutely indispensable to the universe; Plotinus can even speak of it as the "cause of coming into being" (*Enn.* 3.6.14). Its role is to provide a base: "[T]hings only appear on matter;... the reason for their appearance [is] the existence of the real beings" (*Enn.* 3.6.13). He adds:

> Individual things acquire magnitude by being drawn out by the power of the forms which are visible in matter and make a place for themselves, and they are drawn out to everything without violence *because the universe exists by matter.* Each form draws out by its own power which it has; and it has it from the higher world. (*Enn.* 3.6.17; emphasis added)

When Plotinus said, as he once did, that matter is evil, he meant simply that it lies outside the range of the One's emanations. He did not mean that matter exercises any ability to *do* evil. Matter does not suck; it is merely passive, unable to resist form. Forms "enter into matter as their mother," but their powers are directed not toward matter but "toward their opposites" (*Enn.* 3.6.19). At this point, however, Plotinus digresses to explain that the analogy of "mother" for matter is only approximate and somewhat misleading, for mothers are not merely receptacles but also contribute form to the child, while matter is purely receptacle.

Plotinus did not give body and the visible world a permanent value. Bodies must be variously valued *according to the use made of them by the one perceiving them.* It is certainly possible, and an ever-present danger, that one can become immured in the world of bodies and senses, by investing the lion's share of one's attention and affection on it. One can "fall out of beauty and into what is called beauty" (*Enn.* 6.7.33). What is supremely important is that one discerns the entities of the sensible world as *images.* Seen as image, at several removes, of the One, the sensible world becomes not mere image but perfect image:

Surely, what other fairer image of the intelligible world could
there be? For what other fire could be a better image of the intelligible fire than the fire here? Or what other earth could be
better than this, after the intelligible earth? And what sphere
could be more exact or more dignified or better ordered in its
circuit [than the sphere of this universe] after the self-enclosed
circle there of the intelligible universe? And what other sun
could there be which ranked after the intelligible sun and before
this visible sun here? (*Enn.* 2.9.4)

In short, if you revere the One, you must honor the universe created
from its emanations. A person must even recognize that she herself
contains and reflects the universe, for "we are each of us an intelligible universe, making contact with this lower world by the powers
of the soul below, but with the intelligible world by its powers above
and the powers of the universe. You become the All" (*Enn.* 3.4.3).

Beauty

It is time to examine more directly the role of beauty in Plotinus's
universe. In his treatise "On Beauty," he undertakes to discuss "what
the primary beauty in bodies really is":

Our explanation of [the beauty of bodies] is that the soul, since
it is by nature what it is and is related to the higher kind of
reality in the realm of being, when it sees something akin to
it or a trace of its kindred reality, is delighted and thrilled and
returns to itself and its own possessions. . . . [T]he things in this
world are beautiful by participating in form. (*Enn.* 1.6.2)

Because each entity in the universe takes its being from a stronger
reality, it mirrors that reality:

For God the qualities of beauty and goodness are the same,
or the realities, the good and beauty. . . . [F]irst we must posit
beauty which is also the good; from this immediately comes
intellect, which is beauty, and the soul is given beauty by intellect. Everything else is beautiful by the shaping of Soul, the
beauties in action and in ways of life. And Soul makes beautiful
the bodies which are spoken of as beautiful . . . [I]t makes every-

thing it grasps and masters beautiful, as far as they are capable of participation.

To see the universe as beautiful is to understand *at the level of perception* that the beauty one sees is precisely the informing emanations. The quality of beauty is itself the image of the Great Beauty. Plotinus's metaphor is light: when the soul "sees the beauties here flowing past it, it already knows completely that they have the light which plays on them from elsewhere" (*Enn.* 6.7.31).

Porphyry reports that, in his "eager longing for the One," Plotinus attained a vision/touch of the One four times (*Life 23*). Plotinus does not mention these episodes directly, but he does mourn the inability of discursive language to describe the "absolutely simple." He testifies that the intellect can come into contact with the One: "[B]ut when it has done so, while the contact lasts, it is absolutely impossible, nor has it time, to speak.... One must believe one has seen when the soul suddenly takes light" (*Enn.* 5.3.17).

The perception of beauty is a discipline requiring training and exercise. Plotinus describes an oscillation of intense concentrated struggle characteristic of giving birth. Like birth-giving, the experience requires a combination of labor and patient waiting.[8] But to seek the vision is not to seek something alien or external. The vision, when it comes, is a vision of the source of the seer's own being, an awareness of the emanations that give her life and light. There is no separation between vision and seer: the seer "sees suddenly, not seeing how, but the vision fills his eyes with light and does not make him see something else by it, but the light itself is what he sees" (*Enn.* 6.7.36). He describes the vision in greater detail:

> There must be those who see this beauty by that with which the soul sees things of this sort, and when they see it they must be delighted and overwhelmed and excited much more than by those beauties we spoke of before, since now it is true beauty they are grasping. These experiences must occur whenever there is contact with any sort of beautiful thing, longing, and a shock of delight and longing and passion and a happy excitement.... [Y]ou feel like this when you see, in yourself or in someone else, greatness of soul, a righteous life, a pure morality, courage.... [H]e who sees them cannot say anything except that they are what really exists. What does "really exist" mean? That they exist as beauties. (*Enn.* 1.6.4)

Ugliness, by contrast, is caused by an "admixture of evil living [and] a dim life...diluted with a great deal of death" (*Enn.* 1.6.5). Extending the visual metaphor he has used throughout his discussion of beauty, Plotinus suddenly speaks of *moral* ugliness. Yet the visual metaphor does not serve him well here because matter, which must represent utter ugliness, cannot be seen and, indeed, has no more characteristics than does the One. Moral ugliness can, however, be defined:

> Suppose, then, an ugly soul, dissolute and unjust, full of all lusts and all disturbances, sunk in fears by its cowardice and in jealousies by its pettiness, thinking mean and mortal thoughts as far as it thinks at all, altogether distorted, loving impure pleasures, living a life which consists of bodily sensations and finding delight in its ugliness. (*Enn.* 1.6.5)

Plotinus even finds this ugliness poignant. In a misguided search for beauty the soul clutches compulsively at everything that crosses its path, seeking to possess it by joining it to itself. "The soul becomes ugly by mixture, and dilution, and inclination toward the body and matter,...just as pigs, with their unclean bodies, like that sort of thing" (*Enn.* 1.6.5).[9]

Beauty and Art

Plotinus nowhere offers a systematic theory of why some objects are — or appear to be — more beautiful than others. His only comments on aesthetics grant that works of human art can alert their viewers to the presence of beauty:

> The wise men of old, who made temples and statues in the wish that the gods should be present to them, looking to the nature of the All, had in mind that the nature of Soul is everywhere easy to attract, but that if someone were to construct something sympathetic to it and able to receive a part of it, it would of all things receive soul most easily. That which is sympathetic to it is that which imitates it in some way, like a mirror able to catch a form. (*Enn.* 4.3.1)

Works of art, however, are not unique representations of reality, for the One continuously fills the universe, articulating all its forms:

Yes, the nature of the All, too, made all things in imitation
of the intelligible realities of which it had the rational principles, and when each thing, in this way, had become a rational
principle in matter, shaped according to that which was before
matter, it linked it with that god in conformity with whom it
came into being and to whom the soul looked, and whom it
had in its making. (*Enn.* 4.3.1)

André Grabar believed that Plotinus's cosmology held some implications for artists. He suggested, for example, that the artist who
wishes to paint realistically (in Plotinus's sense) must eliminate the
dimension of material depth. Optical illusions occur in the third dimension because that is where matter exists — in the "volume and
separateness of bodies." If three-dimensionality reflects the depth
(*bathos*) of matter, then "realistic" figures should be flattened. They
should also have uniform lighting, eliminating shadows. Grabar
pointed out that the illusionistic art of the classical tradition was
largely abandoned in late antiquity in favor of an art that showed
the "true" size, uncorrected for distance, and the "true" color and
other characteristics of objects. He claimed that Plotinian aesthetics
informed the new Christian iconic art of catacombs, church walls,
apses, and panel painting in late antiquity.

More recently, Alliez and Feher have argued that although the
depth associated with materiality was to be avoided in a Plotinian
aesthetic, a "different kind of depth" — a fourth dimension — was
sought. "True depth" is to be found

> in the luminous intensity of which the One is the primordial
> source and from which proceed, as successive emanations, first
> being-intelligence, then soul and finally nature. These are the
> focal points that express light and propagate it. Extension and
> the bodies that inhabit it can now be seen to be effects of the lu-
> minous radiance that emanates from the One and seem to well
> up from the depths of the soul.[10]

The Plotinian painter must aim at a "translucent world in which the
internal light passes through bodies, and, as it propagates itself, can
thereby abolish the distances that three-dimensional space creates
between the bodies....His task is to celebrate radiance of mind as
he represents bodies." According to Alliez and Feher, the Plotinian
painter must also "dispel the state of dispersion in which physical

bodies live." The translucency of the painted figures must evoke the transparency of souls. But "the separation that it is the artist's task to overcome is a lack of unity not simply between the various components of his picture but above all between that picture and whoever looks at it." The spectator of a Plotinian artist's painting discovers in it "reflections of a light from which not only the work of art but he himself proceeds."[11]

Alliez and Feher's description of Plotinus's aesthetics moves attention from the beautiful object — the painting — to the viewer's act of perceiving beauty. They argue that the stylistic specifications Grabar described are irrelevant to Plotinus's focus on sensible beauty's role in alerting the one who wants to understand the world to the "Great Beauty" (*Enn.* 1.6.4). In fact, Grabar acknowledged that there is no evidence either that Plotinus had any interest in Roman figurative painting or that artists contemporary with him were aware of Plotinus's philosophy. Moreover, so-called illusionistic painting was still done when the resources and skill of the painter permitted.

The Tomb of the Aurelii in Rome bears a small head, variously called "Head of a Prophet" or "Head of an Apostle," that may be a better example of Plotinian aesthetics than iconic representation. This frontal head of a young bearded man is naturalistic, mouth and nose modeled by shadows. Eyes and brow, however, are modeled by light rather than shadow, and the eyes gaze piercingly into the distance. Here, the third dimension — matter — has not been eliminated, but it has been deeply penetrated by the light of the intelligible world and transformed. A more accurate description would be to say that the sensible world has been drawn up into the potent intellect that blazes through the "windows of the soul," the eyes. For matter, according to Plotinus, is to be neither denied nor hated, but ignored. It is a necessary part of the universe, but it must not absorb too much attention. In short, within a Plotinian aesthetics, there is no reason why representation should not be naturalistic. Indeed, "What other fairer image of the intelligible world could there be [than the familiar sights of this world]?" (*Enn.* 2.9.4).

Plotinian aesthetics has a larger role to play in Plotinus's moral universe than to inspire painting. Indeed, for Plotinus, the ability to perceive beauty is the foundation of ethical judgment and behavior.

Beauty and Moral Responsibility

Plotinus says that the recognition of beauty occurs not at the level
of judgment but at the foundational level of perception itself. The
perception of beauty is profoundly moral, an "ethical ability."[12]
But this formula sounds deceptively simple; Plotinus will derive a
metaphysics, morality, and what we might call a "spirituality" from
his cosmology. As we have already seen, perception of the "truly
beautiful," for Plotinus, requires training, concentration, and an eye
"adapted to the vision." If, however, one is content with placing
beautiful objects — art — before one's eyes, "you may fall out of
beauty into what is called beauty" (*Enn.* 6.7.33).

Since recognition of the beautiful constitutes a primary orientation
in the universe, Plotinus said, "all our toil and trouble is for this, not
to be left without a share in the best of visions. The one who attains
this is blessed. . . . [T]he one who fails to attain it has failed utterly"
(*Enn.* 1.6.7). The direct apprehension, *at the level of perception,* of
the interconnectedness of the universe is the quintessential human
activity, the knowledge it would be tragic to miss. The experience,
through contemplation, of the concrete organic unity of the world
requires the integration of intelligence and feeling; it is participation
in beauty.

Plato had similarly identified the goal of rational exercise as a
vision of the beautiful. In Plato's treatise on beauty, the *Greater Hippias,* he set out to find, "not what seems to the many to be beautiful,
but what is so." Yet at the end of the treatise he was forced to ad-
mit, as the only fruit of his labor: "So Hippias, . . . I seem to myself
to know what the proverb means that says, 'The beautiful things are
difficult.' "[13] For Plotinus as for Plato, however, identifying the beautiful *as object* was difficult and elusive. But Plotinus saw, as Plato
did not, that an aesthetics that seeks to identify the properties of
an object that make it beautiful is fundamentally misguided. One
must, instead, exercise and develop one's capacity to see beauty in
its myriad forms. At their best, beautiful objects merely train the eye
to perceive beauty; at their worst, they represent economically or socially "interested" identifications of what *counts* as beauty, blocking
perceptions of livelier and more surprising beauty.

Because perceiving beauty defines human happiness, misjudgments
about what is beautiful are the greatest human danger. Because "we
are what we desire and what we look upon," the formative ef-

fects of contemplation of beauty are crucial to human integration
(*Enn.* 4.3.8). Thus, Plotinus rearticulated Plato's method for developing a discernment of beauty. In so doing, however, he revised it
significantly:

> And what does this inner sight see? When it is just awakened
> it is not at all able to look at the brilliance before it. So that
> the soul must be trained first of all to look at beautiful ways
> of life: then at beautiful works, not those which the arts pro-
> duce, but the works of those who have a name for goodness:
> then look at the souls of the people who produce the beautiful
> works. How, then, can you see the sort of beauty that a good
> soul has? *Go back into yourself and look;* and if you do not yet
> see yourself beautiful, then, just as someone making a statue
> which has to be beautiful cuts away here and polishes there
> till he has given his statue a beautiful face, so you must cut
> away the excess and straighten the crooked and clear the dark
> and make it bright, and never stop working on your statue un-
> til the divine glory of virtue shines out on you.... If you have
> become like this, and see it, and are at home with yourself in
> purity, with nothing hindering you from becoming in this way
> one, with no inward mixture of anything else, but wholly your-
> self, nothing but true light: when you see that you have become
> this, then you have become sight; you can trust yourself then:
> you have already ascended and need no one to show you: con-
> centrate your gaze and see. This alone is the eye that sees the
> great beauty.... For one must come to the sight with a seeing
> power made akin to what is seen. You must first become all
> godlike and all beautiful if you expect to see God and beauty.
> (*Enn.* 1.6.9; emphasis added)

In the *Symposium,* Plato had described a process of abstraction
in which, starting with bodies, the most immediately evident beauty,
one proceeded to less visible beauties, like lifestyles, laws, and conceptual schemes. Yet Plato's invisible beauties were concrete human
creations, external to the soul. Plotinus finds the source of the perception of beauty not in beautiful objects, nor in the socialized eye,
but in the beholder's soul. So far from being an inherently dualistic
venture in which the seeker attempts to find beauty outside herself, in
social practices or institutions or in some heavenly realm, it is rather
a process in which she devotes herself "to exploring her own psychic

space, [her] own internal life deep within which [she] discovers radiant intellect and, even deeper, the One of which intellect is already a reflection."[14] Plotinus continues: "If, then, a soul knows itself...[it] knows that its movement is not in a straight line [but] in a circle around something, something not outside but a center, and the center is that from which the circle derives, then it will move around this from which it is and will depend on this" (*Enn.* 6.9.8).

While Plato's method consisted of abstracting the quality of beauty from the many objects and practices that exhibit it, Plotinus's method entailed a systematic movement from attention to external things to an inner life or subjectivity. For Plato, the practice of beauty depended on and resulted from virtue. For Plotinus, perceiving beauty is more fundamental; it underlies and supports the practice of virtue so that the primary effects of an active and alert perception of beauty are ethical. The one who has "become sight" understands intimately the irreducible connection of all living beings that is the basis of ethical feeling and activity. Plotinus discusses at length the merely apparent "absurdity" of believing that all living beings share the same soul:

> It must, no doubt, seem strange that my soul and that of any and everybody else should be one thing only: it might mean my feelings being felt by someone else, my goodness another's too, my desire her desire, all our experience shared with each other and with the one universe, so that the very universe itself would feel whatever I feel. (*Enn.* 4.9.3)

But this "strange" sharing, Plotinus repeats, exists, and we already recognize it, if we think more profoundly and honestly about everyday experience: "We are in sympathetic relation to one another, suffering, overcome at the sight of pain, naturally drawn to forming attachments; and all this can be due only to some unity among us" (*Enn.* 4.9.3).

Soul, Plotinus insists, is the source of that unity. It is because "all souls derive from the same from which the soul of the All derives too, [that] they have a community of feeling." But we also know that every individual does not share the feelings of every other individual, for individual souls are also differentiated from one another. This occurs because human beings do not consist of soul alone but consist of the composite of body and soul. Thus, they are differentiated from one another in two ways: by different bodies and by the objects of their active attention and affection: "Different souls look at different things and are and become what they look at" (*Enn.* 4.3.8). Plotinus urged that the most fruitful direction one might look is toward the One and that what one sees when one does so is the all-pervasive beauty of the universe:

> But if someone is able to turn around, . . . he will see God and himself and the All; at first he will not see *as* the All but then, when he has nowhere to set himself and determine how far he himself goes, he will stop marking himself off from all being and will come to the All without going out anywhere, but remaining there where the All is set firm. (*Enn.* 6.5.7)

The most immediate effect of this inclusive vision appears in the seer; the Great Beauty "makes its lovers beautiful and lovable" (*Enn.* 1.6.7). But the vision's effects go beyond personal enhancement.

Plotinus recognized that the community to which humans are responsible is that of life, manifested in all living beings. More than a century later, Augustine would argue — against the Manichaeans, who held something like Plotinus's view — that humans were ethically responsible only for the community of rational minds, but Plotinus would have found this (literally) shortsighted.[15] For him, life, like light, circulates through the whole universe.

Plotinus himself did not write about how he translated this ethical vision into concrete practices. But Porphyry, his biographer, reports that Plotinus was a vegetarian, that he took numerous orphans into his home, that he conducted business on their behalf, and that he taught while maintaining a virtually invulnerable inner recollectedness. Moreover, many of Plotinus's closest friends and followers were engaged in public life; they were medical doctors, rhetoricians, and senators (Porphyry, *Life* 7). Clearly, Plotinus's teachings were considered useful by those committed to public service.

Beauty and Responsibility

Plotinus's description of the connectedness of living things in a vast, interdependent, and beautiful universe challenges the individualism that has characterized much of Western culture and philosophy since the Enlightenment. As Plotinus put it, "there is no place to draw a limit, to say, 'this and no further is I' " (*Enn.* 6.5.7). A person's primary self-identity is with the universe, a finely textured relationship of parts to whole in which none of the parts could *be* without the whole. Moreover, Plotinus's idea that perceiving beauty is *the* most formative activity challenges the potential quietism that might be implied in claiming that to see beauty is to see reality. Plotinus, valuing contemplation as Plato and Aristotle did, has given it a broader definition; for Plotinus, "every action is a serious effort towards contemplation" (*Enn.* 3.8.1).[16] What if participation in the Great Beauty were to be understood, then, not solely (or perhaps not even primarily) as what we might be inclined to call "contemplation" — self-isolated and individual — but as activity in the world of bodies and society?

If the universe is irreducibly interconnected for damage, it is also interwoven through veins of energy and delight. Plotinus recognized and endeavored to reveal to his friends and students the fundamental generosity of the universe, the continuous, amazing circulation of gifts, of love, of light. And he said that this knowledge could become the centerpiece of one's identity so that one actually feels oneself a part of this circulation of wealth.

According to Plotinus, there is enough for all if we will use responsibly the physical and psychological resources of the world. This is the most evident open secret of the universe. To recognize it on the ecological and social level is to work to distribute more equitably the resources of the earth. To recognize it on the psychological level is to recognize that we may finally abandon our frantic efforts to extract what we need from our families, lovers, and friends. The world contains enough, and realizing this comes as an awareness of beauty, a relaxing. When individual isolation is overcome *on the level of perception,* one can only respond with gratitude and responsibility.

This experiential knowledge is not esoteric and does not require philosophical training. It actively and openly invites recognition. Even fans of media stars know that the fame, beauty, and money the star has collected are, both symbolically and concretely, theirs. They take pleasure in participating in what the star crystallizes and displays for them. The star's social function is to demonstrate the existence of *so much.*[17] There is enough for all, if we will only cease trying to stipulate and control the channels through which it may flow to us, if we will "await it with confidence, and accept it with gratitude."[18] This is Plotinus's vision.

Interconnectedness, then, is a scientifically demonstrable fact as well as a feature of experience, even though we seldom notice it. Yet there is something abundantly and compellingly energizing in those moments when we do see the interconnectedness, what Plotinus calls the "unity," of the universe and the consanguinity of living beings.

We must, however, still ask: What is the relationship between perceiving the circulation of beauty and attention to social arrangements? Isn't social activism antithetical to the activity of perceiving beauty? For totalizing visions of beauty can be, and have been, compatible with the most egregious social injustice. Indeed, "Neoplatonism" has been repeatedly accused of contributing to the high value accorded contemplation in contrast to action and to the escapist mysticism within Christianity that has neglected the concrete needs of other human beings. It is important to investigate such charges so that we do not import, along with Plotinus's inclusive philosophy, its seductions.

Clearly, articulations of beauty must be scrutinized and the ancient Grail question brought to them, "Whom does it serve?" But the point of developing and exercising the ability to perceive beauty is not individual gratification. To hold together beauty and moral responsibility, then, requires both an energizing and compelling vision of an intimately interconnected world as the identity of the "real self" and continuous investigation and revision of the ways this vision is lived in "human, all too human" societies. Our awareness that attentiveness to developing a capacity for perceiving beauty can divert a person from moral responsibility and action to alter injustice, however, goes beyond Plotinus. Reading for life, we must acknowledge *both* the beauty of Plotinus's enspirited universe *and* his own failure fully to explore its effects.

Although his philosophy supports, and even occasionally articulates, a basis for concern about social and economic justice, Plotinus advocated an elitist attitude fundamentally incompatible with his worldview. The "good and wise man," he wrote, leaves concern for poverty to others. He recognizes and accepts that "there are two kinds of life here below, one for the good and wise and one for the mass of men." The mass of men are on earth "to do manual work and to provide for the necessities of the better sort." Brushing aside the pains and damages of human life, *both his own and others'*, Plotinus tells his disciples to consider the world a sports arena "where some win and others lose — what is there wrong with that?" Winners will not impress the "good and wise man," nor will losers worry him. All that is important for the good and wise man is to be "directed to the highest point and the upper region" (*Enn.* 2.9.9). These words summarize Plotinus's guilt in contributing to the quietism of Western contemplation.

Clearly, Plotinus's philosophy could be read, and indeed, has been read, as a rationale for ignoring blatant social and economic inequities — *both* one's own and others', it is important to add. I hope the fundamental incoherence of this attitude with the rest of Plotinus's gentle philosophy is evident. It was also inconsistent with his own practice of caring for orphans, helping those in need, and counseling his friends. Why did he not simply regard all of these as "losers"? Rather than ignoring Plotinus's elitist statements, however, it is important to see them as a cautionary tale and to deplore the apparent ease with which a great philosophical mind could casually incorporate the common prejudices of his social location.

The perception of beauty is an activity; it is, furthermore, an activity that flows spontaneously from our most fundamental gift, our aliveness. Plotinus was able to picture with equanimity human vulnerability to crushing loss, even to the fact that a moment will inevitably come in which life itself is "simply no longer there" (*Enn.* 4.5.7). He did not, however, articulate quite so clearly that the important and irreducible vulnerability in an interconnected universe is transpersonal. A vivid awareness not of individual vulnerability but of the fragile interconnection of all life must inspire the active love for the beauty of the whole that motivates work for its preservation.

But let us examine more carefully the assumption that while one is absorbed in "seeing" one is not simultaneously struggling to make the world and human society a better place to live for more human beings. Are the perception of beauty and the struggle for social change inevitably alternative postures toward the world? Perhaps this depends on one's theory of vision.

The metaphor of vision does not necessarily emphasize the distance between the seer and the object seen, as some twentieth-century theories of vision have claimed. Plato articulated a theory of vision that emphasized the viewer's activity and the connection of viewer and object in the moment of vision. The so-called visual ray theory states that a quasi-physical ray, created by the same fire that animates and warms the body, is at its most intense in the eyes. The act of vision occurs when the visual ray is directed to an object, *touches its object,* and the object travels back along the ray to imprint itself on the memory. Ancient and medieval folk beliefs about the evil eye, in which a malign look can cause physical and/or spiritual damage, rely on this model of vision as touch. Seeing connects viewer and object through the viewer's activity. Obviously, visual ray theory did not emerge from an entertainment culture, a culture that thinks of seeing as passive; rather it assumes vigorous engagement with the object of vision.

For complex reasons, Plotinus rejected Plato's theory of vision, but he nevertheless spoke of the ultimate spiritual vision as culminating in touch. If visual touch is not caused by a quasi-physical ray, what accounts for it? It is significant that Plotinus speaks of intense vision as motivated by love:

> [T]he soul by a kind of delight and intense concentration on the vision and by the passion of its gazing generates something from itself which is worthy of itself and of the vision. So from the power which is intensely active about the object of vision, and from a kind of overflow from that object, Love came to be as an eye filled with its vision, like a seeing that has its image with it. (*Enn.* 3.5.3)

Plotinus maintained the ancient claim that intensely concentrated vision touches its object, but he found the crude physicality of the visual ray theory incompatible with his description of intellectual/spiritual vision. For true vision occurs when the individual soul focuses its gathered longing on the higher Soul that she has in common with all living beings, and, through the part of the soul that has "remained above," her vision touches, and interlocks with, the One's emanations as they project through Intellect and into Soul. The medium of this connection is love: "[S]ince the soul is other than God but comes from him it is necessarily in love with him" (*Enn.* 6.9.9). "And if someone assumed that the origin of love was the longing for beauty itself which was there before in men's souls, and their recognition of it and kinship with it and unreasoned awareness that it is something of their own, he would hit, I think, on the truth about its cause" (*Enn.* 3.5.1). In his late treatise on love, Plotinus repeats that the "spirituality" of his account of vision does not disparage the beauty of the visible world: "If anyone delight in something and is akin to it, he has an affinity also with its images" (*Enn.* 3.5.1). Recognition of kinship with the One, as well as with its images, and enjoyment of the beauty of the visible world are the appropriate attitudes.

But let us linger a moment more on Plotinus's description of loving vision as capable of touching its object. Although the moment of touch is mediated through Intellect, Plotinus is careful to specify that its content is not "intellectual," in the modern sense of the word, but "only a touching and a sort of contact without speech or thought.... [T]hat which touches does not think" (*Enn.* 5.3.10). Plotinus discusses the experience of touch as "a passionate experience, like that of a lover resting in the beloved" (*Enn.* 6.9.4). Moreover, midway through his discussion of the vision of the One, Plotinus suddenly changes from speaking of the One in abstract terms — "simplicity," "indivisible," "power," "the principle of all things" — to using a personal term: "he." As if to demonstrate the necessity of interweaving both abstract and personal terms, however, he soon returns to the abstract: "something extremely self-sufficient," "the cause."

Language, which can only say one thing at a time, is severely limited when one tries to express simultaneously the intimate and the cosmic effects of the One. The One is at once "the spring of life, the spring of intellect, the principle of being, the cause of good, [and] the root of the soul." Yet it is no less active in maintaining an individual's "true life": "[F]or we are not cut off from him or separate, ... but we breathe and are preserved because that Good has not given its gifts and then gone away but is always bestowing them as long as it is what it is" (*Enn.* 6.9.9).

Over six centuries before Plotinus lived, Plato had looked out at the world, endeavoring to see it as Socrates saw it. Through Socrates' eyes, he saw a world in which death stole nothing of importance from the living soul. Death merely brought the soul closer to real existence by stripping off the biodegradable body. Plotinus, in his turn, trying to see the world as Plato saw it, saw that Plato had found human vulnerability intolerable and had tried to articulate a world in which it didn't matter. But, standing on his shoulders, Plotinus also saw that both vulnerability and the circulation of life depend on the same condition — consanguinity, interconnection, the Great Beauty. It was this, the uprights or sides of the cosmic ladder that hold together all life, that he endeavored to communicate to his friends and disciples in his philosophy.

Over seventeen centuries after Plotinus's death, I endeavor to see the world as Plotinus saw it. But my experience and my world are different from Plotinus's in fundamental ways. In a world that is knit together by rapid transportation and communication, I have seen the faces of people who suffer from economic, social, and political inequality. I have also seen and heard news media representations of those who suffer most from war, famine, and disaster. I cannot dismiss suffering children, women, men, and animals as "losers," no matter how stabilizing and reassuring this might be. In his study, surrounded by his students, Plotinus could apparently more easily subsume individual suffering into his worldview, caring in practical ways for those who suffered in his immediate vicinity, but unconcerned with suffering he did not see.

In a world stratified by economic, political, geographical, and religious diversity, Plotinus's description of an interconnected universe can help to overcome attitudes based on isolation and insularity. It can encourage the "strange sympathy" for all living beings Plotinus advocated. His dynamic and intimately responsive spiritual universe can serve as a basis for social concern and action. To understand Plotinus's failure to carry his vision to the point of working to alter the social, political, and institutional conditions that create suffering is not to forgive his failure but to retrieve what is usable. It is to read both appreciatively and critically — for life.

Chapter 3

LOVE'S BODY—
INTENTIONS AND EFFECTS

Augustine's *Homilies on the First Epistle of John*

———— • ————

Love itself is the soul's beauty.
— AUGUSTINE, *Homilies on the*
First Epistle of John

IN THE PREVIOUS CHAPTER, I retrieved from Plotinus's *Enneads* a
spiritual universe that creates and integrates the physical world,
interconnecting living beings in a thick interdependent network of
life. Beauty, enjoyment, and generosity, characteristics of a rich
human life, were central features of Plotinus's universe. In the next
two chapters, I focus on writings that expose two historical debates.
One of them, Augustine's debate with the Manichaeans discussed in
chapter 4, had pervasive, long-term effects in the West. The subject of this chapter, a group of Augustine's sermons, had no such
extended effects. What they demonstrate most pointedly is the complexity of communication and, thus, of reading and interpretation,
for in these sermons, beauty of language and content leads not to
generosity but to religious coercion. Preached during the Easter season, 415 C.E., Augustine's *Homilies on the First Epistle of John*
illustrates the use of beautiful language and concepts to rationalize
religious oppression.[1]

How is an appreciative and sympathetic reading of a text related
to a critical reading? Must a late twentieth-century reader choose
between asking difficult questions about a text's allegiances, institutional authorization, class and gender loyalties *or* exhibiting a text's
beauty, the profundity of the author's insights, and the relevance of
his or her intentions to the historical situation? Augustine's *Homilies
on the First Epistle of John* raises these issues with urgency. These
questions must be brought to the books we read, but they must also

be asked of readers. The discipline of reading for life must correct one's own tendency either for passionate naive reading or for reductively critical interpretation. Am I in danger of losing my capacity for being powerfully attracted by language and ideas in my zeal to deconstruct? Or am I more prone to notice only the political and institutional loyalties of a text, discounting the author's powerful and profound insights and rhetorical skill?

Augustine's sermons stay close to the scriptural texts he explores; they are, in effect, a public extempore reading of First John. I will describe the sermons before discussing their momentum and effects, paying attention to their power and to the escalating invective interwoven, with Augustine's rhetorical skill, into his insights.

Generosity and Suspicion

Imagine two twentieth-century readers of Augustine's sermons on First John. Both are far removed, in time and space, from the threatening situation in which Augustine worked, as well as from the assumptions and values of his society. The first reader's values and commitments are consciously secular. Critical of abuses within the history of Christianity, this reader is likely to see in the homilies nothing but the coercive rhetoric by which Augustine vilifies his rival Christians in North Africa, the Donatist Church. I will return to this reader's "suspicious" perspective on Augustine's homilies.

The second reader, educated within a Christian perspective and loyal to its doctrinal teachings, is likely to see in the sermons only the magnificent claims that Augustine makes for the power of love. This reader is likely to accept Augustine's assessment of his Donatist rivals and, consciously or unconsciously, to accept his premise that every rhetorical skill at his disposal should be brought to refuting the Donatists' claims and dismissing their religious perspectives. Because Augustine's writings have been powerfully influential in this reader's intellectual and emotional development, he must resist the temptation to concentrate solely on Augustine's explicit description of active and powerful love. He must recognize, first, that Augustine's text has been preserved and has come to our attention because Augustine won the argument. Donatist writings, in contrast, are preserved primarily because Augustine quoted from them as he refuted them.

Imagine now a third reader, one who admires and enjoys the passion and beauty of Augustine's discourse on love and, simultaneously, sees the coercive effects of his dazzling rhetoric. The third reader's task is difficult and complex; it requires historical knowledge as well as textual analysis. It is, nevertheless, the task of this chapter. What do we need to know about Augustine's circumstances in order to understand why he says what he says? What articles of our own historical baggage — assumptions and partial knowledges — do we need to discard in order to get there from here?

Consider Augustine's situation, for the historical context — political, institutional, and geographical — in which Augustine spoke may considerably affect our understanding of the meaning and effect of his words. If, for example, he spoke from a minority and marginalized position, we might hear his attack on Donatists as the desperate words of a frustrated and frightened man. If, however, he spoke as the powerful leader of a dominant institution, the social effects of his rhetoric would inevitably be greater and more deplorable to us.

It is often useful to ask, when confronting a text from the past, whether circumstances can be imagined in which it might be plausible and justifiable to write as the author did. Having imagined such circumstances, research can establish whether they, or similar circumstances, in fact existed. This exercise in imagination and research is potentially valuable in the process of understanding a text not in the abstract but "in the life." I will sketch the historical situation in which Augustine spoke, but that sketch will not, unfortunately, point us to a clear and unambiguous meaning for the homilies. On the one hand, Augustine's Catholic Church was numerically in the minority in North Africa in comparison to the Donatist Church. On the other hand, it was affiliated with, and could call upon the resources of, a strong but distant ally, the Christian Roman Empire. In the face of local harassment and his frustration with the Donatist Church, Augustine appealed for imperial support, and he received it.

Can we get there from here? If we are to do so, we must take into account not only the historical situation but also the baggage with which we travel. To twentieth-century readers, aware of the powerful medieval Catholic Church that systematically persecuted and executed dissidents, the early fifth-century North African church may seem similar. However, Augustine's church was threatened and beleaguered, not an obvious victor in North Africa. In the first decades of the fifth century, it was a church with notable successes, but it was significantly weakened by internal strife and external threat. Moreover, in addition to ecumenical dissidence, North African Christianity itself was fragile. It would disappear in the Islamic invasions of the seventh and eighth centuries.

As Augustine lay dying in August 430 C.E., invaders from northern Europe were at the gates of Hippo, laying siege to the city. Augustine thought his life's work was destroyed. His biographer, Possidius, confirms that indeed it was, at least for the immediate present, as churches and monasteries were razed, clergy and church members killed, and North African society itself demolished. When Augustine preached the homilies on First John in 415, he already anticipated, and feared, the destruction to come. In reading the homilies, then, the generous reader will remind herself that authors are engaged with the present and cannot predict the effects of their words, nor how they will sound to future readers. Augustine did not know that he was setting a dangerous precedent and that his argument would be invoked again and again in vastly different circumstances.

If, however, we resume a "suspicious" twentieth-century perspective, we will see, from this comfortably distant vantage point, that Augustine's advocacy of persecution of dissidents had effects that reached farther than he could have foreseen. It occurred at a time, approximately twenty years after the establishment of Christianity as the official religion of the Roman Empire, when imperial policy in relation to the myriad religious groups of the later empire was still being determined. It was also in *this* context that Augustine pioneered — advocated and rationalized — religious persecution. The homilies on First John represent a crucial moment in that rationalization.

Why bother to identify the precise historical circumstances in which a policy was established that would later be taken for granted? The usefulness of this historical exercise is that it permits one to recognize that the policy, far from being inevitable, was a response to a concrete situation. Augustine's advocacy of persecution represents his judgment of what was called for in particular circumstances. Understanding the original context, then, is preliminary either to criticizing Augustine's historical judgment or to finding it inadequate for the present. Moreover, this can be done without blaming Augustine, who had no access to the "effective history" of his on-location decisions.[2] In other words, one can "understand all" (in a manner of speaking) without forgiving all, without, that is, dismissing one's own sensitivities, questions, and concerns.

The crucial distinction is between intentions and effects. An author's good intentions can be granted, and the effects — rhetorical, institutional, and social — can still be deplored. There are no grounds on which to charge Augustine with intent to deceive his hearers and readers. Lacking other evidence, and adopting his perspective, we must accept his insistent claim to act from love, with nothing but the good of the Donatists at heart. Yet he also bitterly slanders Donatists. For our third reader — the appreciative *and* critical reader — the homilies present a cautionary tale, sad evidence of human self-deception operating under the guise of loving the brother.

The beauty of Augustine's vision of love as center and ground of the universe makes his failure to practice what he preached poignant. For Augustine had both the idea and the experience of beauty. He describes in his *Confessions* his search for, and discovery of, "beauty so old and so new," a vivid and transformative experience (10.27). He was able, in other moments, to envision a generous love that included all the beautiful and love-worthy objects of the world, especially other human beings. "Ask not," he wrote in *The Trinity,* "how much one should love God and how much love one should reserve for the neighbor." When a person loves, she participates in God's love, circulating God's love in the world and localizing it. Even the "enemy" has a place in this love. But a shadow accompanies Augustine's praise of love.

The scriptural injunction to love one's "brother" became a principle of exclusion in a polemical context. Augustine finally urged legalized persecution of dissidents on the grounds that *they* had become unloving; they had separated from the unity of the Catholic Church. I will follow his argument as it proceeds to one of his most notorious injunctions, "Love, and do as you will," and its practical effect, "Compel them to enter."

The Occasion

I will discuss the Donatist controversy, the context in which Augustine's sermons were preached, in some detail because, lacking this context, it is impossible to consider his sermons with relevant generosity and suspicion.

Originating in the Diocletian persecution at the beginning of the fourth century, the Donatist Church was, by Augustine's time, the majority Christian church in North Africa. By the end of the fourth century, a long history of dispute, debate, and violence separated Catholics and Donatists. Yet Donatists and Catholics disagreed not over beliefs but over values. Moreover, Donatists' values had strong historical roots in North African Christianity.

Donatists alleged that a Catholic bishop, Caecilian, ordained in 311 C.E. by Felix of Aptunga, had become a traitor to the faith by surrendering the scriptures to Roman authorities during the Diocletian persecution. Caecilian's ordination was condemned by eighty Numidian bishops but was recognized by a majority of North African bishops. Throughout the fourth century the schism between Donatists and Catholics widened as intermittent persecution by imperial forces polarized the division between a "persecuted church" and a "persecuting church." Donatists accused Catholics of tainted and illegitimate ordinations, following from Caecilian's ordination. At the beginning of the fifth century, when public debates by Catholics and Donatists, conducted under imperial sponsorship, failed to bring the desired unity, imperial laws were enacted against Donatists. Formally, this was the end of the Donatist Church, but underground Donatism persisted in North Africa until the disappearance of Christianity in Africa in the eighth century.

Donatism perpetuated some ancient and thoroughly African Christian values and attitudes. The Donatists held ideas of ritual purity that related to the constant threat and frequent reality of persecution and martyrdom before Constantine extended legitimacy and support to Christianity in 312 C.E. As Christian confessors had rejected the Roman state, so Donatists refused to participate in a Catholic Church they believed to be complicit with the persecuting state, tainted by apostasy, and actively engaged in spreading contamination through its sacraments.

Donatists also valued a self-governing North African church, autonomous in relation to the Roman Empire. They supported the campaigns of two Moorish counts, Firmus in 372–75 C.E., and Gildo in the 390s, to rule Africa. Augustine mocked the Donatists for their nationalism. He ridiculed their view that they alone — a tiny branch of Christianity in relation to a world church — could claim to be a "pure" church. Donatists appealed to the mentality of a time before the empire and the Church were partners in governing society. Maintaining their self-identification with the local martyrs of the earlier North African church, they were unwilling to reconcile with a Catholic Church in partnership with the formerly persecuting Roman state. The radical fringe of Donatism, the Circumcellians, who were especially active in the province of Numidia, dramatized this identification with African martyrs by their use of the first recorded African Christian martyrs' cry, "Deo gratias." They sacked and whitewashed Catholic churches, captured, tortured, and murdered Catholics, and even, in states of ecstatic frenzy, flung themselves to death over cliffs — martyrs, in their view, for Donatist Christianity.

Donatist spirituality and ritual practice were also a protest against a Catholic Church that had become a venue for social and political upward mobility and privilege. Donatists criticized Augustine's acceptance of the church as a *corpus permixtus* (a mixed body), in which blatant sinners and Christians "recovering" from paganism rubbed elbows. Augustine acknowledged: "One who enters [the Catholic church] is bound to see drunkards, misers, tricksters, gamblers, adulterers, fornicators, people wearing amulets, clients of sorcerers, astrologers....[T]he same crowds who press into the churches on Christian festivals also fill the theaters on pagan holidays" (*De cat. rud.* 25.48).

Augustine's favorite metaphor for the Christian church was the parable of the wheat and the tares, lying together on the threshing-room floor until authoritatively separated on the day of judgment. By contrast, Donatists invoked scriptural metaphors that refer to the church as the bride of Christ "without spot or wrinkle." Tyconius, a Donatist theologian, was the first to use a metaphor of the church in the world later made famous by Augustine: the two cities, radically separated by their loyalty either to this world or to God.

Moreover, the Donatists' fierce protection of Christian sacraments derived from the African martyr-bishop Cyprian's insistence that those who had been baptized in dissident Christian groups must be rebaptized upon joining the Catholic Church. Donatists rightfully claimed to be the faithful successors of Cyprian's views. Augustine was very aware that his claim that the sacraments belong to Christ and are not tainted by the imperfection of the minister was in conflict not only with Cyprian's insistence on rebaptism but also with Tertullian, who had been the first to declare non-Catholic baptism invalid. Tertullian had argued, in *On Baptism*, that because the Holy Spirit was not present in "heretical" baptism, it could not be effective. Yet, in Augustine's view, Donatist adherence to the views of the most-honored former leaders of North African Christianity, together with their separation, on principle, from the worldwide Catholic communion, made them liable for prosecution and persecution.

Religious coercion in fifth-century North Africa did not involve imprisonment and execution; rather, it involved fines on laymen who refused to join the Catholics. Augustine was resolutely against capital punishment on the grounds that no one could repent and change after he was dead. Between 412 and 414 C.E. laws stipulated that Donatist church properties would henceforth belong to the Catholic Church. Donatist clergy and laypeople of all classes were fined for refusing to join the Catholics. Yet the Donatist Church refused to fade away. Throughout the fourth and fifth centuries, the Donatists maintained a pope in Rome. Clearly, Donatists were profoundly committed to their beliefs and values.

Augustine as Preacher

A vivid picture of Augustine's preaching can be reconstructed from his sermons. As bishop, Augustine sat ex cathedra while the congregation stood, "lining the walls" of the basilica (*Hom. 5.7*). Clearly, people who came to the lengthy service early chose to lean, while latecomers had to stand unsupported in the center. Augustine's congregation responded as he preached, and Augustine commented frequently on their responses: "The reward is named — what? Eternal life.... You hear, and you cry out with joy!" (*Hom. 3.1*). Or: "You hear the praise of charity and your voices ring out" (*Hom. 7.10*). Like contemporary preaching in African-American churches, this North African congregation expected the sermon to be participatory. They booed at the mention of judgment and at unpopular moral instruction. They wept. They quoted familiar passages of scripture with Augustine after they heard the first words. Throughout his career, Augustine continued to have the problem with his voice that he described in the *Confessions* as the immediate occasion for relinquishing his career as a teacher of rhetoric. He frequently had to beg the congregation for silence so that he could be heard.

Augustine's preparation for preaching was prayer and meditation. He did not preach from a lectionary, except during the important liturgical seasons of the year. His sermons were delivered extempore;

they were copied by scribes — *notarii* — on delivery and circulated across the Roman Empire during his lifetime. Nearly a thousand are extant. His sermons on the Psalms alone are twice as long as his longest written work, the *City of God*.

Augustine's sermons were addressed to a popular audience, not to the educated people who read his written works. They are intentionally informal and without rhetorical devices. And they are long: in antiquity, brevity was considered the sign of a poor education and a weak mind. Although Augustine frequently used colloquial expressions, his speech was grammatically flawless, as one would expect from a former teacher of rhetoric. A great deal of the poetry of Augustine's speech, however, disappears in translation. He loved to use assonance, rhymes, alliteration, and the dramatic juxtaposition of antitheses.

Augustine had received no systematic instruction in preaching, other than the considerable skills of persuasion he had acquired in twenty years as a rhetorician and teacher of rhetoric. He had also observed an excellent preacher, Ambrose of Milan. Typically, as he preached or dictated, an objection would come to his mind, perhaps a question that had actually been raised by a member of his congregation. He would stop to explore the objection, returning to the original point only after he was satisfied that the objection was thoroughly examined. He posed frequent questions that he then proceeded to answer. He advanced his argument by contrasting opposites: light and darkness, old age and infancy, old and new. When Augustine sensed that his congregation was becoming bored, he went on to a different point. The sermon ended when his time was up, when his audience became restless, or when he was tired.

The Christian preacher, he said, is "nothing but a teacher and expounder of holy scriptures." The many obscure passages in scripture heighten the interpreter's engaged struggle with the text. Moreover, it is the exegete's task to show that there is "some harmony, some concord," requiring "a sympathetic ear," in scriptural verses that appear to contradict one another (*Hom.* 9.5). In addition, sermons should explain, edify, and, ultimately, persuade or convert — not merely the mind but, more importantly, the life. The extent to which Augustine recognized and trusted the active listening of his congregation is summed up in his statement: "The noise of our voice can be no more than a prompting; if there be no teacher within, that noise of ours is useless" (*Hom.* 3.13). In another sermon he remarked: "The spoken word has done all it could; the rest must be pondered in the heart" (*Hom.* 4.6).

The *Homilies on the First Epistle of John* are excellent examples of both the style and the content of Augustine's preaching. His preaching, whatever the text, typically revolved around two injunctions: "See that you have love" (*Hom.* 7.8), and, See that you love the appropriate object. Infinite desire must be addressed to an infinite object (*Hom.* 2.8; 10.11).[3]

Augustine's *Homilies on the First Epistle of John*

During the Easter season of 415 C.E., Augustine discontinued a long series of sermons on the Gospel of John in order to engage the lectionary for Holy Week and Easter. He found in First John a short work on which to preach in the intervening days. He chose it, he said, because it not only advocates but also produces increments of love, "like oil on a flame" (*Hom.*, Prologue).

The first homily designates Augustine and his congregation as direct and privileged participants in the event of the "Word made flesh." They enjoy an even greater benefit than those who were present at the original manifestation, in that, "having seen not, [they] believe." Augustine insists, "It is we who are so described and designated" (*Hom.* 1.3). The purpose of the incarnation itself is "that your joy may be full." And joy can be full only in fellowship, charity, and unity. "Have we expounded our text too hastily?" Augustine asked. He has, in fact, not expounded at all but has given a comprehensive summary of his intended agenda in this group of sermons (*Hom.* 1.4).

The text is subtle, rigorously thought through, and carefully worded. It is difficult to believe that it was delivered extempore. Having pondered the scriptural text in advance, he knew, as he began to speak, where he would go with it. But he must keep his audience with him, so he moves slowly. "Love, which 'covers a multitude of sins,'" will be his theme. He urges love for one's brothers but soon introduces an agenda even closer to his heart: "What is love's perfection? To love our enemies, and to love them to the end that they may be our brothers. Love your enemies, desiring them for your brothers: love your enemies, calling them into your fellowship" (*Hom.* 1.9).

This, Augustine says, is what Christ did on the cross. Throughout the sermons he will often reiterate this formula for love's perfection.

But surely, he continues, the injunction to "love your brothers" refers only to those in Catholic unity: "The deserter of the Church cannot be in Christ.... [H]e cannot be in Christ, who is not in Christ's body.... *In the unity of charity brotherly love consists.* [And] what sort of love has been shown in our Donatists?" Suddenly he addresses Donatists: "Was it right for you to condemn [all those practicing Catholic unity throughout the world]?" (*Hom.* 1.12–13; emphasis added). He concludes with a harsh judgment: "There is no blindness like that of those who hate their brothers." Clearly, Donatists are enemies because they hate — formally, if not literally — their Catholic brothers.

In the second sermon, Augustine's preoccupation with the Donatists is again evident in his repeated references to their views. Glossing his text, he says: "We shall not be in darkness if we love the brothers; and the proof of love for the brothers lies in not rending our unity" (*Hom.* 2.3).

In the third sermon, Augustine finds a word in the scriptural text that will advance his polemic against the Donatists: "Antichrist." Antichrists are to be recognized, he says, by the fact that "they went out from us." This is a loss to be lamented, but, Augustine adds rather too quickly, "there is comfort," for "they were not of us" (*Hom.* 3.4). Although Donatists have received the sacraments "with us" — baptism, blessing, and the Eucharist — they are not brothers.

Augustine protests too much; the marks of sibling rivalry accompany his repetitious insistence that the very fellow Christians who might most appropriately be called brothers are not to be so called. In fact, far from calling the Donatists brothers, Augustine calls them heretics and Antichrists (*Hom.* 3.7). Yet Augustine acknowledges that they did not differ from Catholics in their doctrine: "[B]oth we and they confess the same." But the decisive factor is that they have "left us." Their action (setting up their own communion) should be noticed, he says, not their words. In a few paragraphs Augustine has escalated Donatists from enemies to heretics and from heretics to Antichrists and liars (*Hom.* 3.8).

The embattled harassment Augustine felt is visible in his comment that many Antichrists who will eventually "go out" are still concealed within the church. Apparently Donatists were still making converts from the Catholic fold. Those within who will eventually "go out" can be known only by the fact that they "slander Christ's ministers." The slander, however, has apparently gone the other way. Augustine grumbles: "Tell a man that he is Antichrist and he gets angry and thinks an outrage done him" (*Hom.* 3.10).

From this unpromising base, Augustine proceeds to one of the richest panegyrics on love ever written. "A new commandment give I unto you, that you love one another. Consider. This command- ment of Christ has the name of love; and through that love are sins absolved" (*Hom.* 5.3). Augustine reached the powerful core of the homilies on First John in his sermon on 1 John 4:17–21: "Love your brother; in loving the brother whom you see, you will see God at the same time. For you will see charity itself, and there within is God dwelling" (*Hom.* 9.9). Augustine emphasizes the strong claim that by loving, the Christian participates directly in God-who-is-love. He repeats: "Now our vision is by faith, then it will be by sight; and if we love while we do not see, with what ardor shall we embrace when we have seen! But how are our hearts to be trained? Through love of the brothers" (*Hom.* 5.7). In a later sermon he repeats, "If God is love, whoever loves love, loves God" (*Hom.* 9.10).

But even love, as Augustine has defined it, damns the Donatists: "A man that acts contrary to charity, contrary to brotherly love, may not dare to boast that he is born of God" (*Hom.* 5.3). Augustine here refers here to love not as feeling but as action, the one action by which one proves or gives the lie to one's love, that is, under what roof one takes communion.[4] Augustine acknowledges the Donatists' virtues: "Look among those who for lack of charity have brought di- vision upon our unity: you will see many who give much to the poor; you will see others so ready to face death that when the persecutor stays his hand they hurl themselves to destruction." But they do all this, he says, without love. Thus, they merely commit suicide; they are not martyrs.

How can Augustine be so certain that his judgments are accurate? Discussing the verse, "Beloved, if our heart feel no evil, we have con- fidence unto God," Augustine professes to "feel no evil. "The love in us is true love, sincere, not feigned, seeking our brother's good, look- ing for no profit from our brother but his own well-being" (*Hom.* 6.4). He seeks to persuade, and to persecute, for the Donatists' own good. "Ask your heart," he repeats. But we might reflect that all a person can get from asking his heart is his own intentions; how one's actions affect others is not revealed.

Potential trouble appears at the verse: "Every spirit that confesses that Jesus Christ is come in the flesh is of God" (1 John 4:2). Can Augustine deny that the Donatists believe this and thus are of God? Again he insists that the Donatists' action in withdrawing from Catholic unity must be noticed, not "the noise of their words." In fact, he says, if one asks why Christ came in the flesh, it becomes clear that he came in the flesh in order to reveal God's love by dying for humanity. Those who lack love *effectively* deny his coming in the flesh. One expression of this lack of love is tearing at the unity of the Catholic Church. Therefore, "whoever 'rends the body of Christ' denies Christ's coming in the flesh" (*Hom.* 6.13). If the argument fails to satisfy, one must at least acknowledge its ingeniousness. It is skillful, cunning — and profoundly sad — exegesis. Once again, his argument has led him to the point of reiterating: "Whoever violates charity, let his tongue say what it will, by his life denies Christ's coming in the flesh; and that man is Antichrist" (*Hom.* 6.12, 13; 7.1).

If it is difficult for a twentieth-century reader to hold together both Augustine's exuberant rhetoric on love and his use of the concept to rationalize persecution of Donatists, it must have been at least equally difficult for his congregation to do so. The practical application of Augustine's instructions must have been especially difficult to discern, for Donatists were not enemies at a distance but people who interacted with Catholics on a daily basis, in the marketplace, on the streets, and as neighbors. Perhaps some were, literally, brothers.

Beauty and Love

Augustine's first, now lost, work was *De pulchro et apto* (The beautiful and the fitting). In this treatise, Augustine reports that he worked on the following questions: "Do we love anything except what is beautiful? What, then, is the beautiful? And what is beauty? What is it that attracts us and wins our affection for the things we love? For unless there were grace and beauty in them, they could not possibly draw us to them" (*Conf.* 4.13).

Here, Augustine connects beauty and love; we love things, he says, because they have beauty. Love is the affect accompanying the perception of beauty. He continued to relate love and beauty throughout his career. From *De pulchro et apto* (written in 380 C.E.: i.e., before his conversion) to the *Homilies on the First Epistle of John*, written thirty-five years later, his analysis deepened and became specifically Christian. He now introduces the idea that there is one object of love that both is beautiful and renders its lovers beautiful. That object is God. One passage is well worth quoting at length:

> An ugly and misshapen man may love a beautiful woman, or an ugly and misshapen woman of dull complexion may love a beautiful man; but love can make beautiful neither the man nor the woman. The man loves a fair woman, and when he looks on himself in the glass, he is ashamed to raise his face to the beauty of her he loves. He can do nothing to make himself beautiful; if he waits for beauty to come to him, waiting will make him old and his face plainer. There is nothing he can do, no advice you can give him but to restrain his passion and venture no more to set his love upon an unequal match.... But our soul, my brethern, is ugly through its iniquity: through loving God it is made fair. What manner of love is this, that transforms the lover into beauty! God is ever beautiful, never ugly, never changing. He that is ever beautiful, he first loved us — and loved none that were not ugly and misshapen. Yet the end of his love was not to leave us ugly, but to transform us, creating beauty in place of deformity. And how shall we win this beauty, but through loving him who is ever beautiful? Beauty grows in you with the growth of love; for love itself is the soul's beauty. (*Hom. 9.9*)

Yet this passage does not contain the full claim Augustine makes for love. It even overlooks his argument that whenever one loves, one participates in God, who *is* love. Would not the (visibly) ugly man's beauty of soul be capable of recommending his suit to the (visibly) beautiful woman? Why does Augustine suddenly confine erotic love to surface appearances? The answer must lie in his personal rejection of erotic love. Yet what Augustine called "carnal love" *might*, and often does, contain large, even majority, shares of the empathic esteem for the other that Augustine called "brotherly love."

The seventh sermon, on 1 John 4, authorizes precisely this suggestion, though Augustine fails to apply it to erotic love: "Love is of God, and everyone that loves is born of God and knows God.... For God is love." He raves: "My brothers, what more could be said? If nothing else were said in praise of love, in all the pages of this epistle, nothing else whatever in any other page of Scripture, and this were the one and only thing we heard from the voice of God's spirit — 'For God is love' — we should ask for nothing more" (*Hom.* 7.4). Moreover, love is active and powerful. It even has a body: "Love has feet, which take us to the Church, love has hands, which give to the poor, love has eyes which give information about who is in need. Love has ears.... To see love's activity is to see God. Love alone makes the difference between a person being good or evil: 'to have love and be an evil person is not possible' " (*Hom.* 7.6). Moreover, Augustine originated what has been thought of as a twentieth-century invention, "tough love":

> You must above all avoid thinking of [love] as a poor, inactive thing, wanting no more than a sort of gentle mildness for its keeping, or even a careless indifference.... You are not to suppose that you love your servant when you do not beat him, or love your son when you relax your discipline over him, or love your neighbor when you never find fault with him. That is not charity, but weakness.... Love the man, not his errors. (*Hom.* 7.11)

In speaking of God as love, however, Augustine has not forgotten the Donatists. Discussing his own position in opposition to the Donatists, Augustine focuses on intentions: "Some actions seem harsh or savage, but are performed for our discipline at the dictate of love." Thus, he continues, "a short and simple precept is given you once for all: Love, and do what you will." In other words, the final arbiter of one's intentions is one's own heart, honestly and deeply examined. Speaking to Catholics, he repeats "ask your own heart" at least seven times in the course of three sermons (*Hom.* 6.3; 6.9; 6.10; 6.12; 7.7; 8.9; 8.12). As we have seen, however, when speaking of the Donatists, Augustine demands that *their* intentions, indicated by their testimony, be dismissed. Considering Donatists, he looks solely to effects, to actions, and their action of breaking with Catholic communion is the only evidence Augustine allows.

Now he comes to the difficult — some might think, impossible — job of rationalizing persecution of Donatists, and he will do so purely on the basis of intention: "Love, and do what you will." Invoking a dangerous principle, he says, "You need not fear doing ill to anyone; for who can do ill to the person he loves? Love, and you cannot but do well" (*Hom.* 7.11).

A host of contemporaries, ours and his, recovering from domestic and sexual abuse would question this principle. Medieval tyrants used it to rationalize their actions. Countless women have been seduced by its (no doubt unfootnoted!) invocation. In short, its effects have, from its first use, been disastrous. Given the general human lack of self-knowledge, together with original sin — another doctrine developed by Augustine — "Love, and do what you will" has every possibility of leading to exploitation and little chance of leading to the other's good.

Yet Augustine was well aware of the compulsive and consuming propensity of human love. He described it vividly in his own *Confessions*. In fact, he reuses the metaphor of *Confessions* 9.2: "People are not to be loved as things to be consumed, but in the manner of friendship and goodwill, leading us to do things for the benefit of those we love" (*Hom.* 8.5).[5] The model of love is not that of the man who says, "I love partridges," or, as someone recently remarked, "I love animals. I think they're delicious." Nevertheless, Augustine does not recognize the vulnerability of the principle he invokes and its inability to protect others from one's well-intentioned damages.

In the eighth sermon, another awkward text requires careful exegesis: "Love your enemies." Although First John says nothing about this, Augustine deliberately imports a gospel verse (Matt. 5:46) in order to discuss it. If he does not acknowledge and integrate this injunction, this well-known verse might undermine his argument for persecuting Donatists. For if the Donatists are not to be considered brothers, surely the clear injunction to love one's enemies covers them. Watch Augustine work the passage: the command to love addresses first those nearest and then spreads to those farther off. But "love for those who are linked to you is much the same as love for yourself," which is also commanded. But, Augustine says, it is not really much of a stretch. Love for enemies, however, is not only an extension; it is almost a contradiction. In what sense should the enemy be loved?

Augustine returns to the premise that intention defines an act. It is impossible for an observer to define an act; the same act can be done from love or from pride: "In the works themselves we can see no difference." Judgment on what an act represents can come only from the actor: "See as [God] sees, the intention of your acts." "Look for the spring; search out the root from which [actions] proceed." Again, one's own heart is the final judge of intention.

Augustine claims that the command to love one's enemy is *implied* in First John by the injunction to love the brother, for "it is always the brother that you love." The enemy is to be loved as a potential brother: "Let your desire for him be that together with you he may have eternal life: let your desire for him be that he may be your brother."[6] Augustine counsels his congregation to love, in the enemy, the man made in God's image and to pray that God will "put fear in him and change him" (*Hom.* 10.7).

Fear is a new and pivotal element in his argument. Augustine begins his discussion of 1 John 4:16, "Perfect love casts out fear," by remarking that all love begins in fear: "Fear prepares the place for love....Fear is a goad." Fear wounds like a surgeon's knife, but love heals the wound (*Hom.* 9.4). Quoting from memory, Augustine misquotes Eccl. 1:22, which reads: "Unrighteous anger shall not be able to be justified." Augustine says: "He that is without fear shall not be able to be justified."

Augustine returns to the Donatists, those "violators of charity," "brigands," and "usurpers of Christ's estate." "Against such, love can be angry." With this, Augustine concludes perhaps the greatest sermon on love ever preached. Ironically, he chose a scriptural passage on love, using it to call fellow Christians Antichrists. Augustine has "harmonized" the epistle's strong and literal admonitions to love "the brother" with condemnation of the Donatists. He has not, in the sermons on First John, however, provided a rationalization for persecution of fellow Christians as a loving act. I must go to another text to recount the sad sequel to the *Homilies on the First Epistle of John*.

Two years after Augustine preached on First John, in a letter to the governor of North Africa, he described the process by which he came to support persecution of dissidents. Letter 185 addresses Count Boniface as a "beloved son" who has asked Augustine to clarify for him "the difference between the error of the Arians and that of the Donatists." Augustine does that in a paragraph and then hastens on to a matter that lies rather closer to his present preoccupations, namely, a lengthy explanation of his own thinking in relation to the Donatist schism. Love demands, he writes, that "we provide for [the Donatists'] amendment to the extent of our power" (*Ep.* 185.2). As we will see, the principle that underlies this statement was worked out in the homilies Augustine had preached two years earlier.

Augustine explains to Boniface that he changed his mind regarding persecution of dissidents. He had thought initially, he writes, that "it is better [for the Donatists] to be led to the worship of God by teaching rather than forced to it by fear of suffering" (*Ep.* 185.21). He was finally persuaded by converted Donatists' testimony that they were grateful for the legal intervention that brought them to "conversion [and] deliverance from that raging destruction." He concludes that "it is a blessing to many to be driven first by fear of bodily pain, in order afterwards to be instructed, or to follow up in act what they have learned in words" (*Ep.* 185.21). Convinced of their former error, former Donatists worried about their former fellows and urged Catholic officials to "put pressure on them lest they perish" (*Ep.* 185.7).

In fact, Augustine continues, many Donatists would have converted long since had they not been restrained by "fear of those among whom they lived." Now, "helped by imperial decrees," they have happily joined the Catholic congregation. Coercion alone is not enough, of course; teaching must follow, by which the Donatists' hearts, as well as feet, are turned to the Catholic Church. Thoroughly convinced by this evidence and testimony, Augustine exults:

> If you were to see the effects of the peace of Christ: the joyful throngs; their eagerness to hear and sing hymns and to receive the word of God; the well-attended, happy meetings; the sentiments of many among them — their great grief in recalling past error, their joy in contemplating the known truth. . . . I repeat, if you were to see in one glance these flocks of people in many parts of Africa now delivered from that destruction, you would say that it would have been excessively cruel for all these to be abandoned to eternal loss and to the torments of everlasting fire. (*Ep.* 185.32)

Augustine insists that coercion to the unity of the Catholic Church, far from cruelty, is actually a "great mercy" to Donatists (*Ep.* 13). He repeats several times that if Catholics had not appealed for imperial support, they would have been "negligent" (*Ep.* 185.18, 28).

Can the other side of this conflict be glimpsed? It is possible to reconstruct several Donatist allegations against Catholics from Augustine's rebuttals. First, Donatists allege, with scriptural warrant and precedent, that the persecuted church is the real church. Here Augustine finds himself in the dubious position of contesting an ancient and highly honored North African Christian principle, namely, that martyrdom proves commitment. He replies that only when persecution is "for righteousness' sake" is it praised by scripture. Augustine—the rhetorical heir of his African predecessor, Tertullian— twists the accusation and returns it toward the accusers: "Are they not the persecutors," who, without proof, accuse Caecilian of the crime of surrendering the sacred books to imperial agents? Are not they the persecutors who break the unity of the Catholic Church? Anyway, Augustine states, Donatists persecute out of hatred, while Catholics are motivated to persecute by brotherly love (*Ep.* 185.14).

Donatists, the majority of Christians in North Africa, apparently persecuted in more direct ways also. Augustine lists atrocities committed by Donatists, especially on bishops and clerics: "Some had their eyes put out; one bishop had his hands and tongue cut off; some were even massacred. I say nothing of the inhuman beatings, of looting of homes in nightly raids, of fires set not only to private houses but even to churches; and into these flames some even cast the sacred books" (*Ep.* 185.30).

There is no record that similar atrocities were committed by Catholics. This could be the result of systematic destruction of this evidence by the victorious party. Lacking evidence, we cannot speculate. It is perhaps more likely that a majority denomination, fortified by local strength in numbers, and represented by a fanatical fringe, resorted to "civil disobedience" to make their point. Catholics, in contrast, their position secured by imperial and legal backing, found legal means of reinforcement more congenial.

Second, Donatists accuse Catholics of innovation in calling upon imperial reinforcement for their position: "The Apostles did not call on the kings of the earth for such services." Augustine contents himself with remarking tersely that "times were different then" (*Ep.* 185.19). Nevertheless, the accusation disturbs him. In the tradition of Roman legal argument, he finds a precedent for requesting imperial help. The Apostle Paul, he says, called on a Roman magistrate to protect him from a plot against his life (*Ep.* 185.23:12, 32).

However, the letter's most triumphal (for Augustine) and dismal (for me) argument occurs when Augustine cites the ultimate precedent for persecution of dissidents. Christ, he says, persecuted in order to convert. He "not only compelled [the Apostle Paul] by words, but used his power to strike him prostrate, in order to force him to leave off the savagery of his dark unbelief and to de-

sire the light of his heart." Christ "first compelled and afterward
taught, first struck and afterwards consoled" (*Ep.* 185.22). "Paul
was forced by Christ; therefore the Church imitates her Lord in
forcing [Donatists]" (*Ep.* 185.23).

The gospel parable of the feast unattended by the invited guests
provides the final warrant for going out "into the highways and
byways" and compelling them to come in:

> If the Church, in the era of kings, exercises, as she ought, the
> power which she has received as a divine gift, together with
> religion and faith, and if those who are found in the highways
> and hedges, that is, in heresies and schisms, are compelled to
> come in, she is not to be blamed for compelling them, but they
> for waiting to be compelled. (*Ep.* 185.24)

In the face of the established Roman virtue of tolerance, Augustine
argues that there are situations in which tolerance is nothing more
than laziness and negligence.

Clearly, tolerance as an attitude of respect and willingness to learn
from others' beliefs, practices, and values was not a goal of any of
the passionately committed Christians I have discussed in this chapter. Donatists and Catholics simply used different kinds of power
to compel the other. In the historical moment in which Augustine
preached his homilies on First John and composed his letter to Count
Boniface it was not evident which kind of power would carry the
day. The power of the state to coerce religious belief is, even Augustine acknowledged, a poor second to belief by attraction. Yet
violence is perhaps an even poorer way to missionize.

It must be acknowledged, then, that even to notice the element
of coercion in Augustine's argument is profoundly unhistorical. It
reveals a twentieth-century sensibility, a religious tolerance that be-
lievers up to our own time, and many in our time, would not
consider a virtue. For if one is confident of authorization by God
through scripture and/or interior communication, it is sheer laziness
not to exert every effort to convert the other to one's view. In the
Homilies on the First Epistle of John, Augustine exhibits the full
force of his trained power of persuasion to establish the Donatists'
guilt. It seemed to him evident that the full continuum of power,
from strong power, the power to attract, to weak power, or force,
should be brought to bear on so important a matter as the eternal
salvation of his fellow Africans. It was obvious to Catholics and Do-

natists alike that ownership of the truth warranted, even required, pressing that truth on others.

The *Homilies on the First Epistle of John,* I have said, is a cautionary tale. Yet there are, I believe, some detachable conclusions. For example, Augustine's emphasis on love as method and goal insists that to see accurately is to see lovingly. Moreover, the idea that love entails participation in God, who *is* beauty and love, is powerfully exhilarating. The caution to be learned comes from the fact that Augustine articulated the connection between love and beauty so powerfully but effectively evaded it in practice.

At first I refused to think that it was possible to understand something thoroughly enough to explain it precisely and forcefully, yet to be unable to act on that insight. It is frightening to think otherwise. Anyone who has endured high school education has been told repeatedly that if she cannot explain something, she does not understand it. Yet Plato drove a wedge between the ability to articulate and understanding. He claimed that it is not the ability to articulate an insight but one's ability to incorporate it into one's behavior that proves that one understands it.

Augustine articulated, but could not live, his own insight about the power of love. This, of course, was sad for all those affected by his failure. But it does not necessarily invalidate the usefulness of his insight on love for me. Thinking as honestly as I can about my own experience, I realize that occasionally I have, and can articulate persuasively, a vision that I cannot fully inhabit. Is that vision or insight worthless, then? I think not, for once articulated, in print or in the classroom, others, who do not have my particular limitations, can and will incorporate — give body to — that insight. That human beings can understand but sometimes lack the ability to act on the understanding is, I believe, simultaneously the poignancy and the glory of human being.

To love the "brother" is to love the awkward, imperfect people closest at hand, the "drunkards, misers, and fornicators" Augustine described elsewhere. One's love may not bypass those nearest at hand in order to fasten on more worthy recipients: "The reaching to enemies does not mean the passing over of brothers. Our love, like a fire, must first take hold of what is nearest, and so spread to what is further off" (*Hom.* 8.4). According to Augustine, the "brother" of one's religious group has a first claim to love. Everyone else must be "loved" as an enemy; that is, to the end that the person or group may be brought, through fear, to change. The sibling who differs strongly enough to "vote with her feet," who "goes out" from one's religious company, must be regarded no longer as a sister but as an enemy one loves — if this is still the right word — conditionally.

But I must reconsider Augustine's conclusions. The gospel reports that Christ said, "Love your enemy." Christ apparently did not specify who should be regarded as enemy. Presumably, then, "my enemy" is anyone toward whom I feel enmity. The act of exerting myself to love that person or group is, or should be, a generous effort to see the "enemy" in the light of her own perspectives, circumstances, and values rather than as illuminated by mine.

It is precisely this kind of "loving the enemy" that Augustine must discourage. For Donatist Christians' religious values, as we have seen, were closer to the tradition of African Christianity than were Augustine's Catholic values. They were attractive to North African Christians. A church in cahoots with emperors was distinctly at odds with the formative years of African Christianity.[7] Augustine learned the ecclesiastical allegiances he advocated not in North Africa but during his years in Italy, in close proximity with an international culture and a confidently universal church.

Martyrdom for nonnegotiable convictions, separation from the secular world, and sacramental purity: these traditions were the heritage of North African Christians. Augustine argued that they were no longer relevant. Times had changed; it was presently more important, he said, to maintain the unity of a worldwide church supported by the Roman state than to adhere to either the "times of the apostles" or to the views of earlier leaders of Christianity in North Africa. In his *Homilies on the First Epistle of John*, Augustine faced the difficult job of simultaneously reversing his congregations' possible sympathies with Donatism and interpreting the epistle's strong and repeated admonitions to love "the brother." To do so, he found it necessary to supplement First John with a verse from Matthew that supplied an alternative to loving the brother. "There is scarcely a word in the whole Epistle about the love of enemies," but this is, Augustine says, because love of enemy is implicit in the command to love the brother. When you love your enemy "that he may be your brother, you love a [potential] brother" (*Hom.* 8.1; 8.10).

Where did Augustine acquire his notion of how to love someone with whom one disagrees? In the *Confessions*, he describes his mother's anguish over his youthful refusal of Catholic Christianity. He credits his conversion to her ceaseless tears and prayers for his salvation:

> You [God] saved me, full as I was with the most execrable uncleanness, from the waters of the sea and brought me to the water of your grace, so that, when I was washed in this water, the rivers that flowed from my mother's eyes, tears daily shed for me that watered the ground below her downcast looks, should be dried up. (*Conf.* 5.8)

When Augustine was a member of Manichaean Christianity, Monica was so distressed over his erroneous beliefs that she permitted her nineteen-year-old son to live with her only after she had a dream in which she, weeping as ever, was standing on a ruler. An angel came and instructed her to notice that Augustine was standing close to her on the same ruler. The dream comforted and reassured her that Augustine would come to Catholic Christianity (*Conf.* 3.11).

Augustine's model of love for the enemy appears to have been informed by Monica's intransigent concern for his salvation from what she considered heresy. In his sermons on First John, he twice invokes a revised version of the parable of the son to urge the "prodigal" Donatists to return to the Mother, the Catholic Church (*Hom.* 1.11; 3.1). For in his experience, it is the mother that is capable of tenacious labor to recover lost "sons." Monica's labor to bring him to spiritual birth was more arduous, Augustine said, than that with which she gave him physical birth (*Conf.* 5.9). Her love for him was expressed as commitment to bringing him to stand with her on the same ruler, to share the same communion.

Augustine could not, and did not, imagine a kind of love that could accept and respect religious difference. He did not envision a humble and generous love that acknowledged that the human institutions and beliefs by which people endeavor to express the sacred and its operation in the world remain human, even as they seek to define and actualize a relation to the divine. We have considered some personal and historical reasons why this was so. He saw, and powerfully articulated, his conviction that human affiliation with divinity occurs only in the activity of love. But he generalized the idea of love to include harshness, anger, and persecution of the "enemy," even when the "enemy" was a brother or sister who worshiped the same God, practiced the same sacraments, and maintained a principled allegiance to time-honored North African Christian values.[8]

Clearly, Augustine's exuberant description of love does not include a suggestion that Christians ought to love those not of their own immediate religious family. Indeed, in the history of the West, sibling rivalry has frequently been more destructive than has opposition to people of other religions. Augustine seldom advocated love for the common good, including people with different beliefs, values, practices, and institutional affiliations. No doubt Augustine would have his readers love all these as "enemies," that is, in order to cajole or coerce them to his own position.

Perhaps Augustine was able to imagine unconditional love when he described love as participation in God, but, diverted by the immediate pressures in which he lived and worked, he was unable to sustain that vision. His frustratingly interwoven passages on love and on Donatist "Antichrists" support this suggestion. Augustine was unable to act on the principle of love, but that does not cancel his powerful description. Critically retrieved, his vision of love can ground commitment to the common (pluralistic) good, despite his own on-location sabotage of it.

Chapter 4

WHO IS "WE"?

Augustine's Debate with the Manichaeans

———— • ————

It must, no doubt, seem strange that my soul and that of any and everybody else should be one thing only: it might mean my feelings being felt by someone else, my goodness another's too, my desire his desire, all our experience shared with each other and with the one universe, so that the very universe itself would feel what I feel. We are in sympathetic relation to one another, suffering, overcome at the sight of pain, naturally drawn to forming attachments; and all this can be due only to some unity among us.

— Plotinus, *Enneads*

Historians are often asked to comment on the relationship of historical understanding to contemporary problems, another way of asking whether historical texts can be read "for life," to illuminate or comment on present concerns. In spite of our discomfort with such questions, it also seems unaffordably luxurious to study history for its own sake. On the one side, presentism threatens; on the other, irrelevance. How, then, to negotiate between the two dangers? Perhaps the sensitivities of the present can legitimately provide critical perspectives on historical texts and events. Might it also be possible to gain insight into our own lives from study of the past? This chapter will attempt such a hazardous double enterprise.

Present ecological crises have prompted many late twentieth-century people to examine dominant Western conceptualizations of the natural world. In this chapter I explore the distant historical moment in which the beliefs, values, and loyalties that have supported the undisciplined use of natural resources and the abuse of animals were formulated and argued. I will ask whether the defeated position has some valuable suggestions that can be critically recovered.

At the end of the fourth century of the Common Era, Augustine, bishop of Hippo, argued for an understanding of "human community" and responsibility against his opponents, the North African Manichaeans. In the debate, Augustine stated that human community, and therefore human responsibility, is limited to rational minds, that is, to human beings. Because of his rhetorical skill and institutional power, as well as the force of his argument, Augustine's understanding became the dominant Western view.

Against Augustine's definition of community, Manichaeans taught that humans participate in a wider community of living beings. They included animals, plants, and even soil and rocks in their idea of community, thereby proposing a vastly enlarged province of human responsibility. The Manichaean view of human community and responsibility was not a peculiar feature of their religious sensibility but a view shared by Stoics and Neoplatonists. Yet, despite widespread adherence to this view in late antiquity, it failed to enter the mainstream of Western attitudes and values. Even so, remnants of Manichaeans' empathy with all living beings are to be found in the later history of Christianity, especially in Saint Francis's idea of the need for "mutual deference" between humans and animals (thirteenth century)[1] and in Anabaptists' "gospel of all creatures" (sixteenth century).[2]

The effects of Augustine's idea that humans can and should be indifferent to the suffering of any but rational beings and his intense and detailed focus on human suffering are, I suspect, writ too large to yield to the microscopic scrutiny to which responsible scholarship is adjusted. Moreover, it would be reductionistic to imply that Augustine's theory of human community is solely responsible for Western attitudes toward the natural world; historical effects are too various to be explained by a single idea. Nevertheless, the decisive defeat of the Manichaean view has had long-term effects in the history of the West.

In the last decade of the twentieth century, newscasts enumerate the effects of congenital inattentiveness to living beings. How the twentieth-century world might have been different if the Manichaean vision of community had carried the day must be conjecture. Yet it is likely that if the doctrine of a suffering Jesus, "hanging on every tree," symbol of the struggle and suffering of the whole creation, had woven itself into mainstream Christianity, the exploitative anthropocentrism of Western societies might have been significantly modified.

Examination of these two different religious sensibilities and value systems reveals their historical construction and opens dominant Western ideas of nature, the natural world, and living beings to *de*construction and *re*construction. For centuries of hindsight suggest that Augustine's understanding of human community and responsibility does not adequately serve the desperate ecological needs of the present. It is important to understand the place of the Manichaeans' doctrine of human responsibility within their beliefs, so in what follows I discuss these in some detail. But it is not necessary to accept all the Manichaeans' beliefs to appreciate their insistence that human beings are responsible for the welfare of the whole. To read Augustine's conflict with Manichaeans "as if for life," then, is to understand the historical contingency of our received notion of human community. Having done so, we may want to revise our understanding of human community, extending our responsibility to all living beings with whom humans are interdependent. I will describe Manichaeanism as a religious movement before examining its beliefs and values.

Manichaeanism in North Africa

Mani, a Persian who called himself the "apostle of Jesus Christ," claimed to offer a revelation that superseded that of Christ's earthly teachings. He taught that the Holy Spirit, promised three centuries before, had finally descended on him. Mani was martyred by crucifixion in 276 C.E. at the instigation of Zoroastrian priests. Manichaeanism was a secret religion, but it was also a missionary religion with claims to universality.[3] Within Mani's lifetime it had spread beyond Mesopotamia to Iran and adjoining parts of the Roman Empire. Advancing along commercial routes, Manichaean groups were also in Arabia, Armenia, Syria, Asia Minor (including Palestine), the Balkans, Italy, Spain, and Gaul. Manichaeanism spread from Egypt to North Africa at an early date, "nearly twenty years earlier than the first reference to Manichaeanism in Rome."[4]

Manichaeanism was syncretistic, incorporating features of Buddhism, Zoroastrianism, Taoism, Confucianism, and Christianity. It was suspect in the Roman Empire, however, not only for its ideas but also for its place of origin — Persia, the third-century "California" of new religious movements. This "most persecuted of heresies" was not accepted by the religions with which it sought to affiliate, perhaps largely because Mani claimed to have the only true interpretation of each.[5] Nevertheless, despite Mani's claims to possess Truth, the virtual absence of polemical literature in Manichaeanism is striking in comparison with the volume of anti-Manichaean literature.

Latin translations of Manichaean texts appeared at the end of the third century, less than a century after the first North African Christian writings in Latin. The great tomes containing Mani's teachings were inscribed with graceful calligraphy and lavishly illustrated. Tradition has it that Mani himself was a skillful painter; he is reported to have said of his teachings: "I have written them in books and pictured them in colors; let him who hears them in words also see them in an image, and let him who is unable to learn them from words learn them from pictures."[6]

Only twenty years or so after Mani's death, sometime between March 31, 297, and the same date in 302, Emperor Diocletian dispatched the first prohibition of Manichaeanism to Julianus, the proconsul of Africa. The rescript demanded that "Manichees and magicians and their sacred books" be burned. Yet, in the West, the fourth century was the time of the greatest numerical and geographical development of Manichaeanism, as well as its greatest persecution. Following Diocletian's edict outlawing Manichaeanism, emperors throughout the fourth century reiterated and attempted to enforce the edict, but Manichaeanism survived both the Arian Vandal rulers of fifth-century North Africa and Justinian's (sixth-century) reconquest of North Africa. As late as 724, "Pope Gregory II would still warn against the ordination of Africans who had fled to Italy from Islamic invaders because many of them were either still Manichaeans or former heretics who had been rebaptized."[7] Manichaeanism existed in North Africa until Christianity itself was extinguished by Islamic invasions.[8]

At the time of its encounter with Augustine, Manichaeanism had been established in North Africa for almost a century.[9] It flourished within Catholic congregations,[10] claiming to be an intellectually sophisticated and rigorously ascetic version of Catholic Christianity,[11] a Christianity of the inquiring mind.[12] Augustine acknowledged that one of his subdeacons had been a Manichaean hearer for years without being detected by the Catholic congregation to which he ministered (*Ep.* 236.1–3). Although historians have emphasized the differences between Catholics and Manichaeans, these differences seem to have been less evident on location. Both the popularity of Manichaeanism and its compatibility with Catholic Christianity made it especially difficult to extirpate from North Africa.[13]

Ironically, Augustine himself was repeatedly and throughout his life accused of Manichaeanism.[14] His ordination was delayed while these suspicions were investigated. In fact, in his youth, he had been a Manichaean hearer for nine years; his *Confessions* describes both his attraction to Manichaeanism and his subsequent disenchantment. As a Catholic priest and bishop, his commitment to ascetic monasticism and his teaching that sex is implicated in the transmission of original sin repeatedly sparked accusations that he had never completely departed from the religion of his youth.[15] Perhaps his personal vendetta against Manichaeanism was motivated at least in part by his eagerness to demonstrate his orthodoxy.

Manichaean Beliefs

Manichaeans were dualists, positing a kingdom of light and a kingdom of darkness eternally at war with each other. Their primary appeal to the young Augustine lay in their clear and satisfying answer to the question of the origin of evil. The kingdom of darkness, eternally at odds with the kingdom of light, was the cause of pain and evil; it was also the home of bodies and the natural world. However, Manichaeans' metaphysical dualism was tempered by their recognition that, *in experience,* the kingdom of darkness and the kingdom of light, the material and the spiritual worlds, were intertwined.[16] All material things contain sentient particles of spiritual light, suffering in their entrapment in the material world of bodies and yearning to reunite with their spiritual homeland.[17]

Materiality was seen as the creation of an evil Demiurge. The experience of alienation was thus an intimate and urgent aspect of embodiment. As a Manichaean hymn puts it: "Who shall take off from me this...body, and clothe [me] in a new body?"[18] The *Cologne Codex* relates that Mani's divine mission became clear to him in a revelation that distinguished his spiritual from his material origin. It revealed "who is my father in the height and in what way I was separated from him" and "through what woman I was brought into birth and delivered according to this flesh." Embodiment — and its inevitable suffering — is explicitly gendered and devalued in this association of spirit and light with the father and flesh with the mother.[19] The revelation further instructed Mani to remember "what command and instruction He gave to me before I was clothed with this organ and before I fell into error in this loathsome flesh and before I put on this intoxication and its habits."[20]

Manichaeans had a vivid and concrete sense of the suffering of living beings. The *Cologne Codex* relates that before Mani organized his own religion, while he was still a member of another sect, he was forced to do agricultural work. He withdrew from the sect and founded his own religion when he discovered, as he worked, that "blood oozed from the places where the plants had been hurt by the blows of the sickle. They also cried out with a human voice because of the blows they received."[21]

Manichaean literature describes the poignant longing of the light particles to return to the kingdom of light, a longing believed to be at its most acute in human beings. One Manichaean understanding of Jesus — an understanding documented only in North Africa — was that of *Jesus patibilis,* Jesus, the prototypical and quintessential living soul, perennially trapped and suffering in the world of the senses.[22] Augustine quotes Faustus's description of the suffering Jesus: "The Holy Spirit, by his influence and spiritual infusion, makes the earth conceive and bring forth the mortal Jesus, who, as hanging from every tree, is the life and salvation of humanity" (*C. Faust.* 20.11).

A Manichaean text, preserved in Sogdian fragments, contains a confession of sin against the five kinds of living beings, "the two-legged human beings, the four-legged living beings, the flying living beings, the living beings in the water, and the living beings creeping on the ground on their belly":

If we ever, my God, somehow have inspired with fear (or) scared these five kinds of living beings from the biggest to the smallest, if we somehow should have beaten or cut them, somehow have pained and tortured them, somehow should have killed them, we to the same degree owe life to the living beings. (Therefore) we now, my God, pray that we may be liberated from sin. Forgive my sin.[23]

From Augustine's perspective, North African Manichaeans displayed an emotional and virtually neurasthenic sensitivity to suffering — human, animal, plant, and mineral.[24]

Manichaean Practices

Manichaeanism was also a "highly regulated way of life."[25] Augustine is the source of a rich store of information about Manichaean practices in North Africa. These must be described under two categories: those required of hearers and those expected only of the "perfect" or the "elect." Regulations for both were designed to avoid actions that might harm the light particles or further entrench them in matter. For Manichaeans, nothing short of the redemption of God was at stake. The release of the light speeds the "Future Moment" in which the material world will be abandoned to its native evil and strife. The faithful will be translated to the kingdom of light, there to participate in and enjoy this blissful reward: the hearers will be at the right hand of the triumphant Jesus while the elect will be transformed into angels.[26]

Hearers lived as fully functioning members of secular society. They were permitted to marry but encouraged not to bear children. Their duties to the sect consisted primarily of a "soul service" in which they cared for the elect, providing and preparing their daily ritual meal. The *Kephalaia of the Teacher,* a fourth-century Egyptian document, describes the relationship of food practices to the release of light particles: "The alms which pass over to the Elect are made like many Icons, and they are purified, and they depart to the Country of the Living."[27] At their death, hearers expected to be reincarnated, and the body to which they were reassigned was contingent on the quality and faithfulness of their service to the elect.

The lifestyle of the elect was considerably more strenuous. Augustine described the "Three Seals" in *De moribus manichaeorum:* the Seal of the Mouth, the Seal of the Hands, and the Seal of the Breast. The Seal of the Mouth prohibited blasphemous speech as well as the eating of meat and drinking of wine. Vegetarianism was prescribed because the bodies of animals contain fewer light particles than those of plants. Wine was forbidden because it induces forgetfulness of one's home in the kingdom of light, a forgetfulness that Manichaean teachings, doctrines, hymns, and prayers resisted.

The Seal of the Hands stipulated that the elect must not perform any task that might harm the particles of light. They were "forbidden to till the soil, or to pluck fruit, or to harvest any plant or to kill any animal, no matter how small."[28] Bathing was also forbidden, for Manichaeans focused on the pollution of the water by dirt from the body rather than on the cleansing of the body. The Seal of the Breast forbade sexual intercourse because it results in the propagation of more flesh in which light particles are painfully enslaved.

Manichaean rituals were conducted in private homes.[29] Once a day hearers and elect gathered, the hearers to prepare and witness the meal consumed by the elect — it was called "eucharist" in North Africa. At this solemn ritual, the beautiful and haunting Manichaean hymn cycles and psalms were also sung.[30] A weekly confession of sins — hearers to elect, and elect to elect — completed Manichaeans' ritual practice. Since the death of both hearers and elect represented a liberation from the kingdom of darkness, their deaths were apparently not mourned with funeral rites, though there was a "body and soul" rite, which remains obscure.

Throughout his treatise *The Practices of the Manichaeans,* Augustine argues that intentions, rather than actions, are the decisive, indeed, the only, criterion for virtue. He acknowledges that the Manichaean elect practice celibacy, fasting, abstinence from wine, and vegetarianism, but he asks: "What is your goal in this? The end is the thing to look to" (*De mor. mani.* 17.28). He also questions the consistency of their asceticism: "You praise and teach these things without doing them." "During nine full years when I attended you with great earnestness and assiduity," he writes, "I could not hear of one of your elect who was not found transgressing.... Many were caught at wine and animal food, many at the baths.... Some were proved to have seduced other men's wives" (*De mor. mani.* 19.68). He is careful to note that "this we heard only by report." He personally witnessed only one incident in which several Manichaean men harassed a woman "with indecent sounds and gestures." But Manichaeans accused Catholics of similar misdemeanors. Replying to these accusations, Augustine can only point to the likelihood of observing immoral behavior in a group as large as the Catholic Church. The "scanty membership" of the Manichaeans, he says, ought to make it easier for them to monitor scandalous behavior. As with most religious conflicts, mutual accusations of immorality reduce to a draw. In fact, neither Catholic laypeople nor Manichaean hearers had a distinctive lifestyle. Both Catholics and Manichaeans had a two-tiered organization in which considerably more was expected of "full-time" Christians — monks or elect — than was expected of rank-and-file members.

Lacking independent information on Manichaean practices in North Africa, it is difficult to know how to evaluate the accuracy of Augustine's nonsystematic and frankly adversarial descriptions. Yet clearly, the Manichaeans had held a strong attraction for Augustine. He cites their organization (small groups of hearers gathered around several elect) and their friendliness (the sense of belonging he experienced as a member of one of these cells) as part of the attraction of Manichaeanism.

Human Community and Responsibility

Two treatises, both written by Augustine in 388 C.E., shortly after his baptism, are especially helpful for understanding Augustine's conflict with the Manichaeans — *The Practices of the Catholics* (*De moribus catholicae*), and *The Practices of the Manichaeans* (*De moribus manichaeorum*). Augustine's rhetorical skills, newly converted to Christianity, are at their peak in these treatises. They demonstrate that some of Augustine's most characteristic and enduring theological tenets were developed in the polemical context of debate with the Manichees. After a brief exploration of Augustinian and Manichaean hermeneutics, I will focus on what they reveal of Augustine's understanding of human community and responsibility.

Augustine and his Manichaean opponent, Faustus, described the task of interpretation differently. Faustus alleged that Augustine relied naively on the authority of scripture, receiving "everything without examination, condemning the use of reason, which is the prerogative of human nature, and thinking it impiety to distinguish between truth and falsehood, and as much afraid of separating what is good and what is not as children are of ghosts" (*C. Faust.* 18.3). Faustus believed that interpretation and critical judgment are both inevitable and necessary: "Many things which pass in scripture... are spurious, and they must therefore be tested to find whether they are true and sound and genuine." Faustus seems to have characterized Augustine's position correctly. Augustine held that arguments must be found to reconcile whatever in scripture seems to be contradictory or less than exemplary: "If we are per-plexed by an apparent contradiction in scripture, it is not allowable to say, The author of this book is mistaken; but either the manuscript is faulty, or the translation is wrong, or you have not understood" (*C. Faust.* 21.5).

Each, however, caricatures the other's hermeneutics. In spite of Faustus's claim to greater hermeneutical sophistication, Faustus re-verted, at points, to literalistic interpretation. Moreover, not sur-prisingly, Augustine, though literalistic when describing Manichaean myths, was also capable of subtle interpretations of Christian scrip-tures and the Hebrew Bible. For example, he says that Manichaeans' idea of the God of the Hebrew Bible who "repents, or is envi-ous, or needy, or cruel, or who takes pleasure in the blood of men or animals" is not to be taken literally. He calls such literal inter-pretation "mental childishness" (*De mor. cath.* 11.16–18). Yet, in *The Practices of the Manichaeans,* he interprets quite literally the Manichaeans' three symbols.

In *The Practices of the Catholics,* Augustine agrees with the Man-ichaeans that the body is "man's heaviest bond." The soul loves the body merely from "force of habit," and "when the soul has turned completely to God, it will lose its attraction to the body, not only disregarding death, but even desiring it" (*De mor. cath.* 22.40). Au-gustine must disparage the body, in this polemical context, in order to support his deprecation of the senses. Since Manichaeans claimed to be able to quantify the different degrees of light in different ob-jects by their color, hue, and saturation, Augustine insists: "We are forbidden to regard things which are seen" (*De mor. cath.* 20.37). Similarly, in contrast to Manichaean sensitivity to suffering, he min-imizes its significance, stating that the mind can "soar above all torture free and glorious" (*De mor. cath.* 22.41). He seeks to es-tablish the independence of the rational mind over the exigencies of nature and the sufferings of life.

The primary purpose of Augustine's argument, however, is to insist that the Christian's responsibility consists of love of self, neigh-bor, and God: "It is impossible for one who loves God not to love himself.... We can think of no surer step towards the love of God than the love of human for human.... Our love of our neighbor is a sort of cradle of our love for God.... While the love of God is first in beginning, love of our neighbor is first in coming to perfection" (*De mor. cath.* 26.50–51). Indeed, love of neighbor must include concern for both the body and the soul of the neighbor. The neighbor's physical needs should be cared for, he says, with a sort of emotionless charity — the "calm of a rational serenity" (*De mor. cath.* 27.52–53). Doing good to the neighbor's soul entails, first, restraining him from wrongdoing through fear of God and, second, providing instruction that generates love for God (*De mor. cath.* 28.55–56).

This, Augustine's first full exposition of love of neighbor, reveals that his celebrated theological focus was articulated in the context of refuting Manichaeans' claim that the arena of human community and responsibility is nothing less than the whole creation. In rebuttal of the Manichaean appeal, Augustine wrote: "There is no community of rights between us and brutes and trees," and he cited scriptural precedents for the legitimacy of killing of animals (*De mor. mani.* 13.27).

Augustine claimed that the Manichaeans' extension of sympathetic community to plants, rocks, and soil diluted their empathy for human suffering: "You feel so much more for melons than for men" (*De mor. mani.* 17.62). He ridiculed the idea that plants suffer, that "part of God exists in corn, beans, cabbage, and flowers and fruits" (*De mor. mani.* 15.38). Acknowledging that animals suffer, he denied that their suffering constitutes a moral imperative for humans: "For we see and hear by their cries that animals die with pain, although man disregards this in a beast with which, as not having a rational soul, we have no community of rights" (*De mor. mani.* 18.52).

Augustine maintained love of the human neighbor as the centerpiece of his theology throughout his career. He continued to insist that the community of human accountability excludes animals, who exist to serve human beings and to provide food for them:

> When we read "Thou shalt not kill" we assume this does not refer to bushes, which have no feelings, nor to irrational creatures, flying, swimming, walking, or crawling, since they have no rational association with us, not having been endowed with reason as we are, and hence it is by a just arrangement of the Creator that their life and death are subordinated to our needs. (*De civ. dei* 1.20)

Different religious sensibilities underlie Augustine's theological "reality" and that of the Manichaeans. In contrast to Manichaeans' "emotional" view of the suffering universe, Augustine argued that the only "just judgment" results from a mind "composed," rational, and free of emotion. Moreover, Augustine's idea of God's relationship with the universe depends on his view of suffering. Augustine's God is "present by the power of divinity, for administering and ruling all things, undefilably, inviolably, incorruptibly, *without any connection with them*" (emphasis added). According to Augustine, the Manichaeans' God, by contrast, was intimately and integrally engaged in the world and its processes, deeply interior to the universe, "everywhere mixed up in heaven, in earth, in all bodies, dry and moist, in all sorts of flesh, in all seeds of trees, herbs, humans and animals... fettered, oppressed, polluted" (*De boni natura* 46.44).

Conclusions

The triumph of Augustine's construction of "human community" as composed solely of "rational beings" presented an influential rationale for the use of animals and plants for human pleasure and aggrandizement. Along with, and as an interpretation of, the Genesis injunction to "be fruitful and multiply and subdue the earth," Augustine advocated what came to be the dominant Western attitude of indifference to animal suffering and to the exploitation of natural resources.

Ironically, Augustine's argument does not seem to have produced the sensitivity to human suffering that he intended. Indeed, although he professed a vivid empathy for human suffering, his views on society precluded sympathy for many varieties of human suffering. A complex hierarchical structure of human beings based on gender and class privileged "higher" over "lower," effectively isolating Augustine's "community of rational minds" to ruling-class men.

From his earliest description of society, in *The Practices of the Catholics* 30.63, to his mature social theory, in *City of God* 19.13–15, Augustine held the same view. In a fallen world, he saw no other social possibility than domination and subordination. Social order, he wrote, begins within human beings in the soul's obedient subordination to God and the soul's domination over the body. The relationship of ruler and ruled is echoed in all social relationships — in the subordination of wife to husband, subjects to rulers, and slaves to masters. Even when applied solely to human community, then, Augustine's theory of sympathy and responsibility fails to promote inclusiveness. Suffering that results from external domination, he writes, is much to be preferred over internal slavery to some lust, for slaves can transcend their condition by "serving with the fidelity of affection" (*De civ. dei* 19.15).

The metaphysical dualism of the Manichaeans, while objectionable from many twentieth-century perspectives, was, curiously, compatible with a strongly developed sensitivity to the suffering of all living beings. Augustine's "community of rational minds," institutionalized in Catholic Christianity and Western societies, does not seem justified in its effects. Augustine could not have predicted those effects, but they are abundantly visible from late twentieth-century perspectives.

Even if some Manichaean values are useful for our own time, however, they require critical reformulation. Although Augustine's Catholic Christianity defeated Manichaeanism, some distinctively Manichaean values emerged within Catholic Christianity. For example, dualism of body and soul, explicitly rejected by Augustine on the basis of Jewish and Christian scripture and doctrine, survived in the rhetoric surrounding ascetic practices. As Augustine insisted, asceticism need not imply that any of the objects of a world created good must be rejected. Yet devotional manuals consistently emphasized the worthlessness of bodies, objects, and pleasures. In the Christian West, both ascetic practices and a philosophical tradition that privileged rational thought over embodied life have created hierarchical dualisms.

Although twentieth-century opponents of traditional dualism often wrongly name Augustine as one of dualism's historical proponents, it found, in Descartes, an articulate early modern representative. Why have dualistic explanations of human life and experience seemed plausible, even conceptually compelling, to people throughout Western history? Can more fruitful descriptions be found than those that understand human being as an uneasy forced alliance of spirit and flesh? Consider one recent attempt to accomplish this complex task.

In *The Absent Body,* Drew Leder proposes an alternative to Cartesian dualism. He begins by examining why dualistic explanation has proved so attractive to centuries of Western thinkers.[31] He rejects Cartesian dualism and suggests an alternative only after he has shown that features of human experience suggested and recommended dualism as a description.[32]

Leder's phenomenological alternative to Descartes's dualism of mind and body is the "lived body," "an ecstatic and recessive being, engaged both in a leaping out and a falling back."[33] The lived body includes the integrated operation of mind and body, an operation that is not, strangely, a feature of direct experience. We experience our bodies, Leder argues, only when the "machine" dysfunctions, when pain or disease blocks the spontaneous outward intentionality of the lived body. Similarly, the mind is a "ghost" that disappears from experience in the activity of thought. The mind's disappearance in thought and the healthy body's "dys-appearance" explain why Descartes's theory has received intuitive assent.

Aristotle and Plotinus believed that all living beings participate in one soul; Leder proposes that the universe can be seen as one body. In fact, he says, this is precisely what religious ritual celebrates. Religious ritual assumes and enacts the unity of the world of ideas and sensible objects. Moreover, it does not require the disciplined vision of the sage to understand the internal unity of the universe; this experience is intimately and democratically accessible. Leder quotes the Neo-Confucian philosopher Wang Yang-ming's (1472–1529) *Inquiry on the Great Learning:*

> Even the mind of the small man is no different [from that of the sage].... Therefore when he sees a child about to fall into a well, he cannot help a feeling of alarm and commiseration. This shows that his humanity forms one body with the child. Again, when he observes the pitiful cries and frightened appearance of birds and animals about to be slaughtered, he cannot help feeling an "inability to bear" their suffering. This shows that his humanity forms one body with birds and animals. It may be objected that birds and animals are sentient beings as he is. But when he sees plants broken and destroyed, he cannot help a feeling of pity. This shows that his humanity forms one body with plants. It may be said that plants are living things as he is. Yet, even when he sees tiles and stones shattered and crushed, he cannot help a feeling of regret. This shows that his humanity forms one body with tiles and stones. This means that even the mind of the small man necessarily has the humanity that forms one body with all.[34]

Wang Yang-ming's description of an intuitive mystical bond among living beings replicates Manichaean sensitivity to suffering. It contrasts strikingly with Augustine's notion of the community of rational minds as the basic unit of human empathy and responsibility.

Until the second half of the twentieth century, it has not been possible to identify and to map with scientific precision the interconnectedness of living beings. A few Western and Eastern philosophers, like Plotinus and Wang Yang-ming, have intuited an interdependent web of sentient and nonsentient entities. But their vision could not be documented, so those who subscribed to it have been labeled "romantic," "soft," or "nature worshipers" by "hardheaded" philosophers. But a sea change for thought has occurred in our time, brought about by the scientific capacity to measure and the technological capability to circulate descriptions of the tangible effects of environmental crises such as the disappearance of rain forests, the extinction of animal species, and pollution of air, water, and food. The fundamental fact of life at the end of the twentieth century is that the universe is utterly interdependent. This knowledge is no longer intuited or romantic, but factual and concrete.

Sociobiologists, philosophers, science-fiction writers, and ecologists describe the essential interdependence of all forms of life. Secular spiritualities also advocate loyalty to the earth and its resources. Can responsibility to a community of living beings be seen as a Christian commitment?

The dominant Christian tradition certainly contains suggestions for such a mandate. The doctrines of creation, of an incarnate God, and of resurrection of the body imply the religious worth of the sensible world. Yet, for reasons too complex to discuss here, these suggestions have not been effective in bonding Christians' loyalties to the natural world. Judaism and non-Western religions have emphasized more effectively than Christianity the consummate value of the earth and its creatures.

Christian tradition must be revisioned if its resources are to be made visible. It cannot be seen as consisting solely of a coherent and cohesive system of ideas and practices but must also be understood as an intense and continuous conflict over the interpretation and practical appropriation of its ambiguous, often contradictory, content. Historical circumstances rather than timeless truth have decided the outcome of these struggles over interpretation. Seen in this light, faithfulness to "the Christian tradition" requires attention to the perspectives and values of both sides of conflicts. When this is done, Christian traditions can be seen to contain multiple resources for rethinking the dominant Christian tradition.

Manichaean constructions of the community of all living beings contain a powerful mystical appeal, but they also raise two questions. First, the inclusion of soil and rocks in the community of life would seem to dilute drastically the moral imperative of responsibility. In fact, in Manichaeanism itself, this comprehensive community of life was sustained only in belief. Although the elect were protected from agricultural work, hearers provided food for them.

For most people, some constructions of human community are more intuitively accessible than others. To think of human community as coextensive with soil and rocks requires an intense, profound, and inclusive mystical vision that is not likely to be achieved by many people. Thus, although there may be theoretical and practical reasons for doing so, more is lost than gained by insisting that rocks and soil are part of human beings' community. Simple self-interest may be a more honest rationale for advocating the responsible use of soil and minerals.

Second, the notion of community may need revision before the term can indicate the diversity that exists in a community of all living beings. Recently, Iris Young has argued that appeals to community "privilege unity over difference, immediacy over mediation, sympathy over recognition of the limits of one's understanding of others from their point of view."[35] The anthropocentrism of many contemporary ecological groups is often masked and perpetuated by appealing to the self-interest of the human community.

Young's critique of the idea of community assumes a community of human beings, a community closer to Augustine's community of rational minds than to the Manichaeans' community of life. Since some minds are considered more rational than others, the appeal to a community of rational minds has led to exclusionary practices. A community of life, in contrast, can hardly fail to highlight and delight in difference, in "unassimilated otherness" and "inexhaustible heterogeneity."[36] If the notion of a community of life is to correct the abuses fostered by the community of rational minds, a "real universality," that is, an actual interdependency, must replace Augustine's "fictitious universality," or constructed reality.[37] Augustine's formulation selects one human characteristic on which to base community, while, as Plotinus and the Manichaeans contended, living beings are alike only in their participation in the fragile, evanescent, and exuberant property of life.

Despite the dangers inherent in the appeal to community, responsibility to a community of living beings has a rhetorical persuasiveness and popular appeal in a world threatened by ecological and nuclear crises. And popular appeal is necessary to motivate and stimulate political activity to address abuses of the natural world. Unlike fourth-century Manichaeans, twentieth-century people have unprecedented power — for good or ill — to intervene in the conditions of life for humans as well as for other creatures. No fourth-century Manichaean could have imagined a world in which myriad species are moving toward extinction and natural resources are in danger of exhaustion. In a world in which the fate of all living beings depends on human responsibility, religious traditions must be criticized for their damaging ideas and practices, but they can also contribute to vivid and persuasive appeals for empathy with all living creatures.

Part II

INTRODUCTION

FROM THE TEXTS and historical situations described in Part I, I have begun to compile some usable notions for living a simultaneously enjoyable and generous life: a vision of a spiritual universe in which life circulates into and through the many forms that briefly contain it; an inclusive picture of the interdependent world of living beings; and the suggestion that all love participates in, localizes, and embodies the immense universal generosity Christians call God. I have also begun to see a range of possible relationships between perceptions of beauty and moral responsibility. Beauty can seduce observers, masking injustices, or the perception of beauty can be understood as a basis for moral action.

I explored ideas — such as that of human community and responsibility — *as occasions* rather than as intellectual formulations. Seen as occasions, as responses to concrete situations and debates, ideas within religious traditions lose their tyranny. They can be reexamined and evaluated in the light of present experience. Granting that particular ideas held profound attraction for the people whose perspective is represented by our historical text, we can also recognize their inadequacy, risks, or destructiveness in our own situation.

The historical record of living religious traditions must be explored through the writings that inevitably present their authors' intentions in the best possible light. But the social effects of those ideas in particular contexts must also be investigated. Equipped with different sensitivities and living in immensely different situations, we must reevaluate the usefulness of historically victorious ideas and methods for the dilemmas and threats of our own time. Seeing *how they worked*, then, leads not to fruitless condemnation of historical authors, events, and ideas but to critical recovery of the ideas most fruitful for our time.

My image of the seriousness, the intrepid inventiveness, with which one must seek resources for living a humanly rich life comes from the epic *Beowulf*. The hero Beowulf undertakes to slay a monster who by night routinely snatches men from the mead hall. He tracks the monster, Grendel, to her den under a great lake, clutching his sword, Naegling. The sword's recorded accomplishments, including a list of the strong men killed by it, occupies several pages of the epic. Yet when Beowulf reaches Grendel's den, "his flashing blade was harmless and would not bite. Its edge had failed its master in his hour of need."[1] Desperate, Beowulf looks around the walls for a weapon and sees a "fine giant sword hanging from a wall." Grabbing it, he kills the monster.

Beowulf's own sword, his carefully honed weapon, has failed in spite of its documented power. Nothing he brought with him was of any use. Rather, the weapon appropriate to the conflict was provided on the spot and in the moment of need. Just so, the one who seeks the images necessary for imagining and conducting a rich life must accept those images where they appear. She must be on the alert for resources at every moment, in every situation, and in every literary genre.

It should come as no surprise that I do not find, in the literature of late antiquity, everything I need to construct a repertoire of fruitful ideas for my historical moment, ideas that conduce to enjoyment of beauty and moral responsibility. I turn, then, to several twentieth-century authors for their suggestions.

Between 500 C.E. and the end of the twentieth century, the world has grown smaller; distances have seemed to decrease as travel and communication technology have become faster and more effective. Americans have information about events that occur in remote regions of the world; they can also travel there. Media have established global networks. People from distant lands also come to North America, live alongside Americans, and share a highly diverse, but geographically common, society and culture.

American public life is richly complex, both in problems and in resources. For example, while U.S. troops were fighting in a Muslim country during the 1991 Gulf War, Muslims were rapidly overtaking Jews as the second largest religious group in the United States. Americans cannot now understand Muslims only as distant enemies but must also accept them as neighbors.

In this context, many late twentieth-century North Americans struggle toward theorizing and practicing pluralism. Pluralism supports and enjoys the presence and participation in American society of multiple religious, social, ethnic, and sexual-orientation perspectives. A commitment to pluralism does not preclude commitment to particular beliefs and values but includes *in* one's own beliefs willingness to respect, learn from, and delight in others' beliefs and lifestyles. In the light of the present struggles toward pluralism, people of earlier times who were preoccupied with struggling for religious and cultural hegemony, and with defining and rejecting the religious and/or cultural "other," often seem unconscionably chauvinistic.

Nevertheless, twentieth-century authors are not always unambiguous models. Alongside compelling and creative insights, they often present what Jung called a "shadow" aspect. Moreover, we often have more biographical information about them than we do for authors separated from us by fifteen hundred years. Thus, there is a lively current debate over the relevance of biographical information to evaluation of an author's work. I will not join that complex debate. I use biographical information for purposes of contextualizing an author's work, but, as I argued in relation to Augustine's *Homilies on the First Epistle of John* and Plotinus's *Enneads,* an author's ideas may be useful to readers well beyond the author's own ability consistently to apply and practice them.

Four examples of relationships between beauty and moral responsibility will occupy us in the next chapters. I discuss C. G. Jung's autobiography, *Memories, Dreams, Reflections;* Rainer Maria Rilke's *Duino Elegies;* Leni Riefenstahl's *Memoir;* and Toni Morrison's novel *Jazz.* I hope my readers have read these texts. To the extent that this cannot be assumed, however, I will provide enough orientation to make my discussions freestanding. Beyond that, I hope my questions and suggestions will encourage and expedite readers' own critical reading for life.

Chapter 5

READING ONE'S OWN LIFE
C. G. Jung's *Memories, Dreams, and Reflections*

——————— • ———————

The world into which we are born is brutal and cruel, and at
the same time of divine beauty.
                              —C. G. JUNG, *Memories, Dreams, Reflections*

C ARL GUSTAV JUNG'S *Memories, Dreams, Reflections* has been a
profoundly provocative book for me.[1] The autobiography of a
man who professed to live primarily, if not entirely, from his inner
depths has, on each reading, evoked and encouraged a commitment
to understanding my psyche. In this chapter I will not attempt either
a synopsis of Jung's psychology or a biography; both have been done
by experts, and I will refer to them. I will, rather, read Jung's autobiography "for life," for the profound usefulness of some of his
ideas. I will also read critically, with an eye to identifying what I
believe to be limitations and shortsightedness in Jung's vision.

Autobiography constrains the reader to approach an author's
ideas in the context of his life, the social and institutional arrangements within which he worked, and the socially accepted
assumptions of his time. I have suggested that it is entirely possible that an author can think more generously and insightfully than
he can live. Ideas occur in the context of particular social and institutional arrangements and intellectual climates. But the reader who
refuses to glean from any author whose social, political, and institutional conditions are not identical with her own will dismiss many
useful ideas that could be critically retrieved. Ideas must always be
considered in the particular contexts in which their use is proposed.
An idea that was fruitful in one context can be destructive in another.
Conversely, an idea that harmed many people in one context may become a liberating and/or productive idea in another. The beauty —
and the terror — of ideas is that they cannot be evaluated apart

from their particular concrete effects in the situations in which they are used.

Jung's autobiography, *Memories, Dreams, Reflections,* describes his psychological proposals as they occurred in his long, contentious, and productive life (1875–1961). Written when he was in his eighties and finished shortly before his death, it reviews the insights, experiences, and conflicts that together formed his clinical and theoretical work. But the autobiography presents, above all, what Jung calls his "personal myth": "My life is a story of the self-realization of the unconscious. Everything in the unconscious seeks outward manifestation, and the personality too desires to evolve out of its unconscious conditions and to experience itself as a whole." Jung insists that "interior happenings...make up the singularity of my life" (*MDR* 5). Yet the eventful exterior of that life is striking: Jung enjoyed an international reputation and was continuously embroiled in controversy over his ideas. His internal life, then, provided a ballast for his external life. Rather than seeing himself as formed by whatever happened, he used circumstances to weave the rich tapestry of his inner life.

Jung was reluctant to write an autobiography. He insists instead that he *is* his autobiography. Like all autobiographies, Jung's seeks to present a complex and often self-contradictory life as an integrated whole. But integration plays a larger than literary role; for Jung, autobiography — the demonstration of a complex integration — is both his professional and his personal work and goal:

> The "autobiography" is my life, viewed in the light of the knowledge I have gained from my scientific endeavors. Both are one, and therefore this book makes great demands on people who do not know or understand my scientific ideas. My life has been in a sense the quintessence of what I have written, not the other way around. The way I am and the way I write are a unity. All my ideas and all my endeavors are myself. Thus the "autobiography" is merely the dot on the i. (*MDR* xii)

"I am my writings": this is an unusual claim. Most people feel that they cannot fully express their feelings or ideas in writing. Did Jung have no second thoughts when he reread something he wrote many years earlier? Apparently he did not seek to understand himself through writing, as Augustine did. He understood, and then he wrote, and his understanding is articulated, without omission or distortion. Startling as this claim is, it also represents an act of courage. Jung chose to stand behind all of his writings, rejecting the temptation to reevaluate his earlier thinking from the perspective of age and greater wisdom.

Did Jung also seek to present a personality that would encourage others to think well of him? Did he seek to present his life in the "best possible light"? Did he undertake to evaluate or judge himself? On the one hand, he disclaims judgment: "[W]e possess no standards, no objective foundation, from which to judge ourselves" (*MDR* 3). He does attempt, however, at least to analyze his feelings about his own "myth": "I am astonished, disappointed, pleased with myself. I am distressed, depressed, rapturous. . . . I have no judgment about myself and my life" (*MDR* 358; see also 113). Late in his autobiography, Jung summarizes his work: "A man once dipped a hatful of water from a stream. What did that amount to?" At his best, he says, he only "stand(s) and behold(s)" (*MDR* 355). Did he feel he had made a great achievement in mapping the human psyche? Jung says, "[T]he older I have become, the less I have understood or had insight into or known about myself" (*MDR* 358). Yet he also claims to have "reached the bounds of scientific understanding" (*MDR* 221). He reflects on his agenda:

> I have neither the desire nor the capacity to stand outside myself and observe my fate in a truly objective way. I would commit the familiar autobiographical mistake either of weaving an illusion about how it ought to have been, or of writing an *apologia pro vita sua*. In the end, man is an event which cannot judge itself, but, for better or worse, is left to the judgment of others. (*MDR* 113)

No wonder he was reluctant to write an autobiography, yielding to the task only at his colleagues' insistence. Judgment by others is a terrifying prospect, for human judges lack the God's-eye-view that may be willing to understand, and possibly, then, to forgive, all.

Two ideas of the first importance emerge from Jung's autobiography. First, the psyche is a fundamental reality of human life. Consciousness and the unconscious exist, act, and are related to each other in individuals as well as in collective humanity. Almost anything *could* be going on in the psyche, but one dynamic *is* going on.[2]

According to Jung, belief in the reality of the psyche has important consequences, both in an individual and in religion. Jung's God mirrors the psyche, guaranteeing its reality: "God is an obvious psychic and non-physical fact, i.e., a fact that can be established psychically but not physically."[3] I will return to Jung's ideas of God and religion.

The second major idea Jung presents is that understanding the psyche is an individual's primary lifework. Part of this work is understanding one's proclivities and avoidances, one's patterned responses to the world, one's own myth. The other, no less important part, is to understand the personal myth in relation to a collective myth.

From these two Jungian premises come a strong sense of individual life as "objective," grounded in psychic reality. Work on one's psyche, then, is the ongoing work of a lifetime. Throughout Jung's life, inner considerations determined his choices. In 1913, while he was traveling in Italy, for example, he wanted to go to Rome but did not do so because, after seeing Ravenna and Pompeii, he did not feel equal to "the impression the city would have made on me." Pompeii was "more than enough," he wrote; "the impressions very nearly exceeded my powers of receptivity." He recognized, of course, that it is perfectly possible to enjoy a city aesthetically, but "if you are affected to the depths of your being at every step by the spirit that broods there,...then it becomes another matter entirely" (*MDR* 287–88).

Jung states these two ideas, the reality of the psyche and the integration of consciousness and the unconscious as one's primary lifework, with remarkable force and vividness. Although he calls them facts, both are, in the final analysis, beliefs. Like articles of religious belief, once believed these ideas are abundantly demonstrable. Lacking belief, however, they are interesting interpretations of phenomena that could as easily be described otherwise.

Jung's primary ideas have stayed with me for many years during which I apparently forgot Jung and adopted my academic colleagues' disdain for his psychology. He also offered me a way to understand the Christian myth. Since my psyche was formed by Christianity, no matter how much I may deplore the failures of Christian institutions, the horrors of Christian history, the "absurdity" (as Tertullian said) of Christian dogma, and the airlessness of the Christianity of my childhood, I, like Jung, have found the Christian myth to be a powerful psychic reality.

God and Religion

Memories, Dreams, Reflections is the only place in Jung's extensive writings where he speaks of himself in relation to God. The son of a Lutheran pastor, Jung struggled with religious beliefs early in his childhood. He suffered something akin to John Bunyan's preconversion torments, presuming that God had an intention for him and unsure of what it was. Yet, although frequently reassured by family and friends, Jung had a boyhood conviction that he was "a corrupt and inferior person" (*MDR* 41). His father's religion seemed to him stifled by conventional ways of thinking. On the event of his first communion, he expected to be overwhelmed by "vast despair, overpowering elation, and [an] outpouring of grace" (*MDR* 53–54), but he reports simply "nothing happened." As an adult he scorned the phrase "religious community," saying it meant nothing at all to him (*MDR* 75).

Motivated by his childhood experiences of disorientation and disequilibrium, Jung took "penetrating into the secret of the personality" as his life's goal. "I knew so little about myself, and the little I knew was so contradictory that I could not with a good conscience reject any accusations" (*MDR* 44). He had an acute feeling not only of helplessness in the face of external forces — the bullies much bigger than he who beat him up — but also, and especially, of being at the mercy of "a psychic process which we do not control, [and] only partly direct" (*MDR* 4). "I always knew that I was two persons," a No. 1 self, an 1890s schoolboy, and a No. 2, or "true," self. The true self, Jung writes, "knew God as a hidden, personal, and at the same time suprapersonal secret. . . . It was as though the human mind looked down upon creation simultaneously with God" (*MDR* 45). This self, which he entered as soon as he was alone, became his secret possession, "the essential factor" of his boyhood:

> It occurred to me that I was actually two different persons. One
> of them was a schoolboy who could not grasp algebra and was
> far from sure of himself; the other was important, a high au-
> thority, a man not to be trifled with. . . . This "other" was an old
> man who lived in the eighteenth century, wore buckled shoes
> and a white wig. (*MDR* 33–34)

Despite the reassuring presence of the "true self," fragmentation of identity was a continuing and painful problem for Jung, at least partly because he believed that the self should be a unity. Yet he claimed that the split he experienced between personalities No. 1 and No. 2 "is played out in every individual" (*MDR* 45). While No. 1 contains the individual, No. 2 expresses another reality: "Although we human beings have our own personal life, we are yet in large measure the representatives, the victims and promoters of a collective spirit whose years are counted in centuries" (*MDR* 91).

"Society does not exist, there are only individuals," Jung said.[4] Although, in other contexts, he acknowledged the inescapability of community and society, he had no interest in their formative roles in shaping individuals. He omitted the social in his thinking, moving directly from the individual to the human collective. His neglect of the social and his trust of the collective psyche are illustrated in his statement: "I no longer attempted to put across my own opinion, but surrendered myself to the current of my thoughts" (*MDR* 297). When Jung considered community and society, he thought of them as playing a constraining role in the life of an individual. Anyone who endeavors to conform to a community and, at the same time, "to pursue his individual goal," he wrote, "becomes neurotic" (*MDR* 344). In a late work, *The Undiscovered Self*, Jung wrote: "The inner man remains unchanged no matter how much community he has. His environment cannot give him as a gift that which he can win for himself only with effort and suffering.... A favorable environment merely strengthens the dangerous tendency to expect everything from outside."[5]

Jung's neglect of communal and social factors in forming and supporting the individual was decisive for his ideas of religion. Jung's individual, like a good Protestant, confronts God directly. Although the goal of the quest is a collective myth, he omitted the mediating community that is crucial to religious practice.

Jung claimed that he didn't "believe" in God; rather, he had certain knowledge of God: "I cannot believe what I do not know, and what I know I need not believe in."[6] Experience of God, he said, is "the most evident of all experiences" (*MDR* 92). He rejected the God of his Lutheran father-pastor in favor of the "immediate living God who stands, omnipotent and free, above His Bible and His Church, who calls upon man to partake of His freedom, and can force him to renounce his own views and convictions in order to fulfil without reserve the command of God." As for Christian theology, "God himself had disavowed theology and the Church founded upon it....I

was equally sure that none of the theologians I knew had ever seen
'the light that shineth in the darkness' with his own eyes" (*MDR* 93).

As an old man he described a particularly vivid experience of God
that occurred seventy years before. Commenting on this experience,
he wrote: "It was obedience that brought me grace, and after that
experience I knew what God's grace was. One must be utterly abandoned to God; nothing matters but fulfilling his will. Otherwise all is
folly and meaninglessness" (*MDR* 93).

As a youth, his understanding of God resulted in isolation and
depression. Lacking human empathy and support, Jung expanded his
community to include animals, whom he found "dear and faithful,
unchanging and trustworthy, in contrast to people" (*MDR* 67). He
felt an "unconscious identity with animals" (*MDR* 101). Plants also
participated in "God's world:" "They expressed not only the beauty
but also the thoughts of God's world, with no intent of their own
and without deviation" (*MDR* 67).

Like Plotinus, Jung spoke of the interconnectedness of all living
beings. Unlike Plotinus, he extended this vision to seeing an interconnection between good and evil. Since, in Christian Europe, God's
goodness had been thoroughly articulated, Jung thought of the culture hero as one who brings to light God's dark side — by blasphemy,
if necessary. Jung's God "could be something terrible," forcing a
person to obey his commands, however heinous (*MDR* 40).

Books and authors also became allies in Jung's loneliness. They diverted him in depression, some of them affirming and strengthening
his own vision of the world. Schopenhauer was an especially important discovery for Jung. Schopenhauer spoke of the suffering of the
world, rejecting an "all-good and all-wise" Creator for a "somber
picture of the world" that Jung found much closer to his experience and observation than the Christian God. Juxtaposing the social
world to "God's world," Jung wrote: "To 'God's world' belonged
everything superhuman — dazzling light, the darkness of the abyss,
the cold impassivity of infinite space and time, and the uncanny
grotesqueness of the irrational world of chance. 'God,' for me, was
everything — and anything but 'edifying'" (*MDR* 72).

Jung's vision of an omnipotent and unpredictable God — a God
who "fills [humanity] with both good and evil"[7] — was at odds with
the comfortable loving God he was taught in church. Jung's God is to
be both loved and feared, whereas in his boyhood Lutheran church,
"fear of God...was considered antiquated, Jewish, and long since

superseded by the Christian message of God's love and goodness"
(*MDR* 47).[8] His mature description of God equated God with collective psychological truth: "God is a personality and is the ego of
the universe, just as I myself am the ego of my psychic and physical
being" (*MDR* 57). Nevertheless, it is important to develop a relation to this God of personal and collective destiny: "A man should
be able to say that he has done his best to form a conception of life
after death, or to create some image of it — even if he must confess
his failure. Not to have done so is a vital loss" (*MDR* 304).

Throughout his life, Jung worked to translate the figures of theology and dogma into psychic meaning. The Holy Ghost was, for Jung,
God's activity in the world, taking the place of Christ, as Christ himself had predicted. Jung did not "subscribe to the tendency to move
Christ into the foreground and make him the sole decisive figure in
the drama of God and man.... Lord Jesus was to me unquestion-
ably a man and therefore a fallible figure, or else a mere mouthpiece
of the Holy Ghost" (*MDR* 98). Because God is the psyche's ground
and reality, a religious orientation is central to individuation:

> The individual finds the real justification for his existence, and
> his own spiritual as well as moral autonomy, nowhere but in an
> extramundane principle that is capable of relativizing the over-
> powering influence of external factors. The individual who is
> not anchored in God can offer no resistance, on the strength of
> his own resources, to the physical and moral sway of the world.
> For this man needs the evidence of his own inner, transcendent
> experience.[9]

Contesting the "physical" as the only realm of concrete truth,
Jung pointed to psychic truth as synonymous with religious truth,
referring "without exception to things that cannot be established as
physical fact" but that nevertheless have *effects*.

Jung writes of his experiences of beauty as nourishing, reinforcing,
and motivating. Some of his first memories were of sensual beauty. A
visually sensitive child, he recognized beauty first as a physical property of vivid landscapes. Surrounded by mountains and lakes, Jung
as a child lived in an external world that was certainly beautiful,
but, lacking the contrast of flat spaces or monotone cities, it is remarkable that he saw that beauty *as* beauty at such a young age. He
wrote that, as a depressed youth, "I had a vision of unearthly beauty,
and that is why I was able to live at all."[10] In adulthood, he perceived

beauty both in the individual psyche's tortuous struggle toward unity and wholeness and in the "groaning and travailing" of the universe. "Certainly," he wrote, "the world is immeasurably beautiful, but it is quite as horrible" (*MDR* 58).[11] In old age and illness, he experienced visions accompanied by "the purest bliss":

> It was as if I were in an ecstasy. I felt as though I were floating in space, as though I were safe in the womb of the universe — in a tremendous void, but filled with the highest possible feeling of happiness. "This is eternal bliss," I thought. "This cannot be described; it is far too wonderful...." Those inner states were so fantastically beautiful that by comparison this world looked downright ridiculous.... It would be impossible to convey the beauty and intensity of emotion during those visions. (*MDR* 294–95)

Clearly, for Jung, perceptions of beauty played a central role in both motivating and rewarding psychic work.

Psychology

When Jung was a young man, his views were greeted with "utter incomprehension," which confirmed his isolation and his conviction that "in religious matters only experience counted" (*MDR* 98). His turn to the study of psychology represented a search for a religious outlook based on experience. Initially, however, he specialized in psychiatry because of his interest in the occult and because he was financially unable to acquire the necessary training for a specialization in surgery. Prepared for rejection and scorn by his efforts to communicate his religious views, he was well equipped to associate himself with psychiatry, which "at that time was quite generally held in contempt" (*MDR* 108).

At the time of Jung's medical training, a disease model of mental illness was prevalent in which "psychology played no role" (*MDR* 114). Through clinical work with patients, however, Jung realized that mental illness, far from being completely alien to "normality," contained "nothing new," nothing, that is, that is not already a "substratum of our own [sane] natures" (*MDR* 127). He was deeply respectful of the "richness and importance" of the inner experience of the mentally ill (*MDR* 130). The mentally ill, unable to deny the reality of the psyche, expose that intransigent reality. Jung acknowledged that he acquired insight into his own nature from his patients.

He saw that clinical diagnosis helps the doctor to orient himself toward the patient but fails to describe accurately the morphology of the illness (*MDR* 124). Similarly, he said, theories obfuscate rather than enable the task of understanding the psychic reality of the patient. Jung's religious individualism carried over into his psychology: "The solution of the problem is always an individual one" (*MDR* 131). The model of healing Jung described cut through psychiatry's claim to heal by means of the superior knowledge and will of the doctor. Rather: "The crucial point is that I confront the patient as one human being to another" (*MDR* 131). "Unless both doctor and patient become a problem to each other, no solution is found" (*MDR* 143). As an old man, Jung estimated that a third of the patients with whom he worked were cured; a third improved; and a third remained unaffected (*MDR* 143).

At a crucial point in early midlife, Jung journeyed into his own fantasies, visions, and psychic terrors. He describes himself as undergoing this profound and dangerous quest voluntarily:

> In order to grasp the fantasies that were stirring in me "underground," I knew I had to let myself plummet down into them, as it were. I felt not only violent resistance to this, but a distinct fear. For I was afraid of losing command of myself and becoming a prey to the fantasies — and as a psychiatrist I realized only too well what that meant. After prolonged hesitation, however, I saw that there was no other way out. (*MDR* 178)

One of Jung's biographers, John Kerr, suggests that Jung's claim that he explored his psyche voluntarily was somewhat disingenuous. His interpretation is that Jung "nearly went mad," and madness cannot be "summoned up as an experiment." Jung's retrospective accounts, Kerr says, romanticize the episode, which lasted for several years. Moreover, if these "experiments" have any value at all, if they taught Jung anything of use about the unconscious, it must lie precisely in their *in*voluntary nature.[12] Otherwise, they would have nothing to reveal about involuntary mental illness. I will return to this point.

Perhaps one of Jung's greatest attractions for the many people who admire his work is that he had fully as much to say about psychic health as about mental illness. He believed that even the fundamentally healthy psyche needs vigorous work. Barbara Hannah, Jung's colleague and biographer, reports that when Jung was nearly eighty, he remarked that "his whole life had been spent in eliminating his own childishness."[13] Jung's word for this lifelong work was "individuation."[14]

Individuation is not to be confused either with the development of individuality or with individualism, both of which exclude the collective aspects of the psyche.[15] Similarly, individuation is to be distinguished from the *persona,* "the sum total of the ideas an individual adopts because he belongs to certain groups: occupation, social class, caste, political party or nation."[16] The process of individuation includes several stages in identifying and understanding psychic contents that are potentially or actually destructive: "The essential thing is to differentiate oneself from these unconscious contents by personifying them, and at the same time to bring them into relationship with consciousness. That is the technique for stripping them of their power" (*MDR* 193).[17]

The first stage of the work of individuation consists of translating emotions into images: "To the extent that I managed to translate the emotions into images — that is to say, to find the images which were concealed in the emotions — I was inwardly calmed and reassured. Had I left those images hidden in the emotions, I might have been torn to pieces by them" (*MDR* 177).

Gradually, the fragments of the self expressed as images are brought into relationship with one another and hence into a working unity. Jung taught that, without conscious work, it will be left to death to define the individual's life. It is, of course, greatly preferable to accept the task of individuation intentionally, to participate consciously in the shaping of one's life. When this is done, "so much darkness comes to light that the personality is permeated with light, and consciousness necessarily gains in scope and insight."[18] Nevertheless, individuation carries many risks and dangers: "When one follows the path of individuation, when one lives one's own life, one must make mistakes into the bargain" (*MDR* 297).

Jung does not distinguish between individuation and what has traditionally been called the search for God. It was clear to him that God works through the unconscious, while consciousness is simultaneously attracted and resistant. In fact, he said, "We cannot tell whether God and the unconscious are two different entities." Yet "the God-image does not coincide with the unconscious as such, but with a special content of it, namely the archetype of the self" (*MDR* 199).

Jung described the goal of "completed individuation" as

[d]etachment from valuations and from what we call emotional ties. In general, emotional ties are very important to human beings. But they still contain projections, and it is essential to withdraw these projections in order to attain to oneself and to objectivity. Emotional relationships are relationships of desire, tainted by coercion and constraint; something is expected from the other person, and that makes him, and ourselves unfree. (*MDR* 296)

In the second stage of individuation, images and their "ethical conclusions" must be understood.[19] Usually people stop too soon; it is not enough to identify emotions and images:

We do not take the trouble to understand them, let alone draw ethical conclusions from them. This stopping-short conjures up the negative effects of the unconscious. It is an equally grave mistake to think that it is enough to gain some understanding of the images and that knowledge can here make a halt. Insight into them must be converted into an ethical obligation. Not to do so is to fall prey to the power principle, and this produces dangerous effects which are destructive not only to others but even to the knower. The images of the unconscious place a great responsibility upon a man. Failure to understand them, or a shirking of ethical responsibility, deprives him of his wholeness and imposes a painful fragmentariness on his life. (*MDR* 192–93)

Individuation is also a social duty:

[The psychotherapist] is not just working for this particular patient, who may be quite insignificant, but for himself as well and his own soul, and in doing so he is perhaps laying an infinitesimal grain in the scales of humanity's soul. Small and invisible as this contribution may be, it is yet an *opus magnum,* for it is accomplished in a sphere but lately visited by the numen, where the whole weight of mankind's problems has settled. The ultimate questions of psychotherapy are not a private matter — they represent a supreme responsibility.[20]

Jung insisted that his patients take responsibility for the external reality of their lives as they explored their inner reality. For himself, he understood the importance of his home, practice, and family in providing a stable point while he explored the terrifying and disorienting depths of his psyche.[21]

The goal of "completed individuation" is the self, a uniquely configured unity. According to Jung, one discovers, or "comes upon," the self, but although one may intuit the possibility of the self as a young or immature person, the achieved self results from intensive work (MDR 32). "The self is our life's goal, for it is the completest expression of the fateful combination we call individuality."[22] Yet the self is never fully attainable, for the self one experiences is always, to some extent, fragmented. Committed work toward a unified self requires the belief that it is possible to achieve such a self; the unified self is, then, an article of faith and a goal.

Religion or Science?

Jung made a point of claiming that his work is "scientific" and "objective." He distinguished it, on the one hand, from whatever is "theological, frivolous, and irresponsible" and, on the other hand, from an "estheticizing tendency" (MDR 61). Clearly, in Jung's vocabulary, these were all value-laden words. Since science was the model for all knowledge, legitimate work must be scientific: "[F]or me, reality meant scientific comprehension" (MDR 188). John Kerr points out that "[t]his was the age that first accepted scientific materialism as its dominant worldview. It was... commonly assumed that science had decisively triumphed over religion and metaphysics and that a complete materialistic account of the external world was nearly at hand."[23] Yet Jung claimed to "know," rather than to believe, experiment, or hypothesize. If scientific method is indeed the criterion for conclusions that qualify as science, several features of that method are missing in Jung's psychology.[24] A clinical method by which results could be tested and reproduced was perhaps the most glaring lacuna.[25]

Jung's idea of the relationship of scientific knowledge to the psyche's quirky messiness is evident even in his description of the exploration of his own psyche. It is science that redeems the explorer from the chaos of uninterpreted evidence. Describing his fantasies and dreams, he writes:

> My science was the only way I had of extricating myself from that chaos. Otherwise the material would have trapped me in its thicket, strangled me like jungle creepers. I took great care to try to understand every single image, every item of my psychic inventory, and to classify them scientifically — so far as this was possible — and, above all, to realize them in actual life. (*MDR* 192)

Jung sturdily resisted contemporary charges that his psychology was essentially a religion based on faith and belief. He wrote in response to such a charge:

> I practice science, not apologetics and not philosophy, and I have neither the competence nor the desire to found a religion. My interest is a scientific one. . . . I proceed from a positive Christianity that is as much Catholic as Protestant, and my concern is to point out in a scientifically responsible way those empirically tangible facts that would at least make plausible the legitimacy of Christian and especially Catholic dogma.[26]

Similarly, Jung was horrified at the suggestion that his ideas could be categorized as art (*MDR* 491). Someone Jung described as a "talented psychopath" once suggested this to him — a woman who was, by Jung's own account, intelligent and insightful. "Obviously [she thought that] what I was doing wasn't science," he recalls scornfully. "What then could it be but art? It was as though these were the only two alternatives in the world. That is the way a woman's mind works" (*MDR* 185).[27] Curiously, Jung's apparently unconscious inference that all women's minds exhibit psychopathology comes in the context of his description of the anima, a powerful and dangerous female figure in the male psyche. He seems to have been unaware of the irrationality of projecting a figure from his psyche onto actual women. Although later Jung came to understand that, befriended, the anima has a "positive aspect," it initially manifests as "a mouthpiece of the unconscious [that] can utterly destroy a man" (*MDR* 187).

Freud

Perhaps the most decisive factor in Jung's life was his collaboration and friendship with Sigmund Freud. Both men provided different versions of the "great syntheses" of human experience admired by their time.[28] Describing his relation to Freud as complicated and difficult from the beginning, Jung confesses that "it was not easy for me to assign Freud the proper place in my life, or to take the right attitude toward him" (*MDR* 147). Freud, "the first man of real importance I had encountered," became, in Jung's own description, a father and mentor to him in both beneficial and constraining ways.

After the two men had enjoyed a long personal and professional relationship, they parted over Freud's insistence that repressed sexuality lies at the heart of every psychic ill. Significantly, Jung judged Freud to have permitted sexuality to become "a sort of *numinosum*," a quasi-religious dogma requiring faith and loyalty (*MDR* 150). He developed an acute awareness of the mote in his brother's eye: "Freud, who had always made much of his irreligiosity, had now constructed a dogma; or rather, in the place of a jealous God whom he had lost, he had substituted another compelling image, that of sexuality. It was no less insistent, exacting, domineering, threatening, and morally ambivalent than the original one" (*MDR* 151).

Though he officially lost the status of Freud's son and heir, Jung claimed in retrospect to be the only one who "logically pursued the two problems that interested Freud most: the problem of 'archaic vestiges,' and that of sexuality" (*MDR* 168). In his description of Freud's impaired vision, Jung clothed his own perspective in revealing language:

> Freud *never asked himself* why he was *compelled* to talk continually of sex, why this idea had *taken such possession* of him. He *remained unaware* that his *"monotony of interpretation"* expressed a *flight from himself*, or from that other side of him that might, perhaps, be called mystical. So long as he *refused to acknowledge* that side, he *could never be reconciled* with himself. He was *blind* toward the paradox and ambiguity of the contents of the unconscious. (*MDR* 152; emphasis added)

The most genuinely heroic of Jung's struggles may have been one he does not name, for his autobiography hints that he fought a hereditary depression, inherited from his father (*MDR* 63, 68, 94).

His marked preference for solitude and his extreme fragility while working both signal depression.[29] Although family and colleagues collaborated to protect his working conditions on grounds of the importance and value of his work, they may also have been more or less aware that work was also all that stood between Jung and depression. After describing several youthful episodes of depression in *Memories, Dreams, Reflections,* Jung stopped identifying it as a factor in numerous difficulties. Perhaps he did so because depression was certainly incompatible with Jung's self-presentation as culture hero.[30] Moreover, in Jung's time, depression was infrequently diagnosed, perhaps because effective treatments for it had not been discovered.

A pattern of extramarital affairs may also signal depression. Jung's affairs with Sabina Spielrein and Toni Wolff may represent, at least in part, his effort to hold depression at bay; evidently his wife understood his affairs in this way. His biographer writes: "By 1915 Jung's condition had so deteriorated that his wife allowed Toni Wolff openly to become his mistress and a sometime member of the household, simply because she was the only person who could calm him down."[31]

As I have indicated, Jung's alleged "exploration" of his own psyche following his break with Freud has sometimes been seen as a psychotic episode. However, Kerr's interpretation, namely, that Jung "teetered close to the brink of insanity for several years," may be overdrawn.[32] A close reading of his autobiography supports my suggestion that depression is more characteristic of Jung's psychic state in this period. Moreover, with a relatively mild depression, he would have been able to examine the depths of his own psyche, an option he would not have had if he were insane or even "on the brink."

The loss of Freud, a father figure, could have activated unresolved emotions in relation to his own father's death. Jung had little praise for a father he had experienced as intellectually timid, religiously adrift, and ineffective as a husband and father.[33] His terse, even cruel, summary of his father's life shows little understanding or empathy:

As a country parson he lapsed into a sort of sentimental idealism and into reminiscences of his golden student days.... [He] discovered that his marriage was not all as he had imagined it to be. He did a great deal of good — far too much —

and as a result was usually irritable. Both parents made great efforts to lead devout lives, with the result that there were angry scenes between them only too frequently. These difficulties, understandably enough, later shattered my father's faith. (*MDR* 91–92)

When his father died, Jung immediately replaced him as head of the family both literally and figuratively, although he was only a university student. He moved into his father's room, and he took responsibility for the family's finances. At the time of his father's death, Jung's mother remarked, "He died in time for you," a statement Jung understood to mean: "You did not understand each other and he might have become a hindrance for you."[34] Jung mentions no grief in relation to his father's death, recalling only that his father's death awoke in him "manliness and freedom."[35] But the unresolved nature of his relation to his father is evident in the father's appearance in Jung's dreams for years after his death. The shock of losing a second father may have precipitated unfinished psychic business, and a return of the depression he associated with his father.

Conclusion

I have found some suggestions of essential importance in Jung's writings, but I am also dismayed by his limitations, his misogyny, his prejudices, and his use of power. My intent in the following is not to undermine Jung's achievement and its usefulness but to consider his psychology "for life." What dangers and deceptions accompany Jung's appraisal of human life, the world, and other human beings? We should not be surprised to find that Jung, like the ancient authors we considered, talked a better game than he could actually play. I will examine his relationships before returning to his claim to carry out scientific work, as opposed to religious or aesthetic investigations.

Both Jung and Freud achieved their theoretical insights primarily through self-analysis. Their claim to have reached the bottom of the psyche by self-analysis gave both men the authority of an exemplar or culture hero. Jung says of his writings, "[M]any readers would be pulled into the texts in a unique way, for, by virtue of . . . example, they were being invited to examine their own mental processes."[36]

Both, however, refused to describe the method by which the psyche was explored. But "a method that cannot be formalized is like a finding that cannot be replicated. However interesting it may be, it is not scientific."[37]

Self-analysis has, in addition, other important methodological problems. The first problem lies in assumptions about the nature of the psyche. Jung believed in the fundamental unity of the psyche, a unity that could be articulated if one were in possession of the right key. From the age of eleven, his whole life was "permeated and held together by a single goal,...to penetrate into the secret of the personality" (*MDR* 21, 206). He believed that a thorough exploration of the unconscious would reveal — not create — its integrity.[38] Moreover, his belief in a collective unconscious common to all human beings seemed to him to authorize generalization from his own psyche to a universal human psyche. Jung acknowledged, especially in his work on psychological types, that differences among human beings are real, but he believed that they represent nothing more fundamental than patterned selections within the collective repertoire.[39]

But is the psyche a unity? This assumption — or article of faith — requires scrutiny. Postmodern critics posit an irreducibly and permanently fragmented subjectivity. Iris Marion Young writes: "Because the subject is not a unity, it cannot be present to itself, know itself. I do not always know what I mean, need, want, desire, because these do not arise from some ego as origin. Often I express my desire in gesture or tone of voice, without meaning to do so.... Subjects all have multiple desires that do not cohere."[40] Perhaps postmodern thinkers merely describe the self or subjectivity of Jung's dismissively designated "so called normal people," which he said was "very fragmentary."[41] Nevertheless, criticism of the concept of a unified self raises the issue of whether the human task should be to learn a rough working coordination of the fragments or, believing that what I experience as fragments are *in fact* a unity, to wrestle them into unity. The danger of an intransigent commitment to unification is, as Jung himself clearly illustrates, that this unity may be achieved at the expense of lengthening the shadow or enlarging the blind spots that cannot be integrated and must therefore be excluded from consciousness.

A further problem concerns the universalizing or projection of one psyche to all human psyches. Jung's psychological formulations incorporate his own perspectives and agenda. Well-supported male privilege is evident, as is the Lutheran Christianity around which his childhood psyche formed. Yet he seldom acknowledged particularity and the partiality it engenders or showed awareness that every perspective is simultaneously privileged and limited, sensitized and alert to some factors while ignoring others.

Although he introduced some individualization into his psychology by proposing psychological types, he did not take into account any of the external factors — social location, race, or gender — that shape perspectives. Seeing himself as a culture hero, Jung assumed, by contrast, a myopic human mass on whose behalf he discovered truth. He did not grant that, like himself, others also have privileged and limited perspectives, in short, that people are genuinely and delightfully different. This returns us to problems entailed in self-analysis. Self-analysis can perhaps reveal one's own conscious and even unconscious intentions, but self-analysis can never expose the limitations of one's perspective. To understand this, one must listen to others.

Similarly, Jung was unaware of the effects of wealth, power, and institutional authority on his psychological theories. This may have been partially due to the fact that it is difficult for anyone within the sphere of a "great man" to confront him honestly and critically. But Jung also actively avoided criticism. Colleagues commented on his unwillingness to listen to any serious critical discussion of his theories: "If others disagreed with him, he would turn authoritarian, or he would simply employ his technique of bodily escape."[42]

Although the limitations of perspective have been discussed a great deal in the latter half of the twentieth century, the first psychiatrists understood the danger inherent in combinations of perspective and professional power. An effort to mitigate the authority of a leader/father was included in the proposed organizational plan of the International Psychoanalytic Association. The plan was that "[Freud's] pronouncements would not be followed blindly, as if they were divine revelations, but, like everything else, would be subject to thoroughgoing criticism, which he would accept, not with the absurd superiority of the paterfamilias, but with the attention it deserved."[43] The originators of psychoanalysis understood more than they could achieve in their actual interactions, however. The early history of the International Psychoanalytic Association is an unedifying saga of struggles over power and authority. Jung was a central actor in these conflicts.

Jung wrote about the problem of power in *Answer to Job*. He described Job's all-powerful Yahweh as amoral, unconscious, and omnipotent — a bad combination. Job, he concluded, was morally superior to Yahweh:[44]

> What does man have that God does not have? Because of his littleness, puniness, and defencelessness against the Almighty, he possesses... a somewhat keener consciousness based on self-reflection: he must, in order to survive, always be mindful of his impotence. God has no need of this circumspection, for nowhere does he come up against an insuperable obstacle that would force him to hesitate and hence make him reflect on himself.[45]

As the 1995 film *The Madness of King George* put it: "To be curbed, stood up to, in a word thwarted, exercises the character.... It is want of such exercise that makes rulers rigid." But Jung does not notice any parallel between God and the self-styled culture hero. Like Job's God, Jung was protected and cared for; nothing was allowed to disturb his creative process. His wealth insulated him from potentially instructive need. He had many controversies (battles) in his professional world, but such skirmishes are part of the narrative of the hero from the *Epic of Gilgamesh* forward.[46]

Why did Jung assume that he knew all humanity on the basis of knowing himself? What white-racial myopia permitted him to say, for example, that "every child" fears "the black man"? He means, of course, to say that every child fears the unconscious, but his consistent use of race to characterize the danger of the unconscious incorporates his unchallenged perspective as a Swiss burgher (*MDR* 14, 245, 262–64).

Jung represents himself as "a solitary [who must] hint at things which other people do not know, and usually do not want to know" (*MDR* 42). Recognizing his isolation, he gave it a self-serving interpretation: "Loneliness does not come from having no people about one, but from being unable to communicate the things that seem important to oneself.... If a man knows more than others, he becomes lonely" (*MDR* 356). In *Memories, Dreams, Reflections,* Jung mentions friendships, but no distinct *persons* emerge. Other people either "understood" (agreed with) Jung or were quickly dropped: "As soon

as I had seen through them, the magic was gone." An attentive reading of his autobiography, however, reveals that others must have also
"seen through" him!

"I have offended many people."
"I had no patience with people."
"I made many enemies." (*MDR* 356–57)

Jung was frequently difficult for colleagues and demanding and
abrasive, if not abusive, to students. To his patients, he was usually attentive, supportive, and understanding. Even there, however,
he could on occasion be totalitarian, demanding, or seducing. He
acted, in short, as a privileged man of his time and society, filled
with stereotypes about others and their "natures." He should not
be charged in retrospect with special responsibility for the cultural
blindnesses of his time, of course, except on the basis of his own
claim to transcend such socialized assumptions.

Jung's first patients were lower-class institutionalized psychotics.
Later, his patients were upper-class neurotics.[47] The great majority
of these patients were women. Jung's misogyny has been commented
on repeatedly by biographers and critics. I will not repeat their accusations, except to say that Jung's treatment of women was radically
inconsistent with his acknowledgment that he derived "insight into
my own nature" from his women patients. Among them, at least
two, Sabina Spielrein and Toni Wolff, were later to become his
intellectual and erotic muses (*MDR* 145).[48]

Jung was profoundly ambivalent about women. His mother, Emilie Preiswerk, was simultaneously "a good mother to me" (due
largely to her "hearty animal warmth") (*MDR* 48–50) and "innately
unreliable" (due to her hospitalization for several months when he
was three) (*MDR* 8). Although Emilie had a good "natural mind,"
her literary gifts were submerged through disuse throughout her life.

Jung's wife, Emma Rauschenbach, was another matter. Emma became Carl's professional assistant; she also provided the domestic
stability that supported Jung's ventures into the unconscious. Jung's
autobiography focuses on the romantic beginning of his marital
relationship and on its end with Emma's death.[49] There are few references to her busy domestic and professional life or her unstinting
support of Jung's doctrines.[50]

Despite Emma's crucial role in his personal and professional life, however, Jung differentiated women into two dangerous types. The first, the maternal figure, "automatically disqualified herself as Salome, the erotic counterpart [the second type]."[51] Jung's relationships with women reflect these two female figures of his psyche. He maintained a domestic triangle with Emma Jung (the maternal figure) and Toni Wolff (the erotic muse) for forty years. Both were intelligent professional women who struggled to accept the position in which they were placed by their love and concern for Jung as well as by his demands. At one point they even undertook to analyze each other in order to explore the resentments their situation created. Yet both were perceptibly damaged by this arrangement.[52] In old age, Jung was cared for by a family friend, Ruth Bailey, who, to Jung's relief, had never undergone analysis. He claimed that it was restful for him "not to have to worry about making her more conscious as I always have before with everybody around me."[53] In Bailey, Jung finally found the woman who would accept his well-being as her chief concern.

Clearly, Jung's professional and social position effectively guarded him from the possibility that any woman could confront him as an equal. Emma, who might have done so on the basis of her knowledge, energy, and loyalty, always felt herself overshadowed by her husband, both professionally and domestically. Why, then, did Jung identify one of his most important psychic figures as a confrontational, not to say dangerous, female figure, the anima. The anima, his own repressed femininity, is, for a man, the "mouthpiece of the unconscious." The anima figure represents the extreme danger of psychic exploration: "[T]he insinuations of the anima," he wrote, "can utterly destroy a man" (*MDR* 186). Perhaps a suppressed uneasiness about his relationships with women, if not terror at the possibility that the women upon whom he depended might resist or refuse their assigned roles, underlies his construction of the anima figure.

Instead of equal relationships within which Jung's life and work could have been criticized and refined, his professional relationships tended to pattern themselves after struggles between fathers and sons. Although women became followers and practitioners of Jung's theories in record numbers, they seldom participated in these conflicts. Apparently they accepted without complaint his intellectual and social superiority.

It may seem easy to comprehend why men enjoy and benefit from women's passivity and dependence. On closer inspection, however, it is not so obvious that Western gender arrangements are better for men than they are for women. The psychoanalyst Maria Torok writes:

> The insincerity, ambivalence, and the refusal to identify with the other that this type of [asymmetrical] relationship entails should appear to men as so many obstacles thrown in the way of their complete and authentic fulfillment.... What benefit does the male derive from subjecting to his mastery the very being through whom he could both understand and be understood himself? Self-to-self revelation... would be the realization of our humanity, and this is what eludes nearly all of us.[54]

Jung was a modern prophet of interiority. He learned from intransigent self-exploration; in this he was genuinely heroic. But he capitulated to the temptation to set himself beyond criticism, beyond the possibility of relationship with another person he could recognize as equipped with equal intelligence and profundity. When he did, in reality, meet such people, he quickly recast the relationship in terms familiar to him from childhood. Men, like Freud, must be father. Women might be mother or muse, but never both, for a woman who embodied both mother and muse represented the greatest psychic danger — potential engulfment by the unconscious. Unlike the ancient hero Gilgamesh, Jung never wrestled his Enkidu, another self that he could neither vanquish nor ignore. In short, no one was able to block his projections.

Because Jung met no limits, and because he rightly saw that not many people have the strength, courage, and social support for rigorous self-analysis, he complained of loneliness and misunderstanding. He felt himself successful in learning to operate from his interiority, translating external events into psychic conditions for further labor and insight. What he did not recognize was that other people (occasionally or frequently) do so too and that one's own projections must be negotiated with theirs. He concludes his autobiography as a man whose long life confirmed the self-isolation of his youth. In youth his loneliness was compensated by a vivid and sustaining sense of "God's world," a world "of divine beauty." The words that end his posthumously published autobiography repeat his preference for "God's world":

There is so much that fills me: plants, animals, clouds, day and night, and the eternal in man. The more uncertain I have felt about myself, the more there has grown up in me a feeling of kinship for all things. In fact it seems to me as if that alienation which so long separated me from the world has become transferred into my own inner world, and has revealed to me an unexpected familiarity with myself. (*MDR* 359)

Religion

"I had a vision of unearthly beauty, and that is why I was able to live at all," Jung wrote (*MDR* 198). His perception of beauty gave him the strength and courage to journey into the twisted, dangerous paths of the psyche. He recognized the danger that he might never emerge, but he saw the danger and the beauty as intertwined. Like young trees growing in a thick forest, the psyche's convoluted paths, even — or especially — in their darkest, most congested moments, unerringly head for light.

At the end of *Memories, Dreams, Reflections,* Jung comes close to confessing the religious dimension of his quest for individuation. Disclaimers notwithstanding, he was a theologian disguised as a scientist, for God appears at a pivotal juncture: Eros, the "creator and father-mother of all higher consciousness," has no other name, finally, than God.[55] Acknowledging the essentially theological nature of his work, he writes: "Man can try to name love, showering upon it all the names at his command, and still he will involve himself in endless self-deceptions. If he possesses a grain of wisdom, he will lay down his arms and name the unknown by the more unknown, *ignotum per ignotius* — that is, by the name of God" (*MDR* 354). Motivated throughout his life by resistance to the threadbare theology of his fathers and uncles, Jung's agenda came full circle: fleeing the God he inherited, he gave vibrant witness to a God who can be known only by a return to the self.

In Jung's theology, God is to be found at the interstice between consciousness and the unconscious, guaranteeing their connection. But this is precisely the function of religion. Religions seek to answer the Gnostic questions: Why am I here? Where did I come from? Where am I going? What shall I do while I am here? Although most religions, like Jung's childhood religion, are apparently addressed to consciousness, demanding faith, belief, and understanding, the Gnostic questions, like alchemical formulations, ultimately cannot be answered merely in term of consciousness. They negotiate or mediate between consciousness and the unconscious. Nor are these questions answerable in individual terms. They require a collective answer.

"Life has addressed a question to me," Jung wrote. The question was unchosen, bequeathed to him by parents and ancestors: "I answer for them the questions that their lives once left behind" (MDR 237). To one who reads Memories, Dreams, Reflections for life, Jung's life also poses a question. That question is: How can I respect both my own psychic reality and that of others? For a heavily introspective intellectual such as Jung, the path toward an answer to that question must be, as Augustine put it, "I relaxed a little from myself" (Conf. 7.14).

Jung and Rilke, the poet discussed in the next chapter, both emphasize the incontrovertible reality of the psyche. Their biographical facts were also strikingly similar. Both were born in 1845 in German-speaking societies, and they shared the values of educated men of their time. Rilke contributes, however, two ideas of great importance to the project of reading for life. First, he was an acute observer of the benefits and costs of socialization; second, he held a great respect for the productive potential of psychic pain.

Chapter 6

"STAYING IS NOWHERE"
Rainer Maria Rilke's *Duino Elegies*

———— • ————

For Beauty's nothing but beginning of Terror we're still just able to bear.

Staying is nowhere.

—Rainer Maria Rilke, Duino Elegies

A WOMEN'S STUDIES COLLOQUIUM was discussing Barbra Streisand's film *Yentl*. Yentl, a young Jewish woman at the turn of the twentieth century, wants passionately to study Torah. Because women were not allowed to study, Yentl disguises herself as a boy and successfully pursues the education she wants. Every member of the colloquium could easily detect large problems with the film, for example, the film's repeated undermining or trivialization of its radical topic. Then, one woman said, "That film was very important to me at one time of my life. It suggested to me that I too could study. I am here today, in a doctoral colloquium, at least partly because of the encouragement offered me by *Yentl*."

This remark was difficult for the colloquium to understand. Some of the younger women had not seen the film in the context of the early 1980s, when ideas of what women could do were more limited than at present, and the film seemed obviously and abundantly flawed from the perspective of two subsequent decades of feminist analysis.

The dilemma of assessing *Yentl* raises a larger question about the relationship of reading for life to academic study. For the academic enterprise is opposed to reading for life. The systematic critical readings taught in the university replace and mock the "impressionistic" reading done by someone desperate for expanded horizons, for models, for suggestions. Academics routinely underestimate the number of people now devoted to, and skilled at, critical reading whose educational motivation came from naive but passionate reading. Perhaps most people in graduate education are there because they like to read.

Let us ask again: Can the antagonism between a raw reading and a critical reading be overcome? Can the energy and excitement of the raw reading be captured *within* a critical reading? Since all books, even scripture, have human authors, it seems unlikely that anyone reading for life will find a flawless text on which to base her search for a pleasurable and generous life. Even attention to the author's intentions merely — at best — elicits a text whose conscious intention is impeccable. Moreover, often the author actually intended to advocate the very gender relations or religious intolerance that a late twentieth-century reader may deplore. Does a critical reading, then, inevitably kill a book's potential usefulness by exposing its political, gender, class, or racial loyalties?

My discussion of Rilke's *Duino Elegies* addresses these questions. It tests the suggestion I have developed in earlier chapters that it is not only possible but imperative to integrate appreciative and critical readings. The *Duino Elegies* combines powerful insight with social blindness; the beauty of its poetry masks its gendered message. Once exposed, however, its plea for the care and protection of the (male) creative artist can, I believe, be acknowledged without requiring that the critical reader ignore Rilke's vision of a spacious world of human agency. In fact, I believe that the "best revenge" for the sexism of the *Duino Elegies* is the appropriation of its insights by people the author clearly did not intend to empower.

Rilke was born in Prague in 1875. His father, an army officer, sent the sensitive boy to military school to remove him from the religious influence of his mother. Rilke married a sculptor, Clara Westhoff, in 1901, but they lived together only briefly, and Rilke had many lovers throughout his life. He lived in Munich, served briefly in a war office in Vienna, but spent the most prolific twelve-year period of his life in Paris. Rilke began the *Duino Elegies* in 1912 in the Castle of Duino, on the Adriatic above Trieste, but the text remained unfinished for ten years. In 1919, Rilke moved to Switzerland. Living in a castle at Muzot (near Sierre), he worked in a frenzy, a "nameless storm, a hurricane in my mind.... [E]verything in the way of fibre and web in me split, — eating was not to be thought of." He completed the *Duino Elegies* and *Sonnets to Orpheus* in 1922.[1] Four years later, in 1926, he died of leukemia, at the age of fifty-one.

Rainer Maria Rilke's *Duino Elegies* have some common interests with the psychology of his contemporary, C. G. Jung.[2] Given the similar political and social setting shared by Jung and Rilke, resonances in their preoccupations are not surprising. Moreover, both suffered from chronic depression that affected both the kind of working conditions each found essential and the tone of driven urgency in their work. I will describe Jung's and Rilke's common interests briefly before I discuss two distinctive foci in the *Duino Elegies*.

Surrounded by the turmoil of World War I, Rilke, like Jung, insisted on interiority. Also, because the mass movements of his day — later exemplified by German National Socialism — addressed herd instincts, both men called for individual responsibility. The steadily increasing mechanization of modern life alarmed Rilke as it did Jung.[3] To designate either author as "romantic" misses the historical moment in which each accurately assessed the danger to the human spirit of mass allegiances.

Beginning with oneself is the first theme common to Jung and Rilke. Jung once remarked that all change in society begins with change in oneself. And Rilke believed that the artist can help others only as a result of his work on himself:

> Art cannot be helpful through our ... specially concerning ourselves with the distresses of others, but in so far as we bear our own distresses more passionately, give, now and then, a perhaps clearer meaning to endurance, and develop for ourselves the means of expressing the suffering within us and its conquest more precisely and clearly than is possible to those who have to apply their powers to something else. (*DE*, intro., p. 15)

Yet, as this quotation shows, Rilke sought, in the expression of his suffering, to give others a more fruitful approach to their own suffering. Jung and Rilke worked on themselves, then, with the faith and confidence that the personal is vehicle of the universal. Moreover, as we have seen in Jung, Rilke conceived of work on the self as social responsibility. In 1919, in the wake of World War I, he wrote that the particular task of the intellectual is "to prepare in men's hearts the way for those gentle, mysterious, trembling transformations, from

which alone the understandings and harmonies of a serener future
will proceed" (DE, intro., p. 14).

Jung and Rilke were preoccupied with a mode of being (Rilke) or
individuation/self (Jung) that transcends socialized attitudes and behavior. Acutely aware of the way every culture trains its members to
attitudes and behavior, both men sought to spring open constricting
social definitions of roles and worths. The "cupboard-love loyalty of
a habit that liked you, and stayed, and never gave notice," is not the
arena of human life and the meaning of the individual (DE, intro.,
p. 1). However, neither man scrutinized his own gender, race, and
class assumptions.

Both Jung and Rilke pointed to archetypal experience circulating
in the bloodstream of the presently living. Each advocated recovery
of the awareness of primordial human being, crowded with ancestors. Both sought to set tiny time-and-space-bound human lives in a
larger frame, to open the already existing connections to ancestors,
cosmic spaces, springs, and death that give human life weight, meaning, and size. Both insisted that a human being is not defined by his
adaptation to habit and achievement or by the shriveling of modern
life among machines:[4]

> Look, we don't love like the flowers with only a single
> season behind us; immemorial sap
> mounts in our arms when we love. Oh, maid,
> this: that we've loved, *within* us, not one, still to come, but all
> the innumerable fermentation; not just a single child,
> but the fathers, resting like mountain ruins
> within our depths; — but the dry river-bed
> of former mothers; — yes, and the whole of that
> soundless landscape under its cloudy or
> cloudless destiny: — *this* got the start of you, maid. (DE no. 3)

This insistence on the consummate worth of the individual occurred in the face of the meaningless slaughter of innumerable
human lives in World War I, the defining event of both Jung's and
Rilke's youth. Jung described himself as overwhelmed by the war
and unable to distinguish his personal dreams from dream presen-
timents of collective danger. The war left Rilke "muted, bewildered,
and uncomprehending." His work came to a standstill; he developed
writing blocks and existed in a state of suspended animation.[5] He
wrote in a 1919 letter:

If only for one whole year I could have a [parlor] around me in which to cry....It occurs to me that I have never cried in all of the numbness and torture of these past five years. More and more I recognize why it is that I seek some sort of refuge so desperately: a workroom — for me that means a place in which I can pace back and forth, but also this, a place to scream, a place to cry.[6]

In these circumstances, both men sought the *personal* in the impersonal, the *human* personal, collective humanity, localized in the individual.

The second area of commonality between Jung and Rilke is their concept of the hero, inhabiter of cosmic spaces and primordial time. I will look more closely below at Rilke's definition of the hero. For now it is enough to observe that for both men, the (male) hero is simultaneously dependent on, and uncommitted to, women.

Rilke's work was supported, emotionally and financially, by women. He usually fell in love with much older women in whom he detected and encouraged artistic interests and abilities. It would be presumptuous, indeed impossible, to determine the extent to which the artistic gifts of his benefactresses were genuinely attractive to Rilke. He did seek to promote and further their work whenever he could. But his interest in their undeveloped gifts was also a basis for successful seductions. He wrote, in a letter to a friend, "I am no lover at all, it only touches me from without, maybe because no one has ever shaken me to the very roots of my being, maybe because I do not love my mother."[7]

Nonetheless, his relentless protection of his own solitude (and, whether she wanted it or not, that of his lover) was based — or rationalized — on his insistence on relationships of equality and mutuality.[8] Perhaps his parents' loveless bourgeois marriage had convinced him of the extent to which relationship founded on daily familiarity ("the cupboard-love loyalty of a habit that liked you, and stayed, and never gave notice") inevitably deteriorated, blunting both persons' creativity and energy.[9]

Finally, Jung's interest in consciousness (*bewüssheit*) is similar to Rilke's interest in naming, in finding the word that will translate an object or an image into something recognized, known to human beings, recorded. Rilke suggests that the purpose of human existence is precisely this activity. For neither "the art of seeing, learned here so slowly," nor anything that's happened in life, nor "a handful of earth" can be brought across the slender division between life and death:

> Are we, perhaps, here just for saying: House,
> Bridge, Fountain, Gate, Jug, Olive tree, Window, —
> possibly: Pillar, Tower? (*DE* no. 9)

Rilke shares Jung's sense of the urgency of psychic work. The work of consciousness can *only* be done during life: "*Here* is the time for the tellable, *here* is its home" (*DE* no. 9).

> Because being here amounts to so much, because all
> this Here and Now, so fleeting, seems to require us and strangely
> concerns us. Us the most fleeting of all. Just once,
> everything, only for once. Once and no more. And we, too,
> once. Never again. But this
> having been once, though only once,
> having been once on earth — can it ever be cancelled? (*DE* no. 9)

Rilke's Vision

Within these similarities with Jung's vision of human life, its beauty and responsibilities, Rilke's project differs from Jung's in important respects. While Jung's expansion of human being includes ancient wisdom, Rilke's poetic vision extends forward to, and beyond, death. Rather than conceptualizing death as the absolute limit of the human, Rilke appropriates death to the human realm:

> Yes, but all of the living
> make the mistake of drawing too sharp distinctions.
> Angels, (they say) are often unable to tell
> whether they move among living or dead. The eternal
> torrent whirls all the ages through either realm
> forever, and sounds above their voices in both. (*DE* no. 1)

He blurs the line between the living and the dead, emphasizing the *usefulness* of death within human life. Death, for Rilke, is the other side of life, an integral part of the human. As such, it is to be neither ignored nor feared; it is to be entered into relation with.

But this vision would be conventional poetic fancy if it merely urged the naturalization or acceptance of death. Rilke's description

of the present uses of death have a much more practical meaning.
"Being dead," for Rilke, also means sharing the enviable condition
of the child whose socialization is incomplete, so that social customs
and conventions are still strange, other, incomprehensible:

> True, it is strange to inhabit the earth no longer,
> to use no longer customs scarcely acquired,
> not to interpret roses, and other things
> that promise so much in terms of a human future;
> to be no longer all that one used to be
> in endless anxious hands, and to lay aside
> even one's name like a broken toy.
> Strange, not to go on wishing one's wishes. Strange
> to see all that was once relation so loosely fluttering
> hither and thither in space. And it's hard being dead,
> and full of retrieving before one begins to espy
> a trace of eternity. (DE no. 1)

The inclusion of death within one's concept of life challenges and
dismantles the normalization that confines and cheapens human existence. Solitude, the "hardness of life, the long experience of love":
these are Rilke's prescriptions against the condition of socialized
spectatorship. Spectators perch on the edge of life, onlookers, "always, everywhere, looking *at,* never *out of,* everything!" (DE no. 8).

If socialization constricts the full expression of human being so
dramatically, why is it so universally successful? Because, Rilke
suggests, it is, quite simply, a process of humanization. The child
achieves its place in a family, community, and society by reproducing
the language and gestures, the attitudes and behavior by which the
community defines itself. It procures love and acceptance by learning socialized skills. Moreover, learning entails considerable pleasure.
Yet socialization is also difficult and costly. So society devises attractions, distractions, and titillations ("money's organs on view") to
entice and reward its adherents. Given these enticements, the "bitter
beer that tastes quite sweet to its drinkers" is no longer mysterious
(DE no. 10).

Rilke does not deplore all socialization. On the contrary, it is necessary and important to tame the "interior jungle" that threatens to
overwhelm the child's fragile ego. The inner "ravines where frightful-
ness lurked, still gorged with his fathers," require the ballast of the
"more human space" provided by the mother:

Nowhere a creak you could not explain with a smile,
as though you had long known *when* the floor would behave
   itself thus....
And he listened to you and was soothed. So much it availed,
gently, your coming; his tall cloaked destiny stepped
behind a chest of drawers, and his restless future,
   that easily got out of place, conformed to the folds of the
   curtain. (*DE* no. 3)

But, inevitably, "the pure too-little," the barely achieved contain-
ment of the "floods of origin," becomes the "empty too-much."
The "pure, contained, narrow, own little strip of orchard in between
river and rock" disappears into the marketplace, where "booths that
can please the most curious tastes are drumming and bawling" (*DE*
nos. 5, 10).

Everyone, Rilke believes, has had moments in which she intuited
the full extent of humanness:

For to each was granted an hour, — perhaps not quite
so much as an hour — some span that could scarcely be measured
by measures of time, in between two whiles, when she
really possessed an existence. All. Veins full of existence.
But we so lightly forget what our laughing neighbor
neither confirms nor envies. We want to be visibly
able to show it, whereas the most visible joy
can only reveal itself to us when we've transformed it,
within. (*DE* no. 7)

Lovers experience a temporary reprieve from the condition of rapid
fatigue that governs the world of the senses. For lovers, the caress
persists. Yet even for them, this "pure duration" vanishes quickly,
absorbed in normality. After the "startled first encounter,"

[w]hen you lift yourselves
up to each other's lips — drink unto drink:
oh, how strangely the drinker eludes his part! (*DE* no. 2)

Moreover, socialization continually betrays those who depend on
its rewards: "Each torpid turn of the earth has such disinherited
children, to whom no longer what's been, nor yet what's coming,
belongs" (*DE* no. 2).

The rewards of attentiveness to the larger compass of human life
are less visible than are those of socialization, but they are more

trustworthy, Rilke contends. These rewards are not the pleasures of "plenty of fresh distractions," but a "loving confident task," patiently done every day. The core of the *Duino Elegies* is the "Seventh Elegy," specifically the following passage, which describes the task of human existence:

> Nowhere, beloved, can world exist but within.
> Life passes in transformation. And, ever diminishing,
> vanishes what's outside. Where once was a lasting
> house, up starts some invented structure across our
> vision, as fully at home among concepts as though it
> still stood in a brain. Spacious garners of power are
> formed by the Time Spirit, formless as that tense urge
> he's extracting from everything else. Temples he knows
> no longer. We're now more secretly saving such lavish
> expanses of heart. Nay, even where one survives, one
> single thing once prayed, or tended or knelt to, it's
> reaching, just as it is, into the unseen world. Many
> perceive it no more, but neglect the advantage of
> building it grandlier now, with pillars and statues,
> *within!* (*DE* no. 7)

The primary task of living, for Rilke, is *imagining* the real: interior *representation* of Chartres, music, night, spring, earth, and tree. This task could also be described as the perception of beauty. Rilke defines beauty in the first lines of the "First Elegy": "Beauty's nothing but beginning of Terror we're still just able to bear." Beauty terrifies because it crosses the thin line that distinguishes living from dead. Beauty, made by humans, can be seen and felt by angels, the wise inhabitants of both realms.[10]

Resisting the forces of socialized desire that "try to hide us," we must stop the evaporation of ourselves that occurs when we react to, rather than interiorize, beautiful objects. The task is to appropriate and incorporate the constant communications from things, transforming them into oneself:

> These things that live on departure
> understand when you praise them: fleeting, they look
> for rescue through something in us, the most fleeting
> of all. Want us to change them entirely, within our

invisible hearts, into — oh endlessly — into ourselves!
Whosoever we are. (*DE* no. 9)

Things *mean* and are full of messages when a person "transforms
them, within." The dead also communicate with the living through
things. They may point to "the catkins, hanging from empty hazels,
or else they'd be meaning the rain that falls on the dark earth in the
early Spring." The dead don't need the living, but the living need
them: "Could we exist without them?" (*DE* no. 1). Without death,
especially early death, we would not be reminded of the brief time we
have to transform "world" to "within": "your holiest inspiration's
Death, that friendly Death" (*DE* no. 9).

In the "Fourth Elegy," Rilke despairs over the divided quality of
human life. How can we be equal to the ancient terrors circulating
in our blood? How can we even keep them from encompassing and
overwhelming us? We are not sure enough of ourselves to keep them
firmly in their place. We are always second-guessing ourselves, not
knowing why we acted as we did, unsure, tentative, ready on the
slightest challenge to retreat and to take a different course. We "don't
know our feeling's shape, but only that which forms it from outside"
(*DE* no. 4).

In the face of the human quandary, Rilke advocates the learned
skill of living as if already dead, recognizing that only what adheres
to me without my grasping belongs to me, and even that, only briefly.
Awareness of death, woven into the fabric of life, is the closest we
can come to the self-abandonment Rilke urges: "But this, though:
death, the whole of death, — even before life's begun, to hold it all
so gently, and be good: this is beyond description!" (*DE* no. 4). In
her novel *Talk before Sleep,* Elizabeth Berg writes: "When you are
aware that you are dying, the path narrows, and there is room eventually for only one person — you, not distracted by anything else and
therefore able to see all that couldn't be seen before. And this can be
such a great gift that you shiver inside at the taking of it."[11]

No achievement or pleasure can match the ecstasy of transforming
"what's outside" into "an invisible re-arising in us" (*DE* no. 8). But
it is a different sort of pleasure than those to which we are socialized
and, by the time we are adults, addicted. The ability to "build the
world within" depends on the perception of beauty, the source of
terror and joy.

The Hero

Rilke calls his protagonist "the hero." Did he contrast the heroism of the one who endeavors to transform world into interior spaces with the popularly recognized heroism of the World War I soldier? Perhaps, but the hero was also the poet himself.[12]

For several years of my life, the *Elegies* provided me with courage and motivation. It is somewhat daunting, then, to reread this poetry, noticing now the hero's insistent maleness. Moreover, as I have already noted, his heroism depends on women's support and encouragement. Yet thirty years ago, I immediately appropriated in imagination the hero's role. How could I have ignored such loud and insistent signals that Rilke's hero was *not* me? I will first look more closely at gender in the *Elegies;* afterward I will try to answer this embarrassing question.

The hero is propelled from his mother's womb toward his destiny: "being opposite, and nothing else, and always opposite" (*DE* no. 8).[13] Engaged from the moment of his conception in a vigorous competition for being, his mode is aggressive: "Thousands were brewing in the womb and trying to be *he,* but look! he seized and discarded, chose and was able to do" (*DE* no. 6). The hero's birth was itself his first conquest: "If ever he shattered columns, that was the time, when he burst out of the world of your body into the narrower world, where he went on choosing and doing" (*DE* no. 6).

Two kinds of women provide the simultaneous support and "opposition" the hero needs for his self-definition, the mother and the girl (*Mädchen*). After the mother passively suffers the hero's cataclysmic birth, her role is to displace "for him, with your slender figure, the surging abyss" (*DE* no. 3). The maiden's role is similar. Because her presence arouses in the hero "more ancient terrors" than herself, she must also soothe and protect him. She must "give him those counter-balancing nights" that "withhold him" from the immensity that circulates in his own blood (*DE* no. 6).[14]

The "Third Elegy" pleads with the young woman to understand the hero's needs. It informs her of the continuity of her provisions with those of the mother and advises her not to think that the hero's need specifies *her* in any personal way:

Do you really suppose your gentle approach could have
so convulsed him, you that wander like morning-breezes?

You terrified his heart, indeed; but more ancient terrors
rushed into him in that instant of shattering contact. (*DE* no. 3)

She must understand that she represents for the hero a function. *Her
horrors* must remain concealed so that she can, with a tender smile,
reassure him. Both Jung and Rilke suggest that they would like to be
able to perform the maiden role for themselves. Rilke refers to the
"maiden within you," while Jung's woman within, the anima, is a
crucial key to individuation. Yet both relied heavily on women for
support, inspiration, and caregiving (*DE,* intro., p. 3).

Commitment is alien to Rilke's poetic hero. Jung described himself
as maintaining relationships only as long as they played a part in
his personal and professional work. Similarly, Rilke insisted that the
hero's passion does not attach to any particular woman. The hero is
much too vast to be constrained by committed love. Before he even
approaches

> maids have already plunged, victims-to-be for the son.
> For whenever the Hero stormed through the halts of
> love, each heart beating for him could only lift him
> beyond it: turning away, he'd stand at the end of the
> smiles—another. (*DE* no. 6)[15]

Rilke's hero exemplifies twentieth-century male gender socialization.
Yet Rilke's description occurred at the beginning of the century, before the phenomenon of the dependent, yet uncommitted, man had
become a popular role model. In this, as in other future events,
Rilke's intuition detected "what's coming" and also helped to rationalize it for the "young poets" who followed him. Curiously, Rilke's
gender constructions in *Duino Elegies* contradict his hope, stated
in *Letters to a Young Poet,* "for a future humanity that will have
transcended, among other things, the distinction between men and
women and all of the conflicts that derive from it."[16] In fact, women
artists have seldom received the attentive and committed care that
Rilke's hero expected and demanded.

The Uses of Pain

The "First Elegy" introduces the second theme that distinguishes
Rilke's preoccupations, pain and its uses. For Rilke, pain plays an

active role in the transformation of world into *"our* spaces" (*DE* no. 7). The "First Elegy" opens with the anguished cry:

> Alas, who is there
> that we can make use of? Not angels, not men;
> and already the knowing brutes are aware
> that we don't feel very securely at home
> within our interpreted world.

The hero mistranslates all the urgent signals he receives to alert him that his longing is matched by an external world that "has need of us." Distracted by socialized expectation, he thinks that things like spring, waves, and violins announce the imminent arrival of someone to love. Thinking of romantic love as the reward of all longing, he misses the fact that the lucky in love are actually those who are unrequited, for their capacity for love increases with their suffering: "sorrow's so often source of blessedest progress." Elsewhere in the "First Elegy" this theme arises again:

> Ought not these oldest sufferings of ours to be yielding
> more fruit by now? Is it not time that, in loving, we freed
> ourselves from the loved one, and, quivering,
> endured: as the arrow endures the string, to become in
> the gathering out-leap, something more than itself? For
> staying is nowhere.[17]

Both the unrequited in love and those who die young suffer from the notorious unfairness of life. But the lesson they teach is one of crucial importance: "I must gently remove the appearance of suffered injustice that hinders a little, at times, their purely-proceeding spirits."

Rilke's answer to the cry "Who is there we can make use of?" is pain. Yet in the "Tenth Elegy," the poet still despairs, "We wasters of sorrows!" We *have* what we need, and we neglect to put it to use. We don't *use* sorrow; we endure it passively, simply waiting for it to end.[18]

Pain is intimately linked to ecstasy. Refusing to use pain, we also reject "the source of joy." In the "Tenth Elegy," Lament, a personification, leads the young dead hero to the "mountains of primal pain" where lumps of "polished original pain" or "drossy petrified rage" were once mined. This place, she tells him, is the source of joy.

It is only, for Rilke, through the knothole of pain that we learn to transfigure the external world, *within*. Does Rilke glorify pain? Or does he merely point out its uses in the context of a social world in which pain is either passively endured or disguised by "fresh distractions"? He has seen that suffering is key to "blessedest progress"; it stretches the psyche, rendering the psyche capacious enough to accommodate sorrow *and* joy.

> Then at last
> can spring from our own turning years the cycle
> of the whole going-on. (*DE* no. 4)

Because popular wisdom conceives suffering as waste and loss, Rilke emphasized its potential. In doing so, he certainly neglected to advocate the alleviation of suffering whenever possible. His strange and powerful novel, *The Notebooks of Malte Laurids Brigge,* documents Rilke's extreme sensitivity to suffering, but it is the sensitivity of an observer, not of a reformer. Rilke was well aware of the difference; he wrote:

> A human compassion, a sense of brotherliness is certainly not alien to me. . . . But what completely distinguishes such a joyous and natural sympathy from the social impulse as we understand it today, is my complete lack of any desire, in fact my reluctance, to change or "better," as they say, the situation of anyone at all. The situation of no one in the world is such that it might not be of singular benefit to his soul.[19]

The insight that pain can be used is profound. Yet it loses its value and trivializes pain when it rationalizes inaction. Like other profound ideas, it becomes dangerous, even poisonous, when it is evoked at the wrong moment, used to justify injustice, or detached from the particular circumstances in which it interprets fruitfully.

The elegies oscillate between praise and lament. Rilke is full of praise for the provisions of the earth. Used well, they are fully sufficient. His emphasis on pain and its profit must be seen in relation to the affirmation, "Life here's glorious."[20] In the final lines of the "Tenth Elegy," lament and joy, pain and ecstasy are interwoven in a final affirmation of human life:

> And we, who have always thought
> of happiness climbing, would feel

the emotion that almost startles
when happiness falls. (*DE* no. 10)

Conclusions

In the *Duino Elegies* and *Letters to a Young Poet,* Rilke envisioned a male hero, himself, supported and nourished by a succession of women, mothers and maids. In life, he offered his lovers nourishment, but he "expected the woman to withdraw the moment the voice chose to call him."[21] This condition of relationship must have precluded reliable delivery on his offer. Indeed, those closest to him threatened his solitude more than casual acquaintances did and thus were firmly distanced. Throughout his life, relations with Clara, his wife, were cordial but remote. When Clara learned of his final illness, she rushed to him but was not permitted to enter his room.[22] He did not live with his daughter after earliest infancy, and he refused to see her on several occasions when she proposed a visit. When she married, several years before his death, he refused to meet his son-in-law or his grandchild.

Yet Rilke's ideas of the primacy of being over socialization and of the uses of pain became, for several pivotal years, my religion. Ignoring the maleness of his hero figure, I took as my own the tasks of unwinding constricting social roles and learning to use pain. Reading desperately for information and vision, I did not wonder whether the author was able to realize his visions in life nor that his vision was embedded in a sexist framework.

I was, at that point, slenderly educated. Since I had not been taught that one must read *all* of the elements of a text in relation to one another, I simply read for what the text could teach me and for its inspiration. So I boldly took what I needed. Rilke assigned me the role of "maid," with all her self-effacement, confident "withholding" of the hero from his terrors, and graceful disappearance when no longer needed. But I preferred the role of "hero." The problem was that I appropriated the hero's role without the support the hero could expect.

In fact, it is not, finally, the male hero who most needs the call to being in the *Elegies.* Surrounded and supported by the institutions of social life, by the care and protection of women who feed him and wash his socks, and by a gender socialization that regards all this

as his unquestionable right, the hero has little need of further affirmation. But I needed that call. Lacking economic agency and social
support, I desperately needed to be assured that my quest was legitimate, that I was entitled to pursue education and a career. At the
time, only Rilke gave me that assurance, and only when I selectively
appropriated his vision. A desperate person can overlook a great deal
if a book enables her to gather the strength and courage not merely
to go on but to go forward.

African-American cultural critic Michelle Wallace gives a similar testimony. Discussing films of the 1940s, Wallace writes that "it
was always said among Black women that Joan Crawford was part
Black." She admits that that statement "makes no sense in current
feminist film criticism." But she goes on to insist that the white
goddesses of 1940s films were used by black women for their own
purposes, for discussing, adopting, adapting, and resisting the skills
of white femininity: "The process may have been about problema-
tizing and expanding one's racial identity instead of abandoning it.
It seems crucial...to view spectatorship not only as potentially bi-
sexual but also multiracial and multiethnic."[23] Wallace's point is a
courageous one in the present climate of critical studies. She points
to the possibility that language and images that specifically exclude
or marginalize a person of one's own race or gender can nevertheless
be adapted to one's circumstances and used. But is the naive reader
not at risk of being seduced to accept, along with the text's power,
its perspective, attitudes, and allegiances? Yes, clearly; for my naive
reading of the Duino Elegies played a large part not only in inspiring
me to appropriate the hero's role but also in seducing me to a long
and less-than-mutual relationship with (literally) a young poet.

This chapter began with the question of whether a critical reading of a work of literature must inevitably destroy any potential it
may have *for life*. It should, I hope, be clear by now that neither a
naive reading nor a critical reading can, without loss, supplant the
other. A naive reading is capable of recovering the book's potential
for life-altering insight. However, the naive reader is vulnerable to incorporating also the book's assumptions and loyalties. Both critical
and naive readings are needed; neither should suppress the other.

Critical readings that have lost the book's excitement and en-
ergy have also lost most of the reason for examining it critically.
For the text's attractions conceal its danger. The French semiologist
Roland Barthes once said that you *get* the cultural message at the

same instant that you get the pleasure. A book's beauty *is* its power of seduction and therefore its potential danger. An adequate critical reading, then, must explicate not only the text's gaps, omissions, indifferences, and injustices, its covert and overt affiliations, but also its skillful rendition of a powerful vision.

In short, one need not ignore a work's gender bias in order to make use of its insights. Indeed, it is only after recognizing textual bias that one can deliberately use a text in defiance of its author's explicit intention. After all, criticism is not done in order to condemn authors long dead and blissfully indifferent. It is done to alert the living to the poignant fallibility of all human labor and achievement. And to reaffirm human labor and achievement, for "staying is nowhere" (*DE* no. 1).

Chapter 7

"WHERE THE GROWN PEOPLE?"
Toni Morrison's *Jazz*

——— • ———

We never feel as grown-up as we expected to feel when we were
children.

—Dorothy Dinnerstein, *The Mermaid and the Minataur*

A MAN SHOOTS an eighteen-year-old girl who has accepted, manipulated, and finally rejected his obsessive love. The police don't
care: the murdered and the murderer are black. So is the murderer's
wife, who watches him cry all day every day and decides to *do* something. She takes a lover; that doesn't last long. She makes herself fall
back in love with her husband; even shorter duration. Finally she
sets out to understand the dead girl. She finds out from people who
knew her what kind of lip-rouge she wore and where she went to
school. She even learns the dance steps the dead girl did. She wants
to "love—well, find out about—" the girl, to know concretely and
in detail how it felt to be the girl her Joe loved enough to shoot.

Jazz is a serious love story, a story about real love, not movie or
fairy tale love. It is about love among people who have made choices
with the best they had to work with at the moment. But life went on;
they changed and society changed, and they kept doing what they
were doing. Their choices were not terrible. They got them a piece
of the way. But then they needed revision: "Staying is nowhere."[1]
Jazz is about *making* love out of what one has. It is about giving and
receiving "the necessary things for the night." Out of the worst of
circumstances—unfaithfulness, a murdered girl, a crying husband, a
silent, crazy wife, bitter memories—out of these, a grown-up love
is made.

Jazz is a big story; I see it on a wide screen. It is about the
city, New York City, its enticements, its inebriations, its dangers,
its beauty, its people, and its music. There is room for everyone

in the city, and *Jazz* reproduces this spaciousness. In this, it resembles Julie Dash's film *Daughters of the Dust,* an account of the African-American Pezant family on the eve of their departure from the Gullah Islands off the coast of South Carolina for the mainland. There is no "hero" in Dash's film; the interactions of the family members provide the narrative. The frame of each scene is a wide landscape. There is room for everyone to stand in her own light.

In the city, most people are as interested in one another's business as readers are. They watch and listen, eager to detect something of interest. The small excitements of their lives are composed of others' misbehavior and misfortune. But

> I've known a few exceptions. Old people who didn't slap the children for being slappable; who saved their strength in case it was needed for something important. A last courtship full of smiles and little presents. Or the dedicated care of an old friend who might not make it through without them. Sometimes they concentrated on making sure the person they had shared their long lives with had cheerful company and the necessary things for the night.[2]

Jazz is Joe's and Violet's story, but their story is interwoven with the city's story and with many other people's stories. There are no incidental characters, no half-people who exist in the novel only to supplement Joe's and Violet's story. The same incident is often narrated from more than one person's perspective. All the characters, no matter how small their part, vibrate with their own lives: Malvonne, Felice, Alice, Henry Lestory, Victory, Golden Gray, Rose Dear, True Belle.[3] The reader must unlearn ingrained expectations that a narrative must focus on several main characters, the rest becoming foliage, backdrop. In *Jazz,* attention is distributed among the characters; visibility is shared.

No one is reduced to the effect she has on someone else. The city, the neighborhood, the people, the times: all are essential to the narrative. Everyone is exactly as important as everyone else, no more and no less. By narrative conventions, the sign that a character is incidental to a novel is that readers see that character only as she touches the central characters. Moreover, readers never learn the fate of ancillary characters and it doesn't matter, because we have never learned enough about them to feel empathy, curiosity, or affection for them. In *Jazz*, we know what happens to almost everyone, not just Dorcas, or Joe, or Violet. We also know what happens to Alice Manfred, Felice, and Victory, as well as Golden Gray.

Predictably, a novel that departs from established conventions receives some uncomprehending reviews. Does *Jazz* "stir the mind more than the heart," as Deborah McDowell claimed in the *Woman's Review of Books?*[4] Edna O'Brien, reviewing *Jazz* for the *New York Times Book Review,* also "missed" "the emotional nexus, the moment shorn of all artifice that brings us headlong into the deepest recesses of feeling."[5] I disagree. If the "deepest recesses of feeling" are not engaged by *Jazz,* I suspect that it is the reader's failure, not the author's. If the characters fade just slightly into the rhythm of the whole going-on, it is because they share the limelight with each other and with the city. Their lives are swept up into the music of the city. Each of its interwoven lives has its own beat, but each also blends into the "snapping fingers, the clicking" of a "music that intoxicates them more than champagne" (*J* 227).

Jazz takes place during the so-called Harlem Renaissance, but it does not focus on the leaders of that movement. Rather, ordinary people — for want of a better term — are the subjects of this cultural history. They are "blackpeople" animated by the music that spills from rooftops, doorways, and dark rooms. It is jazz, "dirty get-on-down music" (58): "Songs that used to start in the head and fill the heart had dropped on down, down to places below the sash and the buckled belts" (56). Jazz has a powerful effect on everyone whether, like Alice Manfred and the Miller sisters, they hate and fear it, or, like Dorcas, they love it: "They believe they know before the music does what their hands, their feet are to do, but that illusion is the music's secret drive: the control it tricks them into believing is theirs" (65). New York is a "city seeping music" (67). Morrison makes her reader hear that finger-snapping music that dances her characters even as they think they choose. And "it makes you wonderful just to see it" (11). "That kind of fascination, permanent and out of control, seizes children, young girls, men of every description, mothers, brides, and barfly women, and if they have their way and get to the city, they feel more like themselves, more like the people they always believed they were. No wonder they forget pebbly creeks and when they do not forget the sky completely think of it as a tiny piece of information about the time of day or night" (34–35).

The city makes Joe forget "a sun that used to slide up like the yolk of a good country egg, thick and red-orange at the bottom of the sky." But it has its own beauty:

There is nothing to beat what the City can make of a nightsky. It can empty itself of surface, and more like the ocean than the ocean itself, go deep, starless. Close up on the tops of buildings, near, nearer than the cap you are wearing, such a citysky presses and retreats, presses and retreats, making me think of the free but illegal love of sweethearts before they are discovered. [At a different time of day, the citysky can also] go purple and keep an orange heart so the clothes of the people on the streets glow like dance-hall costumes. (34–35)

Language among these first generation city "blackpeople" is musical, "an intricate, malleable toy, designed for their play" (33). Language defines community. Words like "hincty," "siddity," "catface," and "sweetback" rely on their context in the novel for meaning. Even the first word of the book is not quite a word: "Sth" is the sound of the tongue sucking a tooth. But words are not always playful; they have power to deceive as well as to heal; they can "lie, heat your blood, and disappear" (37). What begins as banter, wordplay, can "take on weight," can make a man decide to do something he has only fantasized (71). Most frightening of all, words can make you feel you understand something you don't.

Making Love

In the city, there is no middle age, no time when the poverty and urgency of youth are quiescent and you are not yet old. Old age comes at "forty or sixty"; it is defined by "not remembering what things felt like" (11, 29). It is being able to feel in the present only by acting out the bleak dead places desire can't get to directly. Violet sits down in the street; she steals a baby for a few minutes; she interrupts a funeral, tries to slash a dead girl's face. Joe makes love to a girl young enough to be his daughter, shoots the girl when he didn't mean to. Tortured, circuitous desire. Holding the baby, Violet felt "comfort [settle] itself in her stomach and a kind of skipping, running light traveled her veins" (19). Seeing Dorcas and imagining loving her, Joe feels the "ping of desire" (29). The characters act out, rather than act.

By contrast, Dorcas and Felice, the young, feel desire as a "stomach jump" (66). Dorcas is "enchanted by the frail, melty tendency of the flesh" (63). She knows, Alice Manfred says, "better than you or me or anybody just how small and quick this little bitty life is" (113). Violet agrees: "I thought it would be bigger than this. I knew it wouldn't last, but I did think it would be bigger" (112).

The characters didn't come from nowhere and begin their lives when the novel begins. They have parents. Everyone they try to love after these, their first loves, are substitutes. Joe and Violet love phantoms. Joe loves the mother he never knew, in whatever woman's body she appears in. For Joe, girl, wife, and mother seep into one another and become indistinguishable. One chapter of the novel ends as the boy Joe tries to track his mother, Wild, the woman accompanied by red-winged blackbirds. "Where is she?" he asks. The next chapter begins, "There she is," as Joe, a fifty-year-old man, sees Dorcas. Hunting Dorcas, Joe confuses Dorcas with Wild. He imagines how she will be when he finds her: "She'll be alone. Hardheaded. Wild, even. But alone" (182). He hunts Dorcas carrying a gun. He will not use it, doesn't mean to use it. "He is hunting for her, though, and while hunting a gun is a natural companion" (181). Joe says, "I had the gun, but it was not the gun — it was my hand I wanted to touch you with" (130–31).

Helpless, the boy Joe needs his mother; helpless, the man Joe needs Dorcas. He needs Violet too, whom he married because he couldn't find his mother. But he treats her "like a piece of furniture you favor although it needed something every day to keep it steady and upright" (123). In the face of all this need, Joe maintains the illusion of choice. He tells Dorcas: "I *chose* you. Nobody gave you to me. Nobody said that's the one for you. I picked you out. Wrong time, yep, and doing wrong by my wife. But the picking out, the choosing. Don't ever think I fell for you, or fell over you. I didn't fall in love, I rose in it. I saw you and made up my mind. My mind" (135). But the narrator comments, "I imagine him as one of those men who stop somewhere around sixteen. Inside." The narrator continues: "Look out. Look out for a faithful man near fifty. Because he has never messed with another woman; because he selected that young girl to love, he thinks he is free. Not free to break loaves or feed the world on fish. Nor to raise the war dead, but free to do something wild" (120).

Violet also has her unexpurgated phantoms. Her mother, Rose Dear, threw herself into a narrow, dark well. She was raised by her grandmother, True Belle, who postponed her own dying in order to raise Rose Dear's family: "The important thing, the biggest thing Violet got out of that was to never never have children. Whatever happened, no small dark foot would rest on another while a hungry mouth said, Mama?" (102). So Violet aborted whenever she conceived, "more inconvenience than loss." But, when children are no longer possible for Violet, she begins to long for one: "By and by longing became heavier than sex: a panting, unmanageable craving. She was limp in its thrall or rigid in an attempt to dismiss it....Violet was drowning in [mother hunger], deep-dreaming....When she woke up, her husband had shot a girl young enough to be that daughter" (108).

Violet's father was absent except for occasional unexpected appearances when he would laughingly disperse gifts: clumps of candy stuck together in his coat pocket, bottles of rye and cologne, lead pencils, and Jap Rose soap. He expected his children to forget that he had abandoned them in their excitement over his gifts, "both genuine and fake." "In his company forgetfulness fell like pollen. But for Violet the pollen never blotted out Rose" (100).

True Belle, the only character in the novel who lives without the illusion of choice, has regaled Violet with stories of Golden Gray, the biracial son of her owner/employer. He became, for Violet, "my own golden boy, who I never ever saw but who tore up my girlhood as surely as if we'd been the best of lovers....I knew him and loved him better than anybody except True Belle who is the one made me crazy about him in the first place" (139).

How can love be made out of these unlikely people and circumstances? Violet and Joe suffer and squirm, getting up in the sleepless night to stare at a picture of the dead girl. For these people, psychotherapy is, quite literally, unheard of. Yet they perform the "talking cure." They do not talk in a "safe place," with a trained therapist, but they are cured, by which I mean freed for the present, as surely as any psychoanalyst could wish, and by the same method. Violet convinces Alice Manfred, aunt of Dorcas, the murdered girl, to let her sit down in Alice's home. She returns, morning after morning, to talk. Both women are initially inarticulate with pain:

"Why did he do such a thing?"
"Why did she?"
"Why did you?"
"I don't know." (181)

Through much talk, tea-drinking, sewing, and ironing, they find common ground: "We born around the same time. We women, me and you. Tell me something real" (110). A pivotal moment comes when Violet recognizes that no one but she can or will make her life: "Oh shoot!" she says, "Where the grown people? Is it us?" She recognizes that it was precisely this realization that her mother could not act on: "Mama? Is this where you got to and couldn't do it no more? The place of shade without trees where you know you are not, and never again will be loved by anybody who can choose to do it? Where everything is over but the talking?" (110). Violet talks her way through pain and anger to see, "He's what I got. He's what I got." Alice tells her, "You got anything left to love, anything at all, do it." "You saying take it, don't fight?" Violet asks. "Nobody's asking you to take it. I'm sayin make it, make it!" Alice replies, as she burns the shirt she is ironing. And they laugh, "crumpled over, shoulders shaking," the serious, complicated kind of laughter that is "more serious than tears" (113–14).

Joe's retrieval is more complicated: "Meaning to or not meaning to, [Violet] got him to go through it again" (119). Dorcas's friend, Felice, comes to call. She has heard of Joe's grieving and wants to tell him that Dorcas was not worth it, that Dorcas need not have died, but that she insisted that the ambulance not be called, and thus she bled to death. Violet asks Felice to come again, sit down, and talk. She leaves Felice and Joe alone. Felice is uncomfortable, sitting by Joe on the couch while Violet is out of the room: "I wished I hadn't taken my sweater off. My dress stretches across the top no matter what I do. He was looking at my face, not my body, so I don't know why I was nervous in the room alone with him" (212). They talk. Joe's story, he says, has already been told — to Dorcas, to whom he told "things I hadn't told myself?" (123). Sitting with Felice he acknowledges, "Well, if you mean did I like what I felt about her. I guess I'm stuck to that" (212):

"Why did you shoot her if you loved her?"
"Scared. Didn't know how to love anybody." (213)

But Joe and Violet are "working on it." The other stories begin to surface, the stories submerged by their phantoms: Joe and Violet as children, as young lovers. They live with their stories. Perhaps they still do not quite have "the necessary things for the night," but it doesn't matter because they have quit sleeping at night. Joe works nights, and "they take short naps whenever the body insists" (223). They often "stay home figuring things out." They have not exorcised their phantoms; they have befriended them:

> Lying next to her, his head turned toward the window, he sees through the glass darkness taking the shape of a shoulder with a thin line of blood. Slowly, slowly it forms itself into a bird with a blade of red on the wing. Meanwhile Violet rests her hand on his chest as though it were the sunlit rim of a well and down there somebody is gathering gifts (lead pencils, Bull Durham, Jap Rose Soap) to distribute to them all. (225)[6]

Dorcas's attraction to Acton, the boyfriend she chose over Joe, is based on appearances — his appearance, which attracts her, and hers. She dresses to please him, doesn't wear glasses in his presence, plucks her eyebrows, changes her laugh, knots her stockings below, not above, her knees (190). When she is shot, he is annoyed that she bleeds on his jacket. Yet Dorcas is "happy" with him, happier than she has ever been. The other girls envy her, and she has a romance she can tell her girlfriends about (188). Unlike her romance with the married and older Joe, Dorcas's romance with Acton is all show and tell.

Compare Dorcas and Acton's love with the difficult and playful love Joe and Violet are working on. Joe and Violet are "inward toward the other" (228):

> It's nice when grown people whisper to each other under the covers. Their ecstasy is more leaf-sigh than bray and the body is the vehicle, not the point. They reach, grown people, for something beyond, way down underneath tissue. They are remembering while they whisper the carnival dolls they won and the Baltimore boats they never sailed on.... They are under the covers because they don't have to look at themselves anymore; they is no stud's eye, no chippie glance to undo them. They are inward toward the other, bound and joined by carnival dolls

and the steamers that sailed from ports they never saw. That is what is beneath their undercover whispers. (228)

Reading *Jazz* for Life

The books I have discussed offer ideas of central importance for living with enjoyment and generosity. But philosophical, psychological, poetic, and theological books do not provide the fleshed-out picture of how such a life might look and feel that a fine novel does. Rilke, Plotinus, and Augustine do not reveal any *particular* people, their pains, their loves, or their amazing and baffling passions. Their works lack the urgency and the detail supplied by novels. There is something powerfully provocative and evocative in watching people work out the details, on location, of a generous and pleasurable life, as one does in reading a masterful novel. Martha Nussbaum writes, "We need a story of a certain kind, with characters of a certain type in it, if our own sense of life and value is to be called forth in the way most appropriate for practical reflection."[7]

I also find in *Jazz* an identification of what is truly serious. The novel reminds its readers that what people ordinarily think of as serious — scholarship or business, for example — can be laughably trivial, without tangible effects in anyone's life. Similarly, Augustine once described most adult preoccupations as substantially identical to childish arguments over "footballs, nuts, and pet sparrows" (*Conf.* 1.19). By contrast, anger is often serious, and laughter, strong, deep laughter coming up from the belly and spilling out of the lips, can be utterly serious. Laughter can announce healing, offer resources for an impossible situation, or supply the energy simply to go on, to find a way to cope:

Violet was the first to smile. Then Alice. In no time laughter was rocking them both. Violet was reminded of True Belle, who entered the single room of their cabin and laughed to beat the band. They were hunched like mice near a can fire, not even a stove, on the floor, hungry, irritable. True Belle looked at them and had to lean against the wall to keep her laughter from pulling her down to the floor with them. They should have hated her. Gotten up from the floor and hated her. But what they felt was better. Not beaten, not lost. Better. They

laughed too, even Rose Dear shook her head and smiled, and
suddenly the world was right side up. Violet learned then what
she had forgotten until this moment: that laughter is serious.
More complicated, more serious than tears. (*J* 113)

An identification of the genuinely serious is *Jazz*'s first contribution
to reading for life.

Second, the importance of imagination is one of the persistent
themes of *Jazz*. A generous imagination is characterized by willingness to imagine another person's life. Imagination is not simply a
matter of projecting one's own fears and angers onto others. It is
knowing when, and with what limitations, a piece of my experience
might help me understand someone else's experience or perspective. Not sloppiness but a skill. In the *Odyssey*, Kalypso says to the
grieving Odysseus: "My heart is not made of iron, but pitiful, like
yours."[8] She feels, in imagination, his pain. Such a moment occurs
when Violet speculates on Dorcas's attraction to Joe: "Maybe that is
what she saw. Not the fifty-year-old man toting a sample case, but
my Joe Trace, my Virginia Joe Trace who carried a light inside him,
whose shoulders were razor sharp and who looked at me with two-
color eyes and never saw anybody else. Could she have looked at
him and seen that?" (*J* 96).

But perhaps I have glided too easily over the moral responsibility of a novel in which a man can murder an eighteen-year-old
woman without legal consequence. One reviewer wrote, "Why am
I so detached from something that should make me cringe: the unpunished murder of a woman who dares to desire?"[9] I wonder too.
Perhaps it is because this story is a tale not of crime and punishment but of relationship. On the most literal level, Joe is not caught
and punished because the ambulance and the police don't come
when called. Alice, Dorcas's aunt, despairs of justice. "She would
have called the police . . . if everything she knew about Negro life had
made it even possible to consider" (74). Perhaps it is also because
Joe was punished, although he was never arraigned before a court
of law:

In the spring of 1926, on a rainy afternoon, anybody passing
through the alley next to a certain apartment house on Lenox
might have looked up and seen, not a child but a grown man's
face crying along the glass pane. A strange sight you hardly ever
see: men crying so openly. It's not a thing they do. Strange as it

is, people finally got used to him, wiping his face and nose with a red engineer's handkerchief while he sat month after month by the window without view or on the stoop, first in the snow and later in the sun. (118)

In *Jazz*, reward and punishment occur as they often do in life, informally, interiorly. In life there is often the most excruciating punishment for nothing at all or for someone else's decisions and deeds. And sometimes there is none for reprehensible deeds. Legal justice, certainly one of the "necessary things for the night" if one is to sleep in safety, is crude and approximate at best. At worst, as in Harlem in the 1920s — and now — legal justice is so untrustworthy as to fall beneath consideration (74). Joe is punished no less surely, and certainly more productively, than if he had received a jail sentence.

In *Jazz*, characters can imagine the reality of others' lives. Some of them can also imagine across mental categories. Augustine *knew* that animals suffer when they are killed, but he refused to allow himself to *imagine* their suffering. Had he done so, he might have felt a distressing compunction about killing them for human nourishment and pleasure. But in *Jazz*, Golden Gray notices that he is repelled by a naked, wet, black woman; he notices that his horse is also naked, wet, and black and that he feels affection for him. He finds that odd, "is a touch ashamed," and determines to care for the woman (144).

"I strain after images," Plato said. The images provided in *Jazz* show, without having to instruct, that moral action begins at the level of perception, with seeing and noticing that one sees. Detailed perceptions carry the vividness, the unrepeatability, the immediacy. We need novels to teach us how to be, in the words of Henry James, a person "on whom nothing is lost," with "the power to be finely aware and richly responsible."[10]

"All love is...love of fictional characters," Martha Nussbaum writes, "and literature trains us for that element in love."[11] Characters in fiction should help us to imagine ourselves loving imperfect, confused, and lovable people like ourselves. Moreover, novels that help us see characters whose lives are intimately connected with others make us understand that we too, and those we love and live with, are affected by, and deeply affect, one another.

Every newspaper documents the myriad ways people are harmed by one another; children are harmed by parents and teachers, partners by one another, the young by the old, and the old by the young.

This is not "news." But that one character's goodness can affect others in powerful but invisible ways: this is less evident and less regularly documented. *Jazz* gives us characters who affect one another for good, as well as for suffering. For example, Alice's generosity in letting *in* the crazy woman who disrupted her niece's funeral. Alice let her sit down and talk, and come back, and drink her tea, and talk some more. And Violet was healed. Consider also Violet's profound generosity, her spectacular lack of fear, in bringing Felice — another young, awkward, appealing girl like Dorcas — into their living room, letting her talk, listening to her, talking to her, and feeding her catfish. This healed Joe.

Fictional characters matter. They train us to imagine, to look for, and to recognize ourselves and the people we undertake to love. Whether we see ourselves and others as pursuing our goals separately, acting out our hopes and fears privately, and living alone, even when others surround us, or whether we see characters *in relationship,* impossible to describe apart from their relationships, largely depends on the novels we read. For people become good at least partly because someone noticed that quality, saw it clearly, and pointed it out. Morrison makes us *notice* Joe neatly putting away the children's toys that littered the front steps. Yes, he killed a girl, we saw that, but we also notice his goodness.

In the hands of a less skillful novelist, we could have seen Joe either as a scoundrel or as a misunderstood, oppressed victim of rotten circumstances, more sinned against than sinning. But a novel that judged Joe out of sentiment or ideology would not have allowed its readers to enter Joe's and Violet's intimate pain, Alice's pain, Felice's pain, and, yes, Dorcas's pain. It would have been more concerned with exonerating Joe than with *how the relationships worked,* how it was possible for a good man to shoot a girl, how it could happen. Morrison insists that we perceive Joe's goodness through our own ability to love, not through our pity. When we have practiced that kind of complex compassion in reading a novel, it is easier to think that way about ourselves and the people with whom we live. A novel that gives us an image of honest goodness, difficult goodness, is a great novel.

Jazz is about *making* love. And love in American media culture is so seldom made. It is frequently fallen into and fallen out of, but our media myths seldom picture for us the work, the pain, and the dailiness of love. Our imaginations are not stocked with images that help us with long loves. We feel this lack in the most sensitive and intimate places of our lives. I depart from *Jazz* briefly in order to sketch more fully the importance of Morrison's contribution to our repertoire of images of making love.

In her book *The Therapy of Desire*, Martha Nussbaum describes the ancient philosopher Lucretius's attempt to direct his reader "beyond obsession and disgust" in matters of love. Lucretius says that the unrealistic lover is characterized by two attitudes. He divinizes the beloved, and in lovemaking, he endeavors to fuse with the beloved, overcoming separateness, controlling and immobilizing the beloved.[12] These attitudes create a selfish lover, one who ultimately hurts the woman to whom he "makes love." His aims will be frustrated because the beloved's goddess-like status will inevitably be rather easily and terminally undermined by intimate daily life and because he cannot achieve the kind of union he desires. She remains separate, but "if she is going to go on feeling separately, if she obstinately resists being devoured, then pain is what she's going to feel."[13]

Lucretius recognized that the unrealistic lover's attitudes derive from culture: "Since this lover has been brought up on myths of Venus, a Venus is what he must see [when he looks at the woman he is 'in love' with]."[14] Emotions are taught "through stories, pictures, poems — through representations to which we later refer, using them as paradigms that guide our understanding of the signs we perceive in life."[15]

Lucretius recommended another approach to erotic love. The lover could see the beloved "beyond obsession and disgust" as a "separate and fully human being." Lovers could take note of the good properties actually possessed by the other and nonetheless mutually acknowledge "human things" — her menstrual periods, his snoring, as well as each other's flaws and weaknesses. Accurate and realistic recognition of the other could prepare the ground for genuine human relationship. Marriage, or any full-time live-in relationship, "requires the ability to see, every day, the other's daily 'backstage' life, and to see this without disgust or even boredom, *without a constant implicit contrast to some other wonderful excitement*."[16]

Lucretius predicted that this more realistic approach to love would have considerable effects on lovemaking. Rather than "the strong taking what they can, and the weak suffering what they must," the aim of lovemaking will be "the giving and receiving of pleasure on both sides."[17]

Morrison describes precisely this realistic love and the pain and the work, for Joe and Violet, of achieving it. *Jazz* offers new and meticulous images of grown-up love, love whose touches and glances would be invisible if you didn't know how to look for them: "There is another part, not so secret. The part that touches fingers when one passes the cup and saucer to the other. The part that closes her neckline snap while waiting for the trolley; and brushes lint from his blue serge suit when they come out of the movie-house into the sunlight" (*J* 229). Minds are as central to these images of love as bodies. Love's mind is bodied, acted in the slightest glimpse and touch. Joe and Violet imagine the real.

I have already mentioned a third contribution *Jazz* makes to reading for life: it helps me imagine myself more realistically. For Joe, finding himself meant acknowledging the goodness in his love for Dorcas, the privilege of caring for her, of seeing her softness. It also meant remembering his young love for Violet — "what things felt like" — and recognizing his *now* love for Violet. Joe *is* his love; he is the sum of all he has, and has had, of what can truthfully be called love. Similarly, Violet thinks in terms of making her "life." She tells Felice, I "messed up my life":

> "Messed it up how?"
> "Forgot it."
> "Forgot?"
> "Forgot it was mine. My life. I just ran up and down the streets wishing I was somebody else." (208)

At the end of the pain and honesty, there is simply "Me," doing "my life." Felice comments: "The way she said it. Not like the 'me' was some tough somebody, or somebody she had put together for show. But like, like somebody she favored and could count on. A secret somebody you didn't have to feel sorry for or have to fight for" (210).

What Violet and Joe make out of their phantoms and their pain is more like an alertness and a doing than like finding a hitherto undiscovered self. They imagine "a secret somebody" and then *try on* this somebody. Violet takes her "secret somebody" out for air — a somebody her mother would have liked, had she stuck around long enough — letting *her* respond to some things that come up. She watches how that works and feels and, when necessary, revises or reimagines her. In *Jazz,* the self is not a thing but a life, touched and touching, richly responsive to others, formed by its loyalties and its loves.

Perhaps the greatest gift of the novel, however, lies in another direction. In *Playing in the Dark: Whiteness and the Literary Imagination,* Toni Morrison discusses the systemic effect of "Africanism" on American literature. Morrison defines Africanism as "the denotative and connotative blackness that African peoples have come to signify, as well as the entire range of views, assumptions, readings, and misreadings that accompany Eurocentric learning about these people."[18] Blackness is the "other" against which Americans' most cherished self-images have been formed.[19] The components of Americanism, "autonomy, authority, newness and difference, absolute power, not only [became] the major themes and preoccupations of American literature, but each one is made possible by...Africanism," represented as rawness and savagery.[20]

Commenting on a character in a Hemingway story, Morrison writes, "Eddy is white, and we know he is so because nobody says so."[21] Clearly, asymmetrical "othering" harms the people thus categorized. It is less evident, but equally true, that it also harms those who categorize. For the person whose race no author needs to identify because it is assumed will never recognize the limitations of his perspective by being confronted by difference in another human being. Imagining himself as norm, and noticing others' difference only as departures from that norm, he does not see his own race as a factor in his perspective.

In Julie Dash's film *Daughters of the Dust,* as in *Jazz,* there are no white characters, though the presence of whites is palpable, shaping the actions and moving the narrative as much by their absence at crucial moments as by their hinted presence. Absent when black people call the police or fire department or ambulance, white people are present in the two works as bosses and owners, both on the plantations from which the city blacks came and in the businesses and government of the city. White people are there in the wings, but they do not come onstage, except to literally "throw money" at black people for "just being neighborly," for simple acts of kindness like opening a door or picking up a package (*J* 106). In *Jazz,* Felice's father, a Pullman attendant, explains the two kinds of white people: "the ones that feel sorry for you and the ones that don't. And both amount to the same thing. Nowhere in between is respect" (204).[22]

I am "othered" by *Jazz,* as I am by *Daughters of the Dust.* I recognize that my whiteness in the context of a thoroughly racist society is neither innocent nor neutral. It matters; it has concrete effects, and therefore it must become a critical part of my self-image. I am a member of a race that has constructed "a history and context for whites by positing history-lessness and context-lessness for blacks."[23]

But a vague racial responsibility is not all that I must accept when I take *Jazz* seriously. I must also notice that I am personally advantaged every day in myriad ways because I am not black. This awareness creates the discomfort of self-knowledge. I feel as distressed as I *should* feel participating in social and institutional arrangements supported ubiquitously by invisible whiteness. This increment of reality represents a priceless gift that *Jazz* offers to a white person who reads for life.

The Author as Narrator

I have considered the novel's morality in letting a horrible crime go "unpunished." I turn now to another issue of moral responsibility specifically raised in *Jazz,* namely, the author's accountability. Morrison suggests that authorial responsibility should be evaluated according to two criteria: ability to create complex characters and moral imagination.

In *Jazz,* the narrator is the author who makes things happen and comments on them. She confesses the predilections that inform her perspective, for example, her confidence in pain:

> Pain. I seem to have an affection, a kind of sweettooth for it. Bolts of lightning, little rivulets of thunder. And I the eye of the storm. Mourning the split trees, hens starving on rooftops. Figuring out what can be done to save them since they cannot save themselves without me because — well, it's my storm, isn't it? I break lives to prove I can mend them back again. And although the pain is theirs, I share it, don't I? Of course. Of course. I wouldn't have it any other way. (215, 218)

The narrator is not an unseen omniscient voice-over. Like the chorus in a Greek tragedy, she is onstage commenting, advising, and questioning: "Maybe she thought she could solve the mystery of love that way. Good luck and let me know" (5). The narrator/author interprets her characters gently, lovingly, even as she disagrees with some of their beliefs and actions. She rejects, but gently, for example, Joe's claim that he *chose* to love Dorcas:

> Take my word for it, he is bound to the track. It pulls him like a needle through the groove of a Bluebird record. Round and round about the town. That's the way the City spins you. Makes you do what it wants, go where the laid-out roads say to. All the while letting you think you're free... You can't get off a track the City lays for you. (120)

When bystanders give her characters bad advice she cannot help but protest. When Violet's mother, Rose Dear, and her five children are abandoned and evicted, neighbors bring what they can spare, along with advice: " 'Don't let this whip you, Rose. You got us, Rose Dear. Think of the young ones, Rose. He ain't given you nothing you can't bear, Rose.' But had He? Maybe this one time He had. Had misjudged and misunderstood her particular backbone. This one time. This here particular spine" (99). The author/narrator models, by the love and concern she shows her characters, the care, the detailed observation, the tenderness the reader can feel, now that she has the image.

I wonder about the lack of attention to religion in *Jazz*. It appears momentarily in Alice Manfred's oppressive upbringing and in the Miller sisters' rejection of modern life in the big city. Theirs is a doomsday religion that prohibits but never authorizes or empowers. In *Beloved*, Morrison treated religion as an intimate and integral part of her characters' lives, a way they had of explaining things and working them out. In *Jazz*, by contrast, despite Morrison's detailed depiction of New York City in 1926 (thirty-five colored nurses at Bellevue hospital; World War I veterans still in their uniform greatcoats), religion is not part of the scene. Did Morrison think that the credibility of her characters, and the reader's identification with them, could not be expected to extend to their religion? Yet religion was difficult for people to ignore in 1926, even in New York City. Religion was the center of black community, *the* thing everyone would have to come to terms with, to embrace or to resist, even in the jazz age. In *Jazz*, no one prays, no one goes to church, and no one sings gospel (although every woman jazz singer of the time established her credentials by singing gospel). Religion was the quintessential "necessary thing for the night," and almost nobody in *Jazz* has any. Of course, a novel is not obliged to represent history accurately. Nevertheless, without religion the characters lack a larger framework than their personal pasts and the present moment. Have they rejected religion? The novel does not answer this question because the question is never formulated. Religion is simply a lacuna.

The author doesn't merely narrate and comment; it is her story too. Her function in the novel is to wait and watch, as well as to move things around; she has been chosen to do this, she says. In *Jazz*, authorship is moral engagement, and the reader is urged to ponder the author's dilemmas as he does the characters':

> Now I have to think this through, carefully, even though I may be doomed to another misunderstanding. I have to do it and not break down. Not hating him is not enough; liking, loving him is not useful. I have to alter things. I have to be a shadow who wishes him well, like the smiles of the dead left over from their lives. I want to dream a nice dream for him, and another of him. Lie down next to him, a wrinkle in the sheet, and contemplate his pain and by doing so ease it, diminish it. I want to be the language that wishes him well, speaks his name, wakes him when his eyes need to be open. (161)

It is finally the narrator/author-as-character that completes the story. She reveals her attentive interest, *her* needs. She worries; she berates herself with being "careless and stupid...unreliable: How could I have imagined him so poorly?" (160). She has, she claims, not imagined accurately her characters' inner resources: "I was sure one would kill the other. I waited for it so I could describe it. I was so sure it would happen. That the past was an abused record with no choice but to repeat itself at the crack and no power on earth could lift the arm that held that needle" (220). She acknowledges: "It was loving the City that distracted me and gave me ideas. Made me think I could speak its loud voice and make that sound sound human. I missed the people altogether" (220). Yet her characters are "not sepia....For me they are real" (226). By representing them as functions of the city and its music, she worries that she has not done them justice. She has not, she says, understood their thoughts, their motives, or their particular urgencies:

I believed I saw everything important they did, and based on what I saw I could imagine what I didn't: how exotic they were, how driven. Like dangerous children. That's what I wanted to believe. It never occurred to me that they were thinking other thoughts, feeling other feelings, putting their lives together in ways I never dreamed of. (221)

For several of the authors discussed in previous chapters, the goal of life is consciousness. But for Morrison, "something is missing there":

I started out believing that life was made just so the world would have some way to think about itself, but that it had gone awry with humans because flesh, pinioned by misery, hangs on to it with pleasure.... I don't believe that anymore. Something is missing there. Something rogue. Something else you have to figure in before you can figure it out. (227–28)

You have to "figure in" passion, images, the driven urgency in the blood "before you can figure it out." Moreover, in *Jazz* the characters who work through their "something[s] rogue" in order to live a humanly rich life are poor black people, young and old, women and men. Nobody would be likely to point to them as culture heroes. Yet Morrison's characters teach, without appearing to teach, serious and important matters.

Morrison's loving eye and dexterity with language are sufficient evidence that author and characters are profoundly motivated by a perception of complex beauty. Even the narrator's repeated confessions that she has not imagined her characters richly enough testify, finally, to her exacting sense of responsibility to them. Any character, in fiction or in life, however lovingly apprehended and painstakingly described, will always elude complete condensation into language. That the narrator is painfully aware of this reveals not her failure, as she supposes, but her acutely developed sense of responsibility.

In the end, nobody, including the author, has reached a conclusion. But author and characters have *made the best, the very best, of ac*tual — not ideal — human lives. They have *made* love. Even the narrator is, well, not satisfied, but — something more like "happiness falling" — she is content. Speaking of Joe and Violet, she muses:

I envy them their public love. I myself have only known it in secret, shared it in secret and longed, aw longed to show it — to be able to say out loud what they have no need to say at all: *That I have loved only you, surrendered my whole self reckless to you and nobody else. That I want you to love me back and show it to me. That I love the way you hold me, how close you let me be to you. I like your fingers on and on, lifting and turning. I have watched your face for a long time now, and missed your eyes when you went away from me. Talking to you and hearing you answer — that's the kick.* But I can't say this aloud; I can't tell anyone that I have been waiting for this all my life and that being chosen to wait is the reason I can. If I were able I'd say it. Say make me, remake me. You are free to do it and I am free to let you because look, look. Look where your hands are. Now. (229)

Now. The point is finally, now. Living in the now a grown-up ability to *make* love.

Chapter 8

"I TRIED TO OVERLOOK MANY THINGS"

Leni Riefenstahl: A Memoir

———— • ————

I must gently remove the appearance of suffered
injustice, that hinders a little, at times,
their purely proceeding spirits.

—RAINER MARIA RILKE, *Duino Elegies*

LENI RIEFENSTAHL differs from the others I have discussed in
that her work has not been a formative influence in my life.
Rather, her life and work interest me for a compelling present reason.
She was, and is, a woman of enormous ability and creativity who
single-mindedly, and with great commitment and energy, sought to
actualize her visions. Riefenstahl acted in the public world in a way
that no woman of her time was acting, and she suffered the massive resistance encountered by most aggressive women. I admire her
tenacious determination, her energy, her ability to endure suffering,
and her considerable accomplishments. But her memoirs also contain a strongly cautionary tale. The same intransigence that brought
her many projects to completion also blinded her to the devastating
political movement that swept Germany and large parts of Europe,
bringing death to millions. Unwilling to examine her actions or to
acknowledge any wrongdoing, Riefenstahl's reaction to criticism and
harsh disappointment has been to renew protestations of innocence.
Finally, the narration of her life ends in bitterness.

Leni Riefenstahl was a dancer, actress, and filmmaker in Germany
during the 1930s and 40s. Though she thought of herself primarily
as a dancer and actress, she had an avid curiosity that led her to learn
photography and film-editing. Through force of circumstances —
lack of funds and pressure of time — she directed a movie of her

own. From then forward, though she sometimes acted in films, she became known more and more as a director, a remarkable one.

Leni Riefenstahl directed six films: *Das Blau Licht* (The blue light, 1932), *Sieg des Glaubens* (Victory of the faith, 1933), *Triumph des Willens* (Triumph of the will, 1935), the eighteen-minute film *Tag der Freiheit: Unsere Wehrmacht* (Day of freedom: Our army, 1935), *Olympia* (1937), and *Tiefland* (Lowland, begun 1941). The most famous of her films, *Triumph of the Will*, commissioned by Hitler, documented the 1934 Nazi Party congress at Nuremberg. For Riefenstahl, however, the film, like the Third Reich, was about "peace and creating jobs" for six million jobless Germans. *Olympia*, a two-part documentary about the 1936 Olympics in Berlin, was funded by the Third Reich. Yet Riefenstahl continues to insist, in press conferences, in her memoir, and in the 1993 documentary film about her life and work, *The Wonderful Horrible Life of Leni Riefenstahl*, that her filmmaking was not intended to advance the political program of National Socialism.

Riefenstahl and the Nazis

Riefenstahl claims that she never made a propaganda film. Her distinction between a "factual documentary" and a propaganda film rests primarily on her statement of intention: "During my work, I never thought of propaganda for even an instant."[1] Others, however, saw the political significance of her project and its reliance on Hitler's favor. Harassment, the story of the rest of her long life, began immediately, at first from party members prompted, Riefenstahl says, by jealousy of Hitler's esteem for her.

Riefenstahl's filmmaking genius is undisputed. Pauline Kael called her "one of the dozen or so creative geniuses who have ever worked in the film medium." John Simon wrote: "[Leni is] one of the supreme artists of the cinema, the greatest woman filmmaker ever."[2] Even Susan Sontag, who called her films an "anthology of proto-Nazi sentiments," acknowledges that *Triumph of the Will* and *Olympia* "may be the two greatest documentaries ever made."[3] Clearly, Riefenstahl's "beautiful images matched her leader's 'beautiful words' with uncanny precision."[4]

Despite her acknowledged artistry, and because of her association with the Nazis, she has not been able to produce a feature-length film since 1938.[5] Reviewers agree that, as one writer put it, she was "an artist seduced into the service of evil by her blind obsessive dedication to aesthetic principles."[6] She rationalized and dismissed Hitler's anti-Semitism by calling it "nothing but campaign rhetoric."

In addition to producing powerful films, Riefenstahl invented film techniques that have become standard. "All televised sport is indebted to *Olympia*."[7] *Olympia* "pioneered such techniques as cameras in balloons, in ditches, on a track racing with the sprinters, [and] underwater as divers slice into the Olympic pool." Despite its better claim to "art for art's sake" than *Triumph of the Will,* however, *Olympia* was also used by the Nazis "to spread the lie of [Germany's] peaceful intentions."[8]

During and after the war, Riefenstahl was rumored to be Hitler's mistress and to be socially intimate with other party leaders, an allegation she denies vehemently. But the primary charge brought against her is that she was "filmmaker for the Nazis," furthering their political goals with her seductively beautiful films. In his preface to *Hinter den Kulissen* (Behind the scenes of the party rally film), Riefenstahl's book about the making of *Triumph of the Will,* Hitler, who suggested the film's title, said that it was "a totally unique and incomparable glorification of our Movement."[9]

Riefenstahl describes her direction of *Triumph of the Will* as coerced by Hitler and undertaken reluctantly: "I have so often been accused of having made propaganda films, but such charges are misguided. This film was a factual documentary, which is something very different. No one, not even the Party, gave me any sort of instructions on what to do. Nor were the shots posed for the camera" (*LR* 148). Her appeal is to her own intentions. She claims only professional interests in her film projects for Hitler. Her reward was simply "the pleasure of a film-maker who gives cinematic shape to actual events without falsifying them" (160). Throughout, she remained belligerently nonpolitical: "I had never voted,...nor did I do so [when Hitler won the national election]" (126).

Riefenstahl's description of the funding for *Olympia* is a puzzling example of her obfuscation of Nazi support. Joseph Goebbels, Hitler's minister of popular enlightenment and propaganda, wanted a film about the 1936 Olympics because it would be good publicity for the Reich. Riefenstahl set up a firm for making the film in which all the shares were owned by the Ministry of Propaganda (177). She claims, however, that the funding was a loan. One of the conditions of the loan was that "I had to tell the press that Goebbels had commissioned me to make the Olympic film, even though this was not true. But at the time I didn't care" (177). Records of the former Ministry of Propaganda establish that Riefenstahl's film of the 1936 Olympics was financed by the Nazi government.[10] Riefenstahl struggled for complete artistic freedom, but obligations were imposed throughout the film's process. In her memoir, then, Riefenstahl is in a quandary: she cannot complain of harassment and frustration without simultaneously acknowledging the party's financial and political interest in her film.

Hitler's racial fanaticism bothered her, Riefenstahl says, and she tried to confront him about it. Each time she mentioned it, however, he rebuked her or simply ended the conversation by leaving the room. Acknowledging that Hitler "fascinated" her (*LR* 127) and that she "sympathized" with his political project, she cites her Jewish friends as proof that this attitude toward Hitler was common and legitimate in the early days of his bid for power. Josef Sternberg, a Jewish filmmaker said, for example: "Hitler is a phenomenon — too bad that I'm a Jew and he's an anti-Semite. If he comes to power we'll see whether his anti-Semitism is genuine or just campaign rhetoric" (131). Nor was Sternberg her only Jewish acquaintance to express this; Manfred George also remarked that Hitler was "brilliant but dangerous" and agreed with her that Hitler's fascinating "personality" should be distinguished from his "political notions" (294). Riefenstahl adds that his political agenda, in turn, must be differentiated from his racism:

> These were two entirely different things, as far as I was concerned. I unreservedly rejected his racist ideas; and therefore I could never have joined the National Socialist Party. However, I welcomed his socialist plans. The deciding factor for me was the possibility that Hitler could reduce the tremendous unemployment that had already made over six million Germans unhappy and desperate. In any case, his racism, many people thought, was only a theory and nothing but campaign rhetoric. (102)

The number of "unhappy and desperate Germans" roughly parallels the victims of Hitler's extermination camps. After the war, Riefenstahl was investigated and cleared of charges of Nazi sympathy by U.S. authorities; subsequently, she was in French prisons until she was also denazified by the French government. Finally, her fellow Germans turned against her. Perhaps the greatest damage came from a spurious memoir allegedly written by Hitler's mistress, Eva Braun, in 1947. The memoir accused Riefenstahl of an affair with Hitler. Finally, however, it may be her dogged unwillingness to acknowledge complicity, and therefore a measure of responsibility, for the ravages of the Third Reich that continues, even today, to enrage her opponents.

In this chapter I will focus primarily on Leni Riefenstahl's memoirs, examining her narration of her life, her intentions and their effects. I also refer to the feature-length film *The Wonderful Horrible Life of Leni Riefenstahl*, directed by Ray Müller, which was released at approximately the same time that *Leni Riefenstahl: A Memoir* was published in the United States.

In the film, Müller leads Riefenstahl through an extended interview, traversing not only the locations on which she made *Triumph* and *Olympia* but also her editing room. The film begins and ends by showing her present project, underwater filming of ocean life. Her courage and indomitable energy are apparent throughout. Müller asks her difficult questions about her association with the Nazis. She is sometimes evasive, sometimes angry; sometimes she quietly repeats the same rationalizations she has expressed in countless interviews. Müller annoys her; once she responds tearfully. Richard Corliss reports, "Unsurprisingly, Riefenstahl refuses to see *Wonderful Horrible Life*. 'I cried and they filmed it,' she says. 'He was brutal.' "[11] In his review of the film, Vincent Canby writes, "Riefenstahl doesn't come across as an especially likable character, which is to her credit and Mr. Müller's. She's beyond likability. She's too complex, too particular, and too arrogant to be seen as either sympathetic or unsympathetic."[12]

Did Leni Riefenstahl deliberately and knowingly aid the Nazi movement? Reactions of sympathy and condemnation are equally possible. On the one hand, readers of her memoir cannot fail to be appalled and moved by Riefenstahl's incarceration in a mental institution by French authorities at the close of World War II. She was given shock treatment for alleged depression while film footage that constituted her life's work was stolen from her. Incidents of persecution can be multiplied. On the other hand, Riefenstahl's protestations of political ignorance, monomaniacal absorption in her projects, and even the claim that for a decisive period she was too drugged by painkillers to notice world-altering events are patently self-serving.

Whether or not she merited persecution, there is no doubt that Riefenstahl received a great deal of it. Nor has it subsided in the more than fifty years that now separate her (she was born in 1902) from her younger self. Throughout the years, every time success seemed imminent, loud protests arose that effectively canceled her "triumph." As late as April 1995 an invitation to Riefenstahl to appear in San Francisco was canceled when the Goethe-Institut failed to find a cosponsor for her visit.[13] Riefenstahl says that her 1932 film, *The Blue Light,* told her own story in allegory:

> Junta, the strange mountain girl, living in a dream world, persecuted and driven out of society, dies because her ideals are destroyed.... Until the early summer of 1932 I too had lived in a dream world, ignoring the harsh reality of the era, not comprehending events like the First World War or its dramatic aftermath. (*LR* 100)

She describes her disillusionment at the end of World War II in identical language: "My ideals were shattered."[14]

I will not attempt to discuss the Nazi era in Germany in its political and social dimensions. However, one feature of Nazi culture bears directly on understanding Leni Riefenstahl's situation. Filmmaking was an important industry in Nazi Germany. In 1933, Goebbels expressed his hope that "Nazi films would conquer the world ahead of Nazi armies."[15] Each of the eleven hundred movies made in Germany during the war had to be approved by Goebbels. Significantly, he preferred movies to be "entertaining, not didactic."[16] He believed that propaganda worked best when people were not aware of it. Entertainment films comprised 85 percent of films made under the Third Reich. Eric Rentschler, a scholar of Nazi-era films, comments: "When you look at Nazi films by and large what you see are films that look like Hollywood productions. Goebbels recognized the

power of Hollywood films to take over people's fantasy life. His notion was to have a German film industry that could be as effective
as Hollywood in creating captive audiences."[17] In Goebbels's Germany, Jews were labeled "critical," and Goebbels officially forbade
art criticism in November 1936, revealing, Susan Sontag writes, his
"contempt for all that is reflective, critical, and pluralistic."[18]

Riefenstahl participated in Nazi film culture. Her lover, costar,
and professional rival, Luis Trenker, "pioneered Hitler's Hollywood." He made his first film for the Third Reich in New York
in 1934, a "Nazi Western," Der Kaiser von Kalifornien. Though
Riefenstahl insists that Goebbels was consistently opposed to her
projects, her fiction films as well as her documentaries met his criteria. They instructed and inspired while entertaining. Critics have
found the precursors of some of Riefenstahl's visual ideas in the
German eugenics films of the 1920s, such as Fritz Lang's Die
Niebelungen (1924).[19] Mountain films, like Riefenstahl's The Blue
Light, appealed to Nazi dreams of conquering the heights. Perhaps
Sontag exaggerates when she says that Riefenstahl was "the only major artist who was completely identified with the Nazi era," but her
films were undoubtedly the most powerful of Nazi-era films and the
only ones to generate artistic interest beyond the Nazi era.[20]

It has never been clearer than in Nazi Germany that entertainment can encourage a nation to turn a blind eye to massive atrocity
within its borders. "Goebbels saw to it that cinemas were among
the first public buildings to be reopened after air raids."[21] When
people are amused and inspired, they are not likely to question leaders who provide this gratification. Susan Sontag, Riefenstahl's most
articulate critic, defines fascist aesthetics as characterized by "preoccupation with situations of control, submissive behavior, extravagant
effort, and endurance of pain; they endorse two seemingly opposite
states, egomania and servitude."[22] Sontag claims that Riefenstahl's
films epitomized Nazi values. They celebrate, she writes, "the rebirth
of the body and of community, mediated through the worship of
an irresistible leader.... The Nazi films are epics of achieved community, in which everyday reality is transcended through ecstatic
self-control and submission; they are about the triumph of power."[23]
Janet Maslin, film critic for the New York Times, goes further, stating that Riefenstahl's films did not simply exemplify Nazi values —
they actually "defined the exultant physicality that Hitler would later
appropriate as an Aryan virtue."[24]

In addition to escapist entertainment, Goebbels wanted directors to project "Nazi themes and motifs far back into history, to give the impression that these themes had deep roots in all aspects and periods of German culture." Contemporary Nazi themes were avoided; "black SS uniforms, swastikas and the shout 'Heil Hitler!' are far more common in American films of the period than in German ones."[25] Moreover, after 1940, Jews were seldom pictured in Nazi films. The major anti-Semitic feature films produced in Nazi Germany were made in 1940: *Die Rothschilds* and *Jud Suss*. The latter was an enormous box office success. It was "used officially to incite both civilians and military to deport or murder Jews."[26] Although war scenes were rare in Nazi films, actual footage from the invasion of Poland appeared in *Wunschkonzert,* which sold twenty-three million tickets by the end of the war. In short, entertaining and inspirational films were sought in Germany under Goebbels's ministry. Among these films, Riefenstahl's were the finest. She played a crucial part in a culture industry whose importance to the maintenance of a submissive society was recognized by Nazi leaders.

Riefenstahl's Memoir

Initially, I read Riefenstahl's memoir trying, like everyone who reads the book, to determine whether or not she is guilty of knowingly aiding the Nazi Party.[27] Since the book was written specifically in order to deny this, however, it quickly became clear that the reader must either willingly suspend disbelief or at least postpone judgment until the evidence can be considered from another perspective than that of the author. Rather than attempting to take a position on the degree of Riefenstahl's involvement with Hitler and the Nazis, then, I examined the memoir itself, noticing the rhetorical patterns, the predilection for certain explanations, the missing transitions, and the significant interstices, as well as the information she gives.

The English translation of the German text was done by Joachim Neogroschel, who is not credited. It has 656 pages, about 30 percent less than the German book's 914 pages, but there is no explanation in the English version as to which parts were cut and why. A quotation from Albert Einstein occupies the place usually reserved for a dedication:

So many things have been written about me, masses of insolent
lies and inventions, that I would have perished long ago, had I
paid any attention. One must take comfort in the fact that time
has a sieve, through which most trivia run off into the sea of
oblivion.

These words capture, in part, the spirit of the memoir, albeit with
a telling difference. Einstein states that personal and professional attacks are to be ignored; to invest one's life in resentment, rebuttal,
and anger is to "perish" as a creative person. He takes the long-
term view, predicting that his work will survive the test of time,
while petty objections will disintegrate. Riefenstahl, however, wrote
a lengthy book, a book that cost her, she says, five years of her
life, specifically to refute the accusations brought against her. She re-
membered and recounted in detail the rebuffs, insults, and trials that
structured her life.

"Great passions" dominated Riefenstahl's life; she refused, no
matter what the consequences, to be distracted from them. As a
child she worked out a philosophy of life that became her religion
throughout her life. After witnessing a fatal accident, she worried
about the prevalence of evil, but noticing the recurrence of creation
and beauty reassured her that life is, after all, good:

The green grass, the flowers and the trees died and revived
again; human life went on. I began at first to have more faith
and confidence and then suddenly I felt liberated. I knew that
no matter what might happen to me, as long as I lived, I would
say yes to life. Every evening thereafter I prayed that God
would give me the strength to endure everything that fate had
in store for me, and that I would never again condemn life but
always thank God for it. (*LR* 7)

Riefenstahl presents herself as a principled, even a "deeply religious," person, but hers was an idiosyncratic morality, a morality
in which ends justify means (299). Determined to accomplish her
projects, she lied, used seductive wiles, and appealed to powerful
men (like Mussolini and Hitler) to get what she wanted. She insists
that she was forced to do so.

Riefenstahl lived in a world of abusive men. Her domineering
father was the first obstacle she faced as a young woman. Seeing
his treatment of her mother, Riefenstahl "vowed never to become

dependent on another human being" (14). He vigorously opposed her interest in dancing, but she won his support through subterfuge, promises, and appeals. Later, a series of men helped her career, fell in love with her, and betrayed her. These betrayals reaffirmed her childhood resolution for independence: "Never again, I swore to myself, never again would I love a man so deeply" (75). Riefenstahl saw that her society was a man's world. As a young woman she wrote to a friend, "How I wish I were a man. It would be so much easier to carry out all my plans" (19).

Early in her memoir, Riefenstahl confesses "with shame" her complete lack of interest in politics (13). Living in a "dream world," she was able to ignore "events like the First World War and its dramatic aftermath" (100). She heard of Adolf Hitler in 1932. She had never voted, but wanting "to form my own image" of him, she attended a rally at which he spoke. As he began to speak, she experienced "an almost apocalyptic vision that I was never able to forget. It seemed as if the earth's surface were spreading out in front of me, like a hemisphere that suddenly splits apart in the middle, spewing out an enormous jet of water, so powerful that it touched the sky and shook the earth. I felt quite paralyzed" (101). Hitler continued to have a "profound effect" on her; she was "fascinated" and "deeply affected." As an old woman, explaining why she is able to report verbatim detailed dialogues with Hitler and party officials, Riefenstahl says, "Hitler has so left his mark on my life that I can still remember every single word of my conversations with him and with the most important people in his entourage" (655).[28]

Riefenstahl arranged a meeting with Hitler, who had been impressed with her after seeing *The Blue Light*. After arranging the meeting, however, she had paralyzing second thoughts. "Why had I become involved in this? I didn't know. Something was driving me" (*LR* 105). At their meeting, Hitler was respectful, admiring, and enthusiastic over her film. He said, "Once we come to power, you must make my films." "I can't," she responded, "I really can't." She recalls that she said, "After all, you have racial prejudices. If I had been born an Indian or a Jew you wouldn't even speak to me, so how can I work for someone who makes such distinction among people?" (106). His response on this occasion was merely to admire her honesty.

Riefenstahl's alternating fascination with, and resistance to, Hitler thread through her text. "I didn't want to be impolite." "His words

struck at my heart." "My interest in learning more about Hitler..."
"Trying to avoid Hitler..." "Now that Hitler was in power I didn't
want to have any contact with him." "I didn't have the courage to
say no." "I felt less and less able to contradict him. I simply lacked
the courage." "I tried to overlook many things." "I held my tongue"
(107, 123, 124, 135, 136, 144, 250, 294). Her initiative in meeting
Hitler and her continued phone calls to him, however, speak louder
than her hesitations. In short, after one last protest, "I can't, I absolutely can't," Riefenstahl agreed to direct *Triumph of the Will.* The
ambivalence that characterized her relationships with men was reen-
acted with Hitler. Despite her cavils and refusals, she ended by taking
on the projects he urged on her. She reports that when Hitler died,
she wept all night (305).

Riefenstahl in Love

Her first sexual experience, at the age of twenty-one, was rape. Fantasies about a champion German tennis player, Otto Froitzheim, led
Riefenstahl to set up a meeting. Determined to "have an adventure"
with him, she went to his apartment. Once there, however, she became more and more uneasy; she "just wanted to run home," but
Froitzheim insisted that she dance with him. She danced a few steps
with Froitzheim, "as if hypnotized," while telling herself that her
"dreams and longings were coming true." But as he lifted her and
placed her on a couch her "happiness abruptly fled": "All I could feel
was fear, a terror of the unknown, as he virtually ripped the clothes
from my body and, with almost brutal violence, tried to possess me
quickly and totally" (33). Riefenstahl reports feeling "nothing but
pain and disappointment." "I had only one wish: to die. The experience had been so shocking that I didn't think I could go on living."
She wrote a letter to Froitzheim, telling him of her "boundless repugnance" for him. He responded with flowers, apologies, and a
proposal of marriage, which she was, oddly enough, unable to resist:
"In some mysterious way I was a slave to him" (34). The marriage
did not happen, however. After learning that Froitzheim was having
an affair, Riefenstahl managed to withstand his urgent pleas for rec-
onciliation, "the most painful decision I had ever made." She cried
all night after refusing him (45). This pattern of longing, ambiva-

lence, and repugnance was to characterize most of her relationships with lovers and other important men in her life.

Riefenstahl was fascinated by famous men and by economically and politically powerful men, perhaps quite realistically recognizing her dependence on their influence and money to further her pursuits. She married a man who exercised a different kind of power. After noticing the burning stares of Peter Jacob, a young infantryman hired for a small part in one of her films, Riefenstahl recognized her "unusually powerful attraction" to him, but "avoided his eyes." Sensing danger, she "wanted to do whatever I could to keep out of that man's way" (268). Her hesitation was no more effective in this context than it was with Hitler. Riefenstahl narrates the decisive scene with Peter Jacob:

> There was a knock at the door, and when I asked who was there, I got no answer. The knocking grew louder, and still there was no response; then it turned into an ear-splitting pounding. Indignant, I opened the door a crack. Peter Jacob stood there. He shoved his boot into the crack, pushed through the door, closed it — and achieved his purpose after some fierce resistance on my part. Never had I known such passion, never had I been loved so intensely. The experience was so profound that in a way it changed my life. It was the beginning of a great love. (269)

Riefenstahl married her rapist, experiencing, in the years she was with him, continuing betrayal, jealousy, and lies interspersed with passionate sex and contrite apology. After they finally divorced, Jacob told her he hoped that divorce would not end their relationship: "I wouldn't like to lose you. I know I've done a lot of things to you, but you have to believe that I've always loved you" (334). She took him back but did not remarry him, only because she learned of his continuing infidelities at the last moment.

After World War II

Riefenstahl has persistently sought social and professional reinstatement and vindication, but these have not been forthcoming. She has suffered over persecution and abuse, betrayal by friends she helped in the past, and slenderly funded projects she has been forced to abandon. Staggered by these obstacles, her capacity for becoming fascinated with a new interest nevertheless has supported her in the face of obstacles most persons would have been unable to surmount.

She was initially drawn to Africa by a picture she impulsively cut from a magazine. The picture showed a black athlete carried on the shoulders of a friend and was captioned "The Nuba of Kordofan." She recalls that "the black man's body looked like a sculpture by Rodin or Michelangelo" (462). Few Europeans, and no missionaries, had visited the Nuba; Riefenstahl could not rest until she did. She lived among the Nuba for months at a time on several occasions; learning the Nuba language and giving them gifts, she won their trust, admiration, and cooperation. The Nuba built her a house and permitted her to photograph their ceremonies. She found them a people unsullied by the acquisitiveness, dishonesty, and guilt of "civilized" people. On several different occasions she was close to getting the support necessary for making a film about the Nuba, but each time her efforts were thwarted, once by a near-fatal automobile accident. Eventually, she published two magnificent books of photographs, *The Last of the Nuba* and *The Nuba of Kau.*

Riefenstahl was acutely aware, as the title of her first book demonstrates, that the Nuba belonged to a "disappearing culture" (484). She saw unmistakable signs of their decline on her last trip in the late 1960s. The wrestling matches that had so fascinated Riefenstahl were no longer the same when the wrestlers wore "gaudy trousers" and adornments of plastic bottles and empty tin cans. Their ritual clothing, once so beautiful and elaborate, was now soiled and ragged. For the first time it was necessary to lock all her belongings. Discouraged, Riefenstahl departed, to return only briefly five years later. What she encountered on her final visit made her want to "get away as soon as possible." When she showed them film rushes made on her earlier visits, the Nuba were ashamed of their former nakedness and demanded, as tourists had taught them, that she give them money for photographing them (588). "Once the natives start posing," Riefenstahl muses, "a real photographer is doomed" (607). She does not consider the part her photographs may have played in hastening the advance into Nuba territory of "civilization."

On the final day of a photographing trip in East Africa, Riefenstahl saw a word scribbled on a blackboard: "goggling." She learned that the word meant "snorkling." This unremarkable suggestion was to lead to her next "great passion." Beginning at the age of seventy-two, Riefenstahl and Horst Kettner, the young companion of her old age, learned snorkling. In order to be certified, she lied about her age by twenty years. Her next career was in place. In 1993, when the English translation of her memoir was published and *The Wonderful Horrible Life of Leni Riefenstahl was filmed*, she was, at the age of ninety-three, continuing to photograph underwater life. She expected to make a silent film within a year.

One's Own Favorite Character in Fiction

After fifty years of attacks, slights, obstacles, and disappointments, the cancellation of a television interview finally convinced Riefenstahl that she must write her memoir in order to "set the record straight." At least half of the lengthy memoir narrates her experience after the war, but the Hitler era determined the course of her life. Throughout her many ventures, she remained preoccupied with that era, writing in her nineties: "The events of those years run before my eyes like a film, over and over again, and I am repeatedly confronted with the past, even today" (655).

In contrast to the epigram from Einstein with which she prefaced the book, Riefenstahl concludes her memoir: "My aim was to tackle preconceived ideas and to clear up misunderstandings and I spent five years working on [this] manuscript. It was not an easy task since I was the only one who could write these memoirs; it did not turn out to be a happy one" (656).

This is a different agenda than that announced in the opening words of the book: "It is not easy for me to leave the present behind and to immerse myself in the past *in order to understand my life* in all its strangeness" (emphasis added). The book's final words acknowledge that her long and discouraging tale failed to produce the understanding for which she had hoped. She was distracted from the effort to *understand* her life by a conflicting agenda — a desire to write an apologetic. She traded the opportunity of achieving *for herself* an understanding of her life, in order to make a bid for her reader's indulgence. The endeavor to understand ninety years of vivid experience held amazing promise, but the apologetic endeavor was not so fruitful, devouring "five years of my life" and making her "a prisoner, chained to my desk, forced to give up almost everything else" (654). Intent on setting the record straight, Riefenstahl ignored the opportunity to re-vision her own life, crafting personal meaning out of its apparently random events. Buffeted by historical movements and events, Riefenstahl succumbed to the temptation to justify herself in relation to those events. Hers is a repetitious tale of abused innocence and guileless struggle against horrendously unjust misunderstanding.

Even so, partial understandings occasionally slide through her apologetics. Riefenstahl herself seems to have noticed the dogged continuity of her early patterns of action and reaction. She writes: "Certain features of my character emerged very early, determining the course of my life" (654). Riefenstahl has learned nothing and forgotten nothing. Her "favorite character in fiction" does not develop. She has the same indomitable, intransigent will when she is nearing the end of her life that she had at the beginning.

If Riefenstahl's initial agenda, that of self-understanding, has not been achieved, has she, in fact, effectively "set the record straight"? Reviewers have gathered evidence that there are multiple errors of date and fact in the memoir: "Riefenstahl claims to base her *Memoir* on diaries and other archival materials in her possession, but [it is] so unreliable as to dates and events that one must simply conclude that she has no such records."[29] Moreover, the publication of Goebbels's diaries in 1987 called into question, if not falsified definitively, some of Riefenstahl's memories and claims. For example, she stated that she knew nothing about Hitler's decision that she should film the Nuremberg party rally until three days before the rally. Goebbels's diaries tell a different story. They report that Riefenstahl socialized with Goebbels, Hitler, and other party leaders five or six times a month during the summer of 1933, sometimes talking about her ideas for the film with them until three o'clock in the morning. Goebbels also describes his enthusiastic assistance throughout the planning stages for *Triumph of the Will,* in contrast to Riefenstahl's post hoc insistence that Goebbels consistently opposed her.

Other aspects of Riefenstahl's long legal and cultural battle for reinstatement are similarly inaccurately reported in her memoir. For example, Riefenstahl sued an accuser who alleged that she had used Gypsy extras from the Maxglan concentration camp in *Tiefland,* the film she began during the war. Although Riefenstahl reports accurately that she won an initial decision, she does not mention that the decision was overturned on appeal.[30]

At the end of his detailed consideration of the relationship of Goebbels's diaries to Riefenstahl's memoir, David Culbert concludes: "No serious film scholar will continue to depend on Riefenstahl's interview as a factual source.... [The memoir] is useful in learning how Riefenstahl wishes things had happened, and reveals some modest inventiveness in explaining away the 1930s."[31]

Riefenstahl's adamant insistence that every detail of her memories reflects actual events and evidence that she misrepresents those events present a puzzling problem, reflecting the complexity of experience and events. Perhaps it is not even necessary to accuse Riefenstahl of intentional falsification in order to question the adequacy of her memory. In her memoir, her obsession with "setting the record straight" won out over the effort to understand, governing her recall of conversations and happenings. It is quite possible that she reports as she recalls.

It might, however, have been evident to Riefenstahl that her memory might conflict with others' different and equally valid memories or that documentation might disprove her memories. Humility is an important virtue for anyone who works from memory, for it is much easier to deceive oneself than to deceive anyone else. Yet Riefenstahl claims to recall and report dates and conversations verbatim; she neither checked nor qualified her claims to remember.

There is, in addition, the further problem of selection. Since a narrator can never reconstruct the whole context in detail, her choices of relevant features almost inevitably support her perspective and interpretation. She cannot be accused of falsification; she is merely creating a plausible and coherent account. The time- and space-saving omissions in Riefenstahl's memoir act in exactly this way. While she gives many details of her meetings with Hitler — what he was wearing, what she was wearing, details of conversation, gestures — other information that would be important for a complete picture is missing. The omitted details, as well as those Riefenstahl includes, are often equally significant.

But self-vindication is not Riefenstahl's only interest in her memoir. She also recalls, with pleasure and satisfaction, her brief career in filmmaking. The utter fascination — there is no other word for it — that Riefenstahl felt for filmmaking motivated her decisions during the 1930s as surely as it informed her memories over fifty years later. When she describes the making of *Triumph* in *Wonderful Horrible Life,* her exact and detailed memory of every shot, the inventions and intrigues necessary for getting the shot, and the interminable editing of each second in the film reveals her intense preoccupation with the project. The same could be said for *Olympia,* which presented, if anything, even more daunting problems. For Riefenstahl, the beam (Germany's political situation) was obscured by the mote (filmmaking) in her own eye. Absorbed in the countless details of making a film, often with scanty resources at her disposal, she was unconcerned with the uses made of her films.

Riefenstahl's zest for triumphing over seemingly insurmountable difficulties was limitless. In Hitler she encountered, for the first time in her life, an equally intransigent vision and will. Hitler once told Riefenstahl that Schopenhauer, the philosopher of will — not Nietzsche, the artist — "was my teacher."[32] If Riefenstahl's and Hitler's wills were equal in strength, however, Hitler's political and social power enormously outweighed Riefenstahl's. She made his films, even while insisting melodramatically that this was "absolutely impossible" or that she would die if she could not go on with her acting.

The public debate about Riefenstahl's guilt or innocence in relation to the goals of the Third Reich is finally unsolvable. Both her protestations of innocence and the incontrovertible evidence that her films aided the Nazi cause must be accepted. Undoubtedly, Riefenstahl's films also earned her permanent hostility, partly because she represents a collective guilt. Riefenstahl's rationalizations of Hitler's racism and, ultimately, her ability to ignore the death camps have been echoed by many Germans since the close of World War II. It is a position that enrages those who identify with the millions slaughtered during the Hitler regime.

In *The Drowned and the Saved,* Primo Levi discusses his refusal to believe that Germans' could overlook Hitler's racism by labeling it "campaign rhetoric." He writes: "There's neither a page nor a speech of Hitler's in which hatred against the Jews is not reiterated to the point of obsession. It was not marginal to Nazism: it was its ideological center."[33] Riefenstahl's friends' reassurances that Hitler's racism was transitory came from a brief historical moment when it was still possible to ignore Hitler's "embarrassing" anti-Semitism. Clearly, neither others' similar self-deception nor her own good intentions exonerate Riefenstahl from charges of helping the cause of Nazism; they do, however, demonstrate that it was possible for a person to adopt such a position in Nazi Germany.

Riefenstahl's capacity for what Janet Maslin has called "tunnel vision" was probably greater than that of most Germans who did not have her creativity and preoccupations with which to keep political awareness at bay. In her monomaniacal passion for filmmaking, Riefenstahl remembers every camera she or her cameramen ever used, how every shot was achieved, and every editing process she conducted. "She becomes an entirely different person when discussing cinematic technique.... [She can] look at an image from *Triumph of the Will* and see the tiny elevator used to hoist the camera up a flagpole, ignoring the huge swastikas that flank the flagpole."[34]

Riefenstahl was scapegoated after the war because her films had a power that other Nazi filmmakers' movies did not. Ray Müller remarked in an interview with Robert Sklar in *Cineaste:* "She was just so good it's never been forgotten. Her talent was her tragedy."[35] Asked whether the ongoing controversy had anything to do with Riefenstahl being a woman, Müller replied that it had everything to do with *Triumph of the Will* being so good. There was a party documentary every year after 1934, and the films "got nastier and nastier, with more political bias":

> But nobody talks about the men who made them, even though they probably were allowed to work in films after the war, unlike Riefenstahl.... She's certainly an artist who was probably blind. I don't know how blind she really was.... In a period of time like we had in Germany, you had the responsibility to look around and not just do your lazer beam thing.... This burden she will always have to carry.[36]

Riefenstahl's bewildering combination of genius and tunnel vision is irreducible. Stanley Kauffmann gets it right when he concludes his review of *Wonderful Horrible Life:* "No matter how she defends herself, she committed vivid actions that aided the Nazis. No matter how she is attacked, she does have exceptional talent. If she had been just another hack Nazi filmmaker, she would never have become a center of controversy."[37]

A more interesting question to me than that of her complicity or independence from the Third Reich is: How can one make a rich life out of one's provisions, one's talents, misunderstandings, obstructions, and achievements? Possessing striking beauty, enormous talent, determination, and energy, Riefenstahl met a combination of dramatic "triumphs" (her word) and cruel obstructions. She became bitter. Is it possible to expend every effort and all one's skill and energy, encountering (what one interprets as) misunderstanding and dismissal, without experiencing bitterness?

Riefenstahl sought to create beautiful artworks, not to question or protest injustice. She wanted to dance and to act when her father forbade it. She wanted to make films when women filmmakers were unheard of. She certainly struggled against gender bias, but her struggle differed in two ways from those of present feminists: first, while Riefenstahl never expressed a desire to open the doors she had passed through to other women, current feminists struggle both for themselves and so that other women will not encounter the conditions they encountered; second, unlike feminists today, Riefenstahl struggled alone, without the support of others. Nevertheless, the question of how to struggle and meet frustration and achievement, without becoming bitter, is close to the bone for many women. An answer is not to be found in Riefenstahl's memoirs, but it is richly instructive to consider why this is so.

According to Riefenstahl's autobiography, everything happened to her from outside herself. She presents herself as "both master of her fate and its victim; the master of fate becomes a victim of forces beyond her control."[38] Although tenacious determination and fearless pursuit of her goals characterized her entire life, a rhetoric of victimization pervades her memoirs. She does not see her problems as arising from conflicts within herself; similarly, whatever refreshed and empowered her came not from inner resources but from outside: "Often in my life when I have reached rock bottom something delightful has happened" (LR 80). Riefenstahl's "successes" and "triumphs" are public events, as are her failures (LR 9, 37). In short, the reader of her memoir never glimpses an active subjectivity, intentionally cultivated, revised as life exposed its inadequacies, and providing a ballast for "whatever happens."

Riefenstahl presents her choices as *either* acquiescence to her socialization to a bourgeois lifestyle and values *or* the role of a lone woman against the world. Though she occasionally acknowledged others' help, the vision she struggled to actualize was her own. Lacking solidarity with others in a common cause, she ironically both adopted the self-image of a Hitler-style culture hero and maintained, through her evasions and ambivalences, the self-deceiving illusion of resisting Hitler. Attention to "the beauty of the way and the goodness of the wayfarers" (Samuel Beckett's phrase in *Waiting for Godot*) could have displaced Riefenstahl's intense focus on goals. Lacking a shared struggle, she missed the richness of relationships that could have rewarded her struggle in a more ongoing and trustworthy way than did her brief "successes" or "triumphs."

The cautionary tale contained in Leni Riefenstahl's memoir and *Wonderful Horrible Life* is that intransigent independent effort is likely to lead to bitterness. When other people are polarized into either supporters or obstacles rather than sharers in a common enterprise, there is no opportunity for healing laughter, nor for revisions of one's own values, methods, and goals. We have seen, in considering Rilke and Jung, that their high esteem for the individual was a way of resisting the mass movements of their day. A similar motivation may lie at the root of Riefenstahl's independence. In the context of the goose-stepping armies of Hitler's rallies, Riefenstahl placed her confidence solely in herself and her talents. Yet the alternatives are not either to march in perfect coordination with masses of others or self-absorption. Informed participation with others in the political and social issues of one's time lies somewhere between these poles. Community is vastly different from mass.

Lacking interiority and community, Riefenstahl identified with the pain she suffered. That pain, together with her triumphs, constitutes the essence of her life as she told it. She was not able to translate her pain into self-understanding; it remained unassimilated, bitter: "We wasters of sorrows," Rilke laments.

Rilke has a further suggestion:

> I must gently remove the appearance of suffered
> injustice, that hinders a little, at times
> their purely proceeding spirits.[39]

His suggestion is not that injustice should be denied or that the awareness of it should be repressed. Rather, he says that the "appearance of suffered injustice" should be consciously acknowledged and set aside lest it consume energy and block one's forward path. That Riefenstahl was able to pursue new interests while harboring potentially debilitating bitterness testifies to her energy and determination. That her life was damaged by bitterness is also evident. Nevertheless, her memoir represents a missed opportunity; rather than narrating abused innocence, it could have been the occasion of understanding, of grasping with astonishment the unsurpassable beauty of a complex human life, full of error and disappointment, but vividly lived.

Riefenstahl exemplifies preoccupation with beauty as a distraction from moral responsibility more clearly than any of the authors I have discussed:

> I can simply say that I feel spontaneously attracted by everything that is beautiful. Yes: beauty, harmony. And perhaps this care for composition, this aspiration to form is in effect something very German. But I don't know these things myself, exactly. It comes from the unconscious and not from my knowledge....I am fascinated by what is beautiful, strong, healthy, what is living.[40]

Whether or not Riefenstahl's statement reveals her engagement with Nazi aesthetics is finally irrelevant. The quest for beauty blinded Riefenstahl to her responsibility as a political and social being. Beauty is not enough. Perhaps this nagging awareness lurks behind Riefenstahl's vehement protestations of innocence and contributes to her bitterness. For pursuing one's passions without endeavoring to the very best of one's abilities to foresee the effects of one's projects is both morally culpable and personally bleak.

Chapter 9

THE EYE OF THE BEHOLDER
Enjoyment and Generosity

———— • ————

Things don't have to be perfect. In fact, it is better if they
are not.

—JESSICA BENJAMEN, *The Bonds of Love*

To MANAGE OUR LIVES we tell stories about the world and ourselves, about what is important and what should not be missed.
Stories that attract and inspire become religions. They claim to tell
the truth. I seek a humbler goal, a picture of the world that enables and enhances enjoyment and generosity. The ability to perceive
beauty is the basis for enjoyment, and enjoyment makes possible
spontaneous generosity. Generosity, in turn, funds responsibility. I
have found a model for a life whose salient characteristics are enjoyment and generosity in a reading practice that integrates pleasure
with a critical eye. Reading can be practice for life.

A picture of the world that facilitates enjoyment and generosity
responds not only to individual need and longing but also, and even
more urgently, to the needy world in which we make our lives, a
world of hunger, ecological crises, wars, contested values, and struggles for just societies. Responsibility must be imagined in relation to
these issues and crises. A proposed picture of the universe must be
able to demonstrate its potential not only for enjoyment but also for
generous responsibility.

To propose seriously, as I do, that a third-century C.E. philosopher
can provide a conceptually satisfying worldview for a pluralistic society in the late twentieth century is to invite objections. Moreover, to
propose a "Neoplatonist" philosopher's worldview (an epithet synonymous with "hierarchy" and "dualism") invites instant dismissal.
Yet I do so because I think that Plotinus has been misinterpreted
and misrepresented, and thus a generous proposal that could signifi-

cantly help us has been ignored. In the seventeenth century, Thomas Traherne wrote, "What we misapprehend we cannot use."

Worldview

Metaphysics has been suspect since the Enlightenment. In the twentieth century, Ludwig Wittgenstein carried this suspicion further by doubting the possibility of any meaningful metaphysical statement. Although there have been philosophical and theological attempts to resuscitate metaphysical concepts, metaphysics nevertheless remains in disrepute. In the second half of the twentieth century, theologians have concerned themselves either with criticizing traditional theology or with defending the integrity and relevance of the Jewish and Christian traditions. They seldom construct pictures of the whole.[1] "Totalizing" theology is not in style.

Yet without a picture of the whole, theology lacks beauty. Without beauty, theologies lack the "strong power" of attraction.[2] They preach to the already converted, or they enrage opponents, but they seldom convert. Without a vision of the whole it is impossible to describe order and complexity. Detail has no meaning except in reference to a whole. Vividness and pleasure recede, and value becomes rhetorical assertion when we cannot see how it *works* in relation to a whole. Without a vision of the whole, theology cannot reflect a universe characterized as beautiful by many of the West's most profound thinkers.

Plotinus describes the universe as an animating spiritual energy that can effortlessly integrate the bottom-heavy physical world into the constantly circulating power of the creating and sustaining One. If the physical universe did not exist, the One would have nothing to grace with its lifefulness. So Plotinus insists on the foundational character of the physical universe, even as it participates, singing, in the circulation of being.

In Plotinus's universe, all living beings are interconnected through the source of their being. Moreover, living beings share a common soul whose first effect is to circulate life through the universe. Not reason or rationality — life. With body comes individuality and particularity and, necessarily, a degree of separation from other living beings. Because living beings share a common soul, we feel one another's emotional pain, though we cannot feel one another's physical pain. In Plotinus's spiritual universe, living beings are not "related," as late twentieth-century people commonly use that word. "Relationship" implies building bridges across vast gulfs separating one person from another and human beings from the natural world. Relationships are built, but connections are explored. Codependency *is* the case, whether we recognize it or not. It is not a neurosis; it is not even an intuition or a faith; connection is a fundamental fact of life.

In chapter 2, I discussed two misunderstandings that have obscured the usefulness of Plotinus's vision of the universe: his alleged hierarchical arrangement of being, pictured as a ladder, and his description of the "opposition" of soul and body, intellect and matter. Both misreadings rest on highlighting an aspect of a metaphor that Plotinus explicitly rejected. As to the first misreading: while we focus on the ladder rungs on which some entities are placed higher than others, Plotinus focused on the side beams that hold together all living beings.[3] Plotinus corrected his ladder model with that of a circle: "[A]ll things are linked in one sphere to one center; many lines proceed from one center" (*Enn.* 6.5.4–5).[4]

As to the second misreading: resentful of a long Western tradition in which intellect has been valued at the expense of body, *we* notice in Plotinus's idea of the "opposition" of soul and body the higher value he allotted to the soul. But Plotinus described opposition as a hinge on which body and soul operate in relation to the other. He emphasized their irreducible interdependence and cooperation. Plotinus's "soul" is not synonymous with reason, discursive rationality, and logic, which are framed, in the Enlightenment paradigm, by excluding bodies and difference.[5] Living beings are united in participation: "[O]ne soul is not spread out and divided up with the body, but is present everywhere where it is present and is everywhere in the All without being divided." Plotinus locates subjectivity not in rational judgment but in experience, which depends on the body (*Enn.* 6.4.6; 4.7.6–7). Clearly, one person may have a radically different judgment than another person, but we can "acquire an understanding of another's experience" through our own experience (*Enn.* 6.4.6).

Like Plotinus, the Manichaeans with whom Augustine argued pictured a sentient, suffering universe, connected by the circulation of particles of divine light. Their spiritual universe, however, was not powerful enough to integrate the physical universe, which ultimately fell away from the informing light to disintegrate and dissolve.

Nevertheless, every living being contained particles of the divine light, painfully trapped in biodegradable bodies. The Manichaeans' distribution of community beyond Augustine's "rational minds" to a community of all living beings encourages attention to and delight in diversity. Confining human community to rational minds, in contrast, encourages identification with a community of the like-minded, emphasizing uniformity and unanimity. As the proverb says: "Great minds think alike." Giving bodies their full "weight," or importance, however, requires recognition of essential differences of perspective based on diverse sexual, class, race, and age *experiences*. Plotinus respected and accounted for both commonality and difference.

Beauty marks the life that informs bodies: "What does 'really exists' mean? That they exist as beauties" (*Enn.* 1.6.5).[6] "Beauty is reality" (*Enn.* 1.6.6). For Plotinus, beauty is also the mark of the good (*Enn.* 1.6.6).[7] To see beauty *is* to perceive the One. Beauty is not immediately evident to a socialized eye, however. It requires a cultivated, countercultural habit of perception, a commitment to seeing each object or person "in the life." Plotinus did not call the One the "Great Beauty"; the Great Beauty is the whole.

The affect that accompanies, enables, and energizes the perception of beauty is love. Does love precede and motivate perception of beauty? Or does it accompany or follow it? Perhaps the limits of analysis are reached here: the perception of beauty and the affect of love are simultaneous and interlinked.

Perception of beauty is a practice of everyday life. The first step is attentiveness to people and objects, a quality of attention that imagines the real being one looks at. Having learned this attentiveness, one can extend and elaborate this attentiveness to real but invisible beauties, as Plato described.

Plotinus said that the ability to perceive beauty is not based on desire, as is usually thought. In this he differs from his mentor, Plato, who said that "desire leads one to what is outside [oneself] and has deficiency in it; for that which desires is led, even if it is led to the good."[8] Plotinus thought that desire for beauty must be volitional because desire based on need clutches, and beauty cannot be grasped (except in the metaphorical sense). Rather, living beings spontaneously seek their own good, craving deficit satisfactions only when they lose sight of that good. When they explore their connection to a source of life and being, they pursue the good freely and not from lack (*Enn.* 6.8.4). Compulsiveness is poles apart from the relaxed and patient inner attentiveness by which beauty can be perceived.

Plotinus insisted that the cultivation and exercise of the ability to perceive beauty "belong to us," are "in our own power." They do not depend on circumstances, and they never entail "going out from" ourselves (*Enn.* 5.8.5). Seeing the beauty of the world is training for seeing more concentrated interior beauty (*Enn.* 1.6.4). Perception of beauty, then, is the essential inner work of human beings. Plato described a method that Plotinus reiterates, even as he revises Plato's starting point. Rather than starting with "one beautiful body," as Plato did in his search for beauty, Plotinus begins by noticing beauty that is interior to observable phenomena:

> And what does this inner sight see? When it is just awakened it is not at all able to look at the brilliance before it. So that the soul must be trained, first of all, to look at beautiful ways of life: then at beautiful works, not those which the arts produce, but the works of men who have a name for goodness: then look at the souls of the people who produce the beautiful works. How, then, can you see the sort of beauty a good soul has? Go back into yourself and look. (*Enn.* 1.6.9)

Finally, Plotinus offers the ultimately life-affirming conviction that being is inextinguishable. Do individuality and particularity survive death? Plotinus does not say. Without negotiating or stipulating, he trusts the Great Beauty to maintain life in circulation. When body slides away from soul, life is no longer "there," but, since the life of one is the life of all, it is still within Plotinus's universe, utterly and unconditionally safe: "Nothing of real being perishes" (*Enn.* 1.6.9). Plotinus's picture of the world describes a universe within which human beings can live with enjoyment and generosity. The universe is fundamentally and essentially spiritual, intimately connected, and perceived as beauty.

Any discussion of Plotinus's worldview must conclude by recalling a crucially important Platonic insight, namely, that ultimately " 'human wisdom'...consists in knowing that one does not know what is 'good and noble.' "[9] One *always* pursues the good *in the dark,* by faith, *not knowing* what it looks or feels like, yet passionately committed to it. Pursuit of the kind of knowledge that would help us to live well is necessarily and permanently explorative, constantly requiring reassessment and revision. It is a discipline and a lifestyle characterized by humility.

Pluralism

Despite its strengths, Plotinus's universe is not a fully satisfying rendition of the possibilities and resources of human existence. Plotinus's account of energy lacks the rich affect of Augustine's description of love. His curtailment of the realm of human will to inner intention and activity clearly does not motivate advocacy and activity for justice. Nor does his philosophy describe shared and negotiated work, thought, and pleasure with others as intrinsic to "beautiful ways of life." Other authors supplement Plotinus's universe, yet his connected and interdependent universe remains a strong basis for a richly lived life.

Augustine described the generosity of love most explicitly and forcefully. Interpreting 1 John 4:16, "God *is* love," as a literal characterization, he wrote that when people love they participate in God's defining activity and energy. Yet it was in studying Augustine that I first understood the necessity of critical reading, for on several occasions Augustine argued for a circumscription of empathic love. In his debate with the Manichaeans, he claimed that rational minds are the sole basis of human community and responsibility. He argued that human beings have no community of life with plants and animals and thus may use, abuse, and kill them at will. In his sermons on First John, he further limited community not only to rational minds but to those of one's own religious affiliation.

Despite Augustine's generous description of love, he applied that description only to abstract and distant "brothers." In the context of local stresses, it was apparently impossible for him to apply his own definition of love to Donatists, his fellow Christians, and Manichaeans, who were often within his own congregation. Moreover, his suggestion that sympathy should be withdrawn from animals and plants in order to focus it on human suffering was undermined by his conservative ideas of society. He taught that slaves must not question their situation; children and wives must obey fathers and husbands without cavil; and rulers must punish wrongdoers severely in order to frighten others into compliance.[10]

The late classical world inhabited by Plotinus and, a century and a half later, by Augustine was threatened by cataclysmic social and political upheaval. When Plotinus died in 270 c.e., northern European tribes were migrating insistently across the borders of the Roman world, seeking a share in the wealth and resources of that world. In Augustine's time, Rome itself was conquered for the first time in eight hundred years. Threatened both at the center and at the edges of the empire (e.g., in North Africa), Augustine's world was more dangerous than that of Plotinus. The social world Augustine advocated reflected the beleaguered conditions in which he thought and spoke. It was an altogether less generous world than that of Plotinus.

In Augustine's world, threats from unknown and known enemies focused his attention on maintaining a tolerable social environment. The Christian universe he occupied conceptually gave him a position from which to describe a carefully defined and circumscribed community *over against* invading Visigoths (without) and Donatists (within). While Jesus had said, "He that is not against me is with me," Augustine said, in effect, "He that is not with me is against me." Augustine's policy of sorting neighbors and brothers from enemies became the practice of kingdoms and institutions in the West to our own time.

In this social framework, Augustine's insistence that one's love must spread, like a fire, to the nearest scurvy brother and from there to others standing at a greater distance lacked practical application. Like C. G. Jung and Leni Riefenstahl long after him, Augustine thought of others either as obstacles or as supporters of his own agenda. Among the writings I have considered in this book, only *Jazz* actually lifts Augustine's definition of love into a fully fleshed-out demonstration of how it might look and feel to create authentic love with the imperfect and precious people at hand.

Augustine described generosity better than Plotinus did, yet he did not practice what he preached. Plotinus considered the needy as losers, yet, according to his biographer, he cared for orphans, accepted women as students, and maintained a vegetarian diet. Plotinus practiced better than he preached. Moreover, Plotinus's philosophy tolerated religious and social diversity better than did Augustine's theology. Plotinus did not designate a special, favored community, isolated from other living beings. Rather than adopting Augustine's embattled conservatism, we can opt for Plotinus's vivid sense of the interconnection of living beings as a basis for moral responsibility.

Neither Plotinus nor Augustine recognized that his geographical and social location affected his ideas and loyalties. Yet historical position and social location can prompt strange and contradictory mixtures of generosity and judgmentalness, as was the case in Augustine's sermons on First John. Is it possible to transcend the perspective impressed on one by situations and circumstances? Only, I believe, by a serious commitment to listening and reading.

Having drawn a broad conceptual scheme of the universe of living beings that includes Plotinus's and the Manichaeans' awareness that human beings are placed among, rather than ruling over, the natural world, I have begun to picture human relationships within such a world. But the question What is the self? is preliminary to relationships based on enjoyment and generosity, both on the personal level and in society.

Self

Several different proposals about how to conceptualize the self occur in the books I have discussed. For Plotinus, the soul is the person. He imagined a permeable soul, differentiated from the universal circulation only by its attention and affection. If the soul turns entirely toward the fragile and transient body, the self merges with the kaleidoscopic change characteristic of bodies; turned toward its source of life, the soul, absorbed in life, carries its body along.

Augustine identified a particular human capacity as constitutive of self. In order to know who someone *is,* he wrote in the *Enchiridion,* it is only necessary to ask what she loves. "My weight is my love," he wrote in his *Confessions;* "by it I am carried wherever I am carried" (*Conf.* 13.9). Love also defined, for Augustine, the character and energy of God, for "God is love." Moreover, love and will coincide, for love is a "stronger form of will." Augustine's *Confessions* narrate the painful experience of a divided will and its healing by perceiving "beauty so old and so new" (*Conf.* 10.36).

For Augustine, one's love is never fully in one's control. Thus, the "real self" is intimately dependent on factors beyond its control. God is the ultimate and absolute disposer of a person's character and destiny. God graces the one who is predestined to salvation, rescued from the *massa damnata,* with love, the energy by which beauty is perceived. Confident of his own salvation, Augustine could contemplate with equanimity the damnation of others.

Leni Riefenstahl had a different construction of the self. She represented herself as constituted by "great passions." She evidently preferred that romantic expression to an equally accurate description, namely, that her successes were the products of an indomitable will. Her determined will also resulted in the tunnel vision that refused to see the effects of her "triumph[s] of the will." Focused on her own intentions, Riefenstahl ignored their effects.

Although Riefenstahl's willful pursuit of her projects created massive blindness, will need not always act in this way. For a person ensconced in a comfortable life, distracted and unfocused, change can occur only through a powerful attraction that grips and directs the will. Inertia, laziness, habit, and sluggishness are enemies of a rich life.

Riefenstahl's memoir also introduces another proposal for identifying the self. Pain is the spot at which it is perhaps easiest to locate one's uniqueness. Riefenstahl's memoirs often present her pain as the source of her identity. Rilke ("We wasters of sorrows!") and Morrison ("Pain. I seem to have an affection, a kind of sweettooth for it") recognized pain's role in integrating the self. Both, however, understood not pain itself but a person's reaction to pain as a potential source of learning and strength. Suffering, they say, is not, or is not necessarily, all waste and loss. "I know you've suffered much, but in this you are not so unique," Bob Dylan sang in the 1960s. Moreover, we have plentiful resources in one another's empathy. Perhaps pain's potential usefulness has not been better publicized because most influential Western writers were male, but only women experience healthy physical pain, the productive pains of menstruation and childbirth.

Recognizing the potential productivity of pain, however, is not the same as a quietist attitude toward suffering. Only after every attempt has been made to alleviate pain can it be said that pain has uses. Moreover, the usefulness of pain can be affirmed only of one's own pain and probably only some time after the experience. To say it of others' pain, as Plotinus did, is morally irresponsible.

We have collected several ideas of the self: Plotinus proposed the idea, adapted by Augustine, of the self as constituted by the direction of its desires; Augustine saw the self as defined by its love; Augustine and Riefenstahl exemplify the proposal that strongly concentrated

will organizes the self; and Rilke, Riefenstahl, and Morrison suggested that the self is formed by pain and its use. Each of these
ideas carries an important insight into how we should live, but until
we have considered self-deception and the self in relationship these
suggestions are allusive and partial.

Self-Deception

Autobiographies, such as Jung's and Riefenstahl's, construct fictional
characters from real lives. Most of us do not publish our "own
favorite character in fiction," but we may nevertheless maintain a
self-serving self-image. The first fictional feature we maintain of the
self is its natural unity. We seek to discover the "true self." For Plotinus and Augustine, as for Jung and Rilke, however, the unified self is
a *project,* not a given.[11] Jung considered the unification of the self the
most difficult and important project of a lifetime, but he recognized
that a unified self is always based, to some extent, on self-deception.
Because a unified self is the result of organizing contradictory needs
and desires, self-unification inevitably creates what Jung called shadows, unacknowledged, unintegrated desires. Psychic energy must be
spent in keeping shadows from consciousness, where they undermine conscious choice and can even determine behavior. Morrison's
Jazz examines interconnections between people who have powerful
shadows and who learn not to obliterate them but to recognize and
befriend them.

One's shadows are usually abundantly evident to others. In *King
Lear,* Cordelia remarks of her father, "He hath ever known himself
but slenderly." If one knows only the self that can be begged, bribed,
or coerced into unity, one knows oneself "but slenderly." "It's the
richness of the mixture," the protagonist of Saul Bellow's *Henderson the Rain King* groans, describing his own psyche's proclivity
for saying "I want! I want!" and its unwillingness to specify *what*
it wants.

People often perpetuate self-deception by keeping themselves insulated from criticism. The same determination that led to achievement
can make criticism intolerable. Moreover, respect for a person in a
position of authority often prevents honest reaction to his ideas or
behavior. Even if criticism is given, accomplished people frequently
ignore or dismiss the very criticism that would refine their under

takings. Accustomed to proceeding with a project despite objections, Jung (and Hitler, according to Riefenstahl's report) would simply leave the room if anyone questioned his policies or procedures. Recall also Augustine's poignantly transparent comment, in his sermons on First John, that he could identify, in his congregation, whoever is not "of us" because he "criticizes God's ministers." Self-deception is a danger that can never be eradicated, but it can be minimized by inviting, and listening carefully to, others' views. It is also lessened by thinking of the self as a roughly coordinated amalgam of desires and loyalties rather than as a discoverable unity.

Self in Relationship

The self must be conceptualized in relation to an "other." It makes a great deal of difference, however, whether the other is pictured as enemy (even if one is constrained to "love" her) or as an "opposer" with whom one works in order to negotiate a result neither could have imagined in isolation. "Opposition," in the usage of Plotinus, Rilke, and Jung, far from threatening one's own position, is essential to self-definition.

On the rare occasions when he was not pressured by dissent, Augustine could also imagine fruitful opposition. He even recognized, in nonpolemical contexts, that religious dissidents (he called them heretics) provide necessary pressure for the further precision and elaboration of one's own religious position. He could have valued his opponents even more had he thought of *both* opposing proposals as mutually dissident. It is not, however, a simple matter of positing a level playing field where differences can be negotiated. If the power, including institutional authorization, rhetorical skill, and personal support, of the opponents is not equal, productive mutual opposition is not possible. And equal power so seldom exists. The history of Christianity from Augustine forward is full of examples of a powerful institution repressing dissidents.

If the self is, in reality, a conglomeration of restless urgencies, lacking intrinsic unity, does responsibility extend beyond one's conscious intentions to the effects of one's words and works? Michel Foucault wrote: "People know what they do; they frequently know why they do what they do; but what they don't know is what what they do does."[12] If one is to be richly responsive and responsible, I believe, one must attempt to predict the effects of one's words and actions, even if a full knowledge of these effects is elusive. One way to minimize misappropriation of one's ideas is to specify their inescapably "partial, partisan, and motivated" nature.[13] The primary ingredients of one's perspective should be specified, as well as the discussion within which those ideas are formulated and to which they respond. It is irresponsible to omit this honesty in order to claim that one's analyses and prescriptions are universally valid, for the same idea that can, in some circumstances, be used to great advantage (from certain perspectives) can also be destructive in other circumstances and/or from other perspectives.

For example, women who presently struggle for institutional space in which to articulate and examine their perspectives must consider under what circumstances these efforts might be destructive. Imagine, if you can, that male dominance in social institutions were so decisively overturned that design and administration of societies became the exclusive prerogative of women. In such a situation, women would need to reassess their advocacy for women's projects. At present it is difficult to imagine this scenario, but that is not the point. The point is, rather, that we are responsible not only for what we say but also for our interpretation of the particular and concrete historical situation in which we speak and act. Intentions may be — and usually are — impeccable, but one is also responsible for effects, insofar as these can be imagined. Moreover, because one's own intentions are both obvious and worthy (at least to oneself), their effects must be considered. But because it is very easy, especially with the help of hindsight, to detect the effects of others' decisions and actions, one must correct by seeking to understand *their* intentions.

I have considered several proposals for the self, especially the self congealed by its desire, its capacity to love or will, and its suffering. But if the self is not coincident with conscious intentions; if the will, even in it strongest form, can gather, at best, only a majority vote, we are left, it seems, with utter dependence on our ability to perceive beauty and thus to be simultaneously ravished and organized — even propelled — into vision and action. Perception of beauty depends, however, on one's capacity to imagine the real. The question, then,

is: How to *get into the circle?* The answer is that the ability to perceive beauty can be cultivated; it is an accessible spiritual exercise.
Iris Murdoch has written: "The appreciation of beauty ... is not only
(for all its difficulties) the easiest available spiritual exercise; it is also
a completely adequate entry into (and not just analogy of) the good
life, since it is the checking of selfishness in the interest of seeing
the real.... Beauty is that which attracts this particular sort of un-
selfish attention."[14] Perception of beauty is cultivated *not primarily
by placing beautiful objects of art or nature before one's eyes* but by
developing habits of attentiveness by which one can imagine the real
concretely and in detail.

Imagining the Real

In the preceding chapters I have described and illustrated a particular
kind of reading practice, a training of attentiveness and imagination.
Reading for life is reading with a critical eye for what one needs
and can use. By the disciplined use of this reading practice, I have
suggested, one can get from books everything one needs to know
in order to live the richest possible life. The chapters of this book
reconstruct my own collection of life-informing and life-enhancing
"news." I hope that my readings of Plotinus, Augustine, Jung, Rilke,
Morrison, and Riefenstahl have demonstrated that, by reading for
life, one can gather pictures of the world, warnings, and detailed
information and instruction.

I began by reading for aphorisms drawn largely from books I did
not comprehend. Before I returned to college at the age of twenty-
seven, I had read all the translated works of Freud and Jung. I did
not understand them, but I learned from them that it is possible
to think hugely and passionately about the world and to interpret
human life in a way that highlights its vivid color, its amazing privilege, and the responsibility inherent in participation in life. Although
my reading was entirely naive, it was also demanding, motivated by
need and longing. I have tried to say, in my discussions of each of the
authors I have considered here, how each served my life.

I did not interrogate the gender assumptions, the social location,
or the institutional loyalties informing the books I read. Nor did I
ask whether a book addressed *me.* I simply took and used whatever encouragement the book offered. As I have described, however,

I slowly became aware that I was not unaffected by books' assumptions and allegiances. The reading practice I have illustrated grew out of the dawning awareness of my need for reading in a way that holds the hungry excitement of naive reading together with critical reading. Reading for life requires both naive reading's willingness to be enchanted and critical reading's refusal to be seduced.

I have said little about choosing books to read "for life." That is because I do not have a method or criteria. I keep lists of books people suggest to me and read them when I can. But, mainly, I read promiscuously. "Reading around" is, I believe, a highly important corrective practice for an academic like myself whose reading is often oriented to "keeping up with the field." Ultimately, however, it is the practice of reading for life that produces aggressive and intense reading. On the one hand, the most profound and exciting book will not affect a listless or disaffected reader. On the other hand, I have often found valuable insights in unlikely places.

What are the ingredients of reading for life? First, reading for life seeks to identify the serious. It would seem that what is serious is, or should be, immediately obvious. But this has not been so for me. A complicated childhood informed by fundamentalist religion, a bored young adulthood soothed by entertainment: these have not been sufficient to point out to me the truly serious. The serious is not boring, as childhood and youth led me to expect. Though it is helpful (but not necessary) to bring the acquired taste of the academic reader to reading Plotinus and Augustine, Morrison's *Jazz* is a profoundly serious book that does not require specialized skills. But the serious is also sometimes identified by works of philosophy, ancient sermons, poetry, and autobiography. In short, I learned from reading how to identify what is serious. Now I think I can spot it in life. I cannot define it, but, if I am not deceived, I know it when I see it most of the time.

The second ingredient of reading for life is practice in imagining, or reimagining, the self, one's own "favorite character in fiction." "All love," Martha Nussbaum wrote, "is...love of fictional characters."[15] Identification with fictional characters extends the reader's experience, enabling her to experiment with new ways of thinking, feeling, and behaving. Books redescribe the world, subtly or boldly suggesting previously unimagined and untried perspectives.

Having imagined the self, one can also imagine the actual person one sees: her body's brief or long history, the unseen and seldom reflected on interior of her body — the heart beating rhythmically, the blood coursing through veins, digestion, and breath. All happening now in a body that will one day no longer perform all these precision tricks. One can imagine the child — not the cheap truism of popular psychology — but the actual child, who was *in fact* transformed day by day into the person one sees. The person in her whole life — birth to death — or beyond, if your imagination can go that far. The body will reveal the person's particular beauty and integrity to a lovingly attentive eye.

Third, reading for life is generous reading, reading for what the author is *trying* to say. I am learning generosity from books as they enable me to relax my jealousies, to visualize ways of thinking and living with which I am unfamiliar, and to perceive beauty in "beginning of terror we're still just able to bear."[16] Generous reading does not omit critical questions, however. Rather, questions about the author's situation and assumptions enable the reader to understand a book "in the life," that is, to reproduce the book's place in a conversation or debate that went far beyond its covers, engaged other voices, and occupied a particular cultural space. Moreover, generous reading makes it possible to appropriate *for life* a book's detachable suggestions *even though* they come from a demonstrably imperfect author or are addressed to someone other than the reader and, yes, even though the author could not himself apply the implications of his thoughts to his own life.

Fourth, reading for life understands reading as practice for a responsible life.[17] Toni Morrison described authorship as a weighty moral responsibility. Did she present her characters lovingly and richly? she asked herself. The reader should be similarly engaged, noticing and evaluating a book's representation of what is important and what is trivial, assessing the author's ability to stimulate her reader's imagination and evaluating the adequacy of her implicit or explicit recommendations for how we should live.

A work of art, whether text or visual arts, should contribute to our ability to imagine the real. By this criterion, Michelangelo's *Pietà* at Saint Peter's in Rome is a beautiful sculpture but a false work of art. For it hides precisely what it claims to represent, namely, a woman's sorrow over the cruel death of her only son. Yet stark, intolerable pain has been deleted; it has been prettified. The sculpture falsifies human grief and pain, which *place their mark* on the body. Picasso's *Guernica,* in contrast, is a true painting. The grotesque screaming heads, the chaos of torn bodies: *this* is what the pain of war *looks* and feels like. Picasso imagined the reality of human pain, while Michelangelo, in this sculpture, did not.

If the "richness of the mixture" could be sorted and some principles adequate for the good life elicited from the cumulative experience of the human race, we would not need stories, artworks, and books that imagine the real. We do need these cultural offerings, however, for how we imagine directs our responses. A disciplined and richly furnished imagination is a more trustworthy tool than principles, for, as Plato insisted, we *do not know* about the most crucial matters. We do not know what is generously responsible in particular situations.[18] We always pursue the good in the dark, by faith, not knowing what it looks or feels like; frequently we do not even recognize it when we see it. No one *likes* to live by faith; we only recognize and acknowledge that we do, or we conceal this knowledge from ourselves. In either case, we live by faith. Without sure knowledge of the humanly good, we must be passionately, erotically, committed to it:

> Once [an erotic person] has experienced self-consciously what his ignorance means while refusing to ignore, or compromise, or hide from the consequences, his *original passion* necessarily alters. He becomes possessed by a desire to make progress in reducing his ignorance, in remedying his inability to find solutions to his needs and perplexities.[19]

Thus, as Socrates said: "It so happens that this is the greatest good for humans, each day to make discoveries about virtue and the other things about which you have heard me conversing, and examining myself and others; and the unexamined life is not worth living" (Plato, *Apol.* 38a).

"Discoveries about virtue" can be had from books. Reading for life requires that one read not only for support, nourishment, reassurance, and challenge but also to discover the patterns of one's own myopia and blindness, misinterpretations, and habitual distortions of vision and reporting. Moreover, reading for life gives practice in seeing that "real things can be looked at and loved, without being seized and used."[20] Imagining love as based on neediness encourages a kind of grasping possessiveness that seeks to consume the loved one, but it is not necessary to imagine love in this way. Reading for life can produce a settled conviction that everything we need is provided, accessible in the generous universal circulation of life. We have only to "await it with confidence, and accept it with gratitude."[21]

Finally, reading for life, one learns that "the beautiful things are difficult" (Plato, *Greater Hippias* 304e; trans. Pangle). But reading is practice for living in that one enjoys a good book not only because the conclusion is satisfying but because the pleasure of reading is distributed throughout the lines, the paragraphs, and the pages. In *Jazz,* the author's keenly attentive eye and ear are focused on "the goodness of the way and the beauty of the wayfarers." She "argues" that people do not exist in order to serve or hinder one's life (as *The Pilgrim's Progress* taught) but for noticing, for the subtle and critical negotiations that define the self, for opposition, and for pleasure. Without others, one would not be able to say, This is where *I* am. Now.

Religion occurs at the intersection of perceived beauty and moral responsibility. The two are not separate or antagonistic, for together they create orientation to a real world. Religions seek to describe and actualize, through liturgy, ritual, and devotional practices, a morally demanding vision of beauty. Religions orient and train the eye to recognize what is serious, to see the beauty and integrity of the whole, and to particular styles and practices of relationship. Reading for life can function as a religious practice, a commitment to actualizing, localizing, and concretizing a fundamentally religious vision, a vision of the Great Beauty.

Reading for life teaches that there is no objective beauty, in the usual sense of the word. No object compels a listless eye to perceive its beauty. For beauty can be seen only by the attentive inner sense that is its kin; it must be recognized, as one recognizes a dear face in a crowd.[22] Plotinus put it this way: "If you would see God and beauty you must become all beautiful and all God-like" (*Enn.* 1.6.9).

In this sense, the experience of beauty *is* redemptive. Once one has recognized it anywhere, one can recollect that experience in order to return to the inner "place" at which it occurred. Because beauty must be recognized, it is, in the most literal sense, in the eye of the beholder. Its most threatening enemy is socialization to a selective and narrow range of beautiful objects. Socialized beauty is always defined from a position of mastery; the power to identify what is to be thought of as beautiful is an important social power. To cultivate perception of the beauty distributed *as life* in many — perhaps infinite — forms is to resist one's socialization to objects of beauty and desire.

The perception of beauty is intimate and particular. It is also common, for the objects that prompt it are multiple and diverse. It often brings a rush of feeling, even tears. Plato writes of shuddering, and a "strange sweating and fever," a "throbbing with agitation," in the presence of a face or body perceived as beautiful (Plato, *Phaed.* 250d). Plotinus writes:

> But there must be those who see this beauty by that with which the soul sees things of this sort, and when they see it they must be delighted and overwhelmed and excited.... These experiences must occur whenever there is contact with any sort of beautiful thing, wonder and a shock of delight and longing and passion and a happy excitement. (*Enn.* 1.6.1)

"The beautiful things are difficult." Yes, but it is possible, with practice, to perceive rich, intimate, detailed, and vivid beauty. Reading for life, I learn not to fear suffering, old age, and death. These are only some of the occasions on which the beautiful — *my* beautiful — will come clear, will become real.

NOTES

───── • ─────

Preface

1. Adam Phillips, *Terrors and Experts* (Cambridge, Mass.: Harvard University Press), cited by Judith Shulevitz, "It's Not Brain Surgery," *New York Times Book Review,* June 30, 1996, 10.
2. Rainer Maria Rilke, *The Notebooks of Malte Laurids Brigge,* trans. M. D. Herter Norton (New York: Norton, 1949), 88.

Chapter 1: How Should We Live?

1. "Cessavi de me paululum" (Augustine, *Confessions,* trans. Rex Warner [New York: New American Library, 1965], 7.14).
2. *The Odyssey of Homer,* trans. E. V. Rieu (Baltimore: Penguin, 1946), 172.
3. Martha C. Nussbaum also discusses the connection between reading novels and public responsibility in *Poetic Justice: The Literary Imagination and Public Life* (Boston: Beacon, 1995).
4. Rainer Maria Rilke, *Duino Elegies,* trans. J. B. Leishman and Stephen Spender (New York: Norton, 1963), "Ninth Elegy."
5. Ibid., "First Elegy."
6. Abraham Maslow, *Toward a Psychology of Being* (Princeton, N.J.: Van Nostrand, 1962), 19.
7. *Epic of Gilgamesh,* trans. N. K. Sanders (Baltimore: Penguin, 1964), 72.
8. Ibid., 90.
9. Denis Saraut, *Death and the Dreamer* (London: Westhouse, 1946), 106.
10. Ibid., 32.
11. Plotinus, *Ennead* 1.6.1. See also Plato's similar description: "When one who is fresh from the mystery, and saw much of the vision, beholds a godlike face or bodily form that truly expresses beauty, first there comes upon him a shuddering and a measure of that awe which the vision inspired, and then reverence as at the sight of a god.... Next, with the passing of the shudder, a strange sweating and fever seizes him. For by reason of a stream of beauty entering in through his eyes there comes a warmth, whereby the soul's plumage is fostered, and with that warmth the roots of the wings are melted.... [S]he throbs with ferment in every part" (*Phaed.* 250d).
12. Michel Foucault, *Power/Knowledge,* ed. Colin Gordon (New York: Pantheon, 1977), 57–59.

13. For recent examples, see Hans-Georg Gadamer, *The Relevance of the Beautiful and Other Essays* (New York: Cambridge University Press, 1986); Carol Harrison, *Beauty and Revelation in the Thought of St. Augustine* (Oxford: Clarendon, 1992); and Patrick Sherry, *Spirit and Beauty: An Introduction to Theological Aesthetics* (Oxford: Clarendon, 1992).

14. Margaret R. Miles, *Carnal Knowing: Female Nakedness and Religious Meaning in the Christian West* (New York: Vintage, 1992).

15. Cultural critic Ian Hunter has similarly argued for a "politicizing aesthetics." He acknowledges that aesthetics, the study of beauty as a property of objects, has seemed to many cultural critics to be at odds with social and political responsibility. But this animosity, he says, rests on a misunderstanding by which aesthetics is narrowly construed as an elitist interest in works of art, distracting attention from the material bases of human existence, such as economics, social arrangements, and politics. Hunter urges that aesthetics be understood as an activity that is interwoven with, and deeply informs, the realities of material life (Ian Hunter, "Aesthetics and Cultural Studies," in *Cultural Studies,* ed. Lawrence Grossberg, Cary Nelson, and Paula Treichler [New York: Routledge, 1992], 348–64).

16. Mystics have repeatedly attempted to characterize exactly what is revealed, but most, like Lady Julian of Norwich, conclude by invoking metaphor and/or ineffability:

> He showed me something small, no bigger than a hazelnut, lying in the palm of my hand, and I perceived that it was as round as any ball. I looked at it and thought: What can this be? And I was given this general answer: It is everything which is made. I was amazed that it could last, for I thought that it was so little that it could suddenly fall into nothing. And I was answered in my understanding: It lasts and always will, because God loves it; and thus everything has being through the love of God. (Julian of Norwich, *Showings,* ed. Edmund Colledge and James Walsh [New York: Paulist, 1978], "Short Text" 4:130)

17. Without the fragility, we could confidently enjoy what we love without fear of loss and pain. Without the preciousness, it would not matter that all the phenomena of the world are so fleeting. When the fragility *and* the preciousness appear together, the full poignancy and value of human lives are revealed.

Chapter 2: *"Beauty is Reality"*

1. The chapter title is a quote from Plotinus, *Enneads* (hereafter *Enn.*) 1.6.6. Throughout this chapter I have used A. H. Armstrong's translations in *Plotinus, Enneads I–VI,* 7 vols., Loeb Classical Library (Cambridge, Mass.: Harvard University Press, 1966–88). I have sometimes altered Armstrong's translation slightly on the authority of J. J. Sleeman and Gilbert Pollet, *Lexicon Plotinianum* (Leiden and Leuven, 1980).

2. Plotinus innovates here by saying that the forms of individuals exist in Intellect. Second-century Platonists had denied this.

3. Plotinus believed in reincarnation, that is, that the "manifold life that exists in the All circulates through the forms given it in intellect." He speaks of death, then, as a "changing of body, like changing of clothes on a stage, . . . [or as] a putting off of body, like in the theater the final exit [of an actor]" (*Enn.* 3.2.15).

4. See also 4.4.27, where Plotinus says that stones "grow as long as they are attached to the earth but remain the size they were cut when they are taken away from it." The capacity for growth is proof of life.

5. Plotinus's own title is probably "Against Those Who Say That the Maker of the Universe Is Evil and the Universe Is Evil." *Ennead* 2.9 is the most pointed part of a four-part refutation of Gnostic views, including also 3.8, 5.5, and 5.8.

6. Alliez and Feher describe Plotinus's different attitudes toward the body as attributable to whether Plotinus refers to "the civic way" or "the mystic way" (Alliez and Feher, "Reflections of a Soul," *Fragments for a History of the Body*, pt. 2 [New York: Zone, 1989], 47).

7. Similarly, in Aristotle's description of the golden mean, opposites are not mutually diluted to a watery middle state; rather, the opposites are held together in full strength to produce a strong synthesis.

8. On "birth pangs," see 5.3.17; on "waiting patiently," see 5.5.8; "One must not chase after it, but wait quietly till it appears, preparing oneself to contemplate it, as the eye awaits the rising of the sun; and the sun rising over the horizon gives itself to the eyes to see."

9. The most humorous footnote I have ever seen in scholarly literature follows this sentence. Readers should know, Armstrong writes, that, although an earlier translator attributes this analogy to "a remark Heraclitus appears to have made," he thinks it is "at least possible that Plotinus might have thought of pigs at this point for himself, without any assistance from earlier philosophy." See also 3.5.1.

10. Alliez and Feher, "Reflections," 66; *Enn.* 2.4.5.

11. Ibid., 67.

12. Martha Nussbaum, *Love's Knowledge: Essays on Philosophy and Literature* (New York: Oxford University Press, 1990), 37.

13. *Greater Hippias* 304e (trans. Thomas L. Pangle, *The Roots of Political Philosophy: Ten Forgotten Socratic Dialogues* [Ithaca, N.Y.: Cornell University Press, 1987], 339). See also *Republic* 435c, 497d; *Cratylus* 348a–b; *Protagoras* 339ff.

14. Alliez and Feher, "Reflections," 63.

15. See chapter 4.

16. Plotinus differentiates compulsive action, which "drags contemplation more towards the outer world," from voluntary action, but ultimately, "all things aspire to contemplation, . . . and all attain to it as far as possible for them in their natural state."

17. A recent commentator on the rock star Madonna has stated that the social function of stars is to "fill the space of desire — this gap that constitutes the subject in desire for an object" (E. Ann Kaplan, "Madonna Politics: Perversion, Repression, or Subversion? Or Masks and/as Mastery," in *The Madonna Connection*, ed. Cathy Schwichtenberg [San Francisco: Westview, 1993], 152).

18. Isak Dinesen, "Babette's Feast," *Anecdotes of Destiny* (New York: Vintage, 1974), 60.

Chapter 3: Love's Body — Intentions and Effects

1. *Ten Homilies on the First Epistle of St. John* (hereafter *Hom.*), in *Augustine: Later Works*, ed. John Burnaby, Library of Christian Classics (Philadelphia: Westminster, 1955), 9.9. Subsequent citations are from this translation unless otherwise indicated.

2. Hans-Georg Gadamer's phrase, developed in *Truth and Method* (New York: Seabury, 1975).

3. Augustine explains that the usual Latin word for what he calls "carnal love" is *amor*. Speaking of less acquisitive love, he uses either *diligere* (delight) or *caritas* (love without self-interest).

4. See *Hom.* 5.7: "Love is the only final distinction between the sons of God and the sons of the devil."

5. In *Conf.* 9.2, he writes of "people who, under a show of care for us, would try to thwart us and by loving us would eat us up, as [people] do with their food."

6. See *Hom.* 10.7: "You are to love all men, even your enemies — not because they are your brothers, but in order that they may be; so that brotherly love may ever burn within you, whether for him who is already a brother, or for your enemy, that love may turn him into one."

7. The first extant document of North African Christianity, "The Acts of the Scillitan Martyrs," was an account of the trial and execution of a group of martyrs from a small, now extinct, town in North Africa.

8. After 420 C.E., however, Augustine rejected legal enforcement of Catholic Christianity in North Africa; see R. A. Markus, *Saeculum* (Cambridge: Cambridge University Press, 1970), 29–30.

Chapter 4: Who Is "We"?

1. Roger D. Sorrell, *St. Francis and Nature* (New York: Oxford University Press, 1988).

2. *Christian Spirituality*, vol. 2, ed. Jill Raitt (New York: Crossroad, 1988), 340.

3. At the end of the fourth century catholicity was still a contested designation. As Augustine argued in the context of the Donatist controversy, world expansion was a fundamental ingredient of catholicity's definition. Thus, Manichaeanism could legitimately lay claim to catholicity.

4. W. H. C. Frend, "The Gnostic-Manichaean Tradition in Roman North Africa," *Journal of Ecclesiastical History* 4, no. 1 (January–April 1953) 16; François Décret, *L'Afrique manichéenne: Étude historique et doctrinale*, 2 vols. (Paris: Études Augustiniennes, 1978), 176.

5. Samuel N. C. Lieu, *Manichaeism in the Later Roman Empire and Medieval China: A Historical Survey* (Manchester: Manchester University Press,

1985), 154; the only Christian dissidents to be executed in the first five centuries were Manichaeans.

6. Ibid., 139; H. J. Klimkeit, *Manichaean Art and Calligraphy* (Leiden: Brill, 1982).

7. Lieu, *Manichaeism,* 164.

8. Jes Peter Asmussen, *Manichaean Literature* (Delmar, N.Y.: Scholars Facsimiles and Reprints, 1975), 17.

9. Lieu, *Manichaeism,* 85–86.

10. In *Contra Faustum,* Augustine complains of the similarity of Catholic and Manichaean Christianity: "For those whom they [Manichaeans] lead astray are Christians already born of the gospel, whom the Christian profession of the heretics misleads (13.12). See Décret, *L'Afrique manichéenne,* 181.

11. Faustus, the African Manichaean, called Catholic Christianity "semi-Christianity," in contrast to the more detailed and demanding teachings of Mani (Augustine, *C. Faust.* 2.2).

12. Frend, "Gnostic-Manichaean Tradition," 23.

13. "Among the spurs which drove Augustine to write his anti-Manichaean works of the period A.D. 387–399 was the reconversion of Catholics who had gone over to Manichaeism, and in many cases he was successful" (W. H. C. Frend, "Manichaeism in the Struggle between Saint Augustine and Petilian of Constantine," *Augustinus Magister* 2 [1954] 865).

14. Ibid., 859–66; see also Pierre Courcelle, *Récherches sur Les Confessions de Saint Augustin* (Paris, 1950), 238–45.

15. In response to the second charge — that of denigrating marriage — Augustine wrote a treatise, *De bono conjungali* (The good of marriage), specifically to exonerate himself from these accusations. All states of life, he wrote, are gifts from God, whether celibacy or marriage. As gifts, they are not to be compared with one another (8.8; 23.29). His conclusion that nevertheless celibacy is better than marriage, however, did little to demonstrate his respect for marriage or to silence his critics. Similarly, in his old-age controversy with Julian of Eclanum, his harshness toward human sexuality prompted Julian's accusations that Augustine was secretly a Manichaean.

16. Alexander of Lycopolis, an Alexandrian Platonist, found inconsistency in Manichaeans' insistence on the absolute incommensurability of divinity and matter: "Why do they speak ill of matter when from the beginning this is blended with the divine power?" ("Critique of the Doctrines of Manichaeus," in *An Alexandrian Platonist against Dualism, Alexander of Lycopolis' Treatise "Critique of the Doctrines of Manichaeus,"* trans. P. W. van der Horst and J. Mansfeld [Leiden: Brill, 1974], 81).

17. Faustus the Manichaean noticed the similarity of Catholic belief in the sacredness of the eucharistic elements of bread and wine to Manichaean belief in the sacredness of all things (*C. Faust.* 20.2).

18. Asmussen, *Manichaean Literature,* 90.

19. Catholic Christians held a similarly gendered view of the incarnated Jesus Christ: his flesh was derived from a human woman, but a spiritual father, God, defined his divinity.

20. *Codex Manichaicus Coloniensis,* ed. A. Henrichs and L. Koenen (*Zeitschrift fur Papyrologie und Epigraphik* 19 [1975] 23–25). The contemporary resonance of the experience formulated in Manichaeanism is attested by Augustine's most frequently cited scriptural passage: "Videmus nunc per speculum in aenigmate; tunc autem facie ad faciem" (We see now through a glass darkly, then, however, face to face) (1 Cor. 13:12).

21. Lieu, *Manichaeism,* 34.

22. Asmussen, *Manichaean Literature,* 47; see also Augustine, *Contra Faustum* 20.2.

23. Asmussen, *Manichaean Literature,* 72.

24. Augustine wrote: "One of your silly notions is that the tree weeps when the fruit is pulled;...you maintain that the fruit suffers when it is pulled from the tree, when it is cut, and scraped, and cooked, and eaten" (*C. Faust.* 6.4).

25. Lieu, *Manichaeism,* 90.

26. Ibid., 21.

27. Vincent L. Wimbush, ed., *Ascetic Behavior in Greco-Roman Antiquity: A Sourcebook* (Minneapolis: Fortress, 1990), 205.

28. Lieu, *Manichaeism,* 20; Frend suggests that Manichaeans' urban location was part of their motivation for refusing agricultural labor ("Saint Augustine and Petilian," 860).

29. Asmussen, *Manichaean Literature,* 61.

30. Lieu states that collections of Manichaean hymns are "among the largest and oldest collections of religious songs known to us," predating the hymns of Prudentius and Venantius by more than a century (*Manichaeism,* 134).

31. Drew Leder, *The Absent Body* (Chicago: University of Chicago Press, 1990), 149.

32. Ibid., 107.

33. Ibid., 103.

34. Wang Yang-ming, *Inquiry on the Great Learning,* in *A Sourcebook in Chinese Philosophy,* trans. and comp. Wing-tsit Chan (Princeton, N.J.: Princeton University Press), 272, quoted in Leder, *Absent Body,* 159.

35. Iris Marion Young, "The Ideal of Community and the Politics of Difference," in *Feminism/Postmodernism,* ed. Linda J. Nicholson (New York: Routledge, 1990), 300.

36. Ibid., 301.

37. Etienne Balibar, "Ambiguous Universality," *Differences* 7 (spring 1995) 49, 56.

Introduction to Part II

1. *Beowulf,* trans. David Wright (Baltimore: Penguin, 1957), 63.

Chapter 5: Reading One's Own Life

1. C. G. Jung *Memories, Dreams, Reflections* (hereafter *MDR*), ed. Aniela Jaffe, Clara Winston and Richard Winston, trans. (New York: Vintage, 1965); in

conjunction with the epigraph to this chapter, see also 58: "Certainly the world is immeasurably beautiful, but it is quite as horrible."

2. Jung's term for the psyche's reality is "psychic objectivity" (*MDR* 183). He remarks in *Answer to Job*: "What most people overlook or do not seem able to understand is that I regard the psyche as *real*" (*Answer to Job,* trans. R. F. C. Hull [New York: Meridian Books, 1960], 191).

3. Ibid.

4. Henri F. Ellenberger, *The Discovery of the Unconscious: The History and Evolution of Dynamic Psychiatry* (New York: Basic Books, 1970), 682. Jung recognized the historicity of this claim, saying that he emphasized the individual to compensate for the mass movements of his time. "Without history there can be no psychology" (quoted by Barbara Hannah, *Jung: His Life and Work* [New York: Putnam's, 1976], 289).

5. Carl J. Jung, *The Undiscovered Self* (1957), in *The Basic Writings of C. G. Jung,* ed. Violet Staub De Laszlo (New York: Modern Library, 1959), 32.

6. Quoted by Ellenberger, *Discovery,* 665.

7. Jung, *Answer to Job,* 186.

8. Christian supersessionist theology is evident in this reference to an outmoded idea of God as "Jewish."

9. Quoted by Gerhard Wehr, *Jung: A Biography* (Boston: Shambhala, 1987), 491.

10. Ibid., 198.

11. Jung agreed with Rilke that "beauty's nothing but beginning of terror we're still just able to bear" (Rainer Maria Rilke, *Duino Elegies,* trans. J. B. Leishman and Stephen Spender [New York: Norton, 1963], 1.1).

12. John Kerr, *A Most Dangerous Method: The Story of Jung, Freud, and Sabina Spielrein* (New York: Knopf, 1993), 446.

13. Hannah, *Jung,* 74.

14. Ellenberger, *Discovery,* 710.

15. "In Jung as in no other psychologist of his time the superindividual was paramount. A decisive role was played by the transpersonal, not only as a biologically and instinctually grounded driving force, but as an 'archetype,' a physical, mental, and spiritual motive power that points beyond man precisely by engaging him in a lifelong process of maturation. This is 'individuation,' the path to full humanness, which is the central theme of Jungian psychology" (Wehr, *Jung* 4).

16. Ellenberger, *Discovery,* 707.

17. See also Jung's description of his own process, in which "demonic strength ... [and a sense of] obeying a higher will" worked together. His project was "to find the images concealed in the emotions" (*MDR* 177).

18. Jung, *Answer to Job,* 198.

19. Wehr, *Jung,* 191.

20. Quoted by Hannah, *Jung,* 292.

21. Ibid., 189; but see Paul J. Stern's statement that Jung's representation of his family life as redemptive was "mostly windowdressing" (*C. G. Jung — The Haunted Prophet* [New York: Braziller, 1976], 118).

22. C. G. Jung, *Two Essays on Analytical Psychology,* in *Collected Works* 7, par. 274.

23. Kerr, *Dangerous Method,* 6.

24. Ibid., 508.

25. Kerr traces the establishment of psychoanalysis, concluding that psychoanalysis was defined "neither by its methods nor by any exterior criteria of validation. Rather, it was and continued to be defined by membership in its exclusive guild organizations. That privilege, in turn, was granted only to those able to adjust themselves to the existing authority structure and to the prevailing views as to what constituted acceptable interpretation and what did not" (*Dangerous Method* 472–73).

26. Letter to H. Irminger in Zurich, 1944, quoted by Wehr, *Jung,* 302.

27. Kerr points out that "psychopath," in Jung's usage, is a term for someone with "hereditary taint, i.e., someone prone to nervous disorders" (*Dangerous Method,* 504).

28. Ibid., 90.

29. He "strongly encouraged" his pupils, however, not to live alone (Hannah, *Jung,* 293).

30. Stern describes Jung as "withdrawn and inaccessible" to his family and refers to his "disgruntled and gloomy, sullen or irritable morose moods much of the time" (*Haunted Prophet,* 132).

31. Kerr, *Dangerous Method,* 503.

32. Ibid., 10.

33. There is little doubt that Jung's father would have been diagnosed today as suffering from depression. Describing him, Paul Stern uses the following words and phrases within a page: "apathy," "sodden lethargy," "gloomy," "spiritually wounded," "desolate," "broken," "drained," and "hypochondriac" (*Haunted Prophet,* 22–23).

34. In 1925, Jung commented in his seminar on a novel the group was analyzing: "Psychologically we know the father must fade when the hero comes, otherwise the development of the hero is seriously hindered" (William McGuire, ed., *Analytical Psychology: Notes of the Seminar Given in 1925 by C. G. Jung* [Princeton, N.J.: Princeton University Press, 1989], 140).

35. Ibid., 96.

36. Kerr, *Dangerous Method,* 77.

37. Ibid., 89.

38. Jung's hermeneutic of interpretation of the psyche is strangely reminiscent of Augustine's theory of scriptural interpretation. Scripture must be interpreted, Augustine wrote, in such a way that its inner unity is made explicit. Nothing can be excluded in order to achieve this coherence, and nothing may be added. See Chapter 4, above.

39. Stern puts it this way: "He unwittingly codified the rules regulating his own conduct as universal laws of human behavior" (*Haunted Prophet,* 76).

40. I. M. Young, "The Ideal of Community and the Politics of Difference," *Social Theory and Practice* 12, no. 1 (spring 1986) 11.

41. McGuire, *Analytical Psychology,* 36.

42. Stern, *Haunted Prophet,* 151.

43. Quoted by Kerr, *Dangerous Method,* 286.

44. Jung, *Answer to Job,* 88.

45. Ibid., 38–39.

46. Jung augmented the esteem he enjoyed by reporting instances that indicated his superior knowledge, for example, a 1913 vision in which he saw himself as a lion-headed god (see *New York Times,* June 3, 1995).

47. Ellenberger, *Discovery,* 658.

48. Kerr discusses in detail Spielrein's multifaceted contributions to the psychological theories of both Jung and Freud (*Dangerous Method*).

49. Jung comments that Emma's death "wrenched [him] violently out of [himself]" (*MDR,* 175). This description is interestingly similar to Augustine's comment on his loss of his partner of thirteen years, the mother of his child: "The woman with whom I was in the habit of sleeping was torn from my side, . . . and my heart, which clung to her, was broken, and wounded, and dropping blood" (*Conf.* 6.15). Neither autobiographer gave a full portrait of his partner or of his relationship with her, but the rhetorical urgency with which each describes his partner's death indicates how crucial the partner was in stabilizing the author's self-image.

50. Emma Jung participated in her husband's seminars (as a student); when their children were grown, she also lectured and analyzed patients. Her book was unfinished at her death and was published posthumously by Marie-Louise von Franz; see Emma Jung and Marie-Louise von Franz, *The Grail Legend,* trans. Andrea Dykes (London: Hodder and Stoughton, 1971).

51. Stern, *Haunted Prophet,* 137.

52. Both "felt trapped in a situation which Jung declared 'natural' but which did violence to the nature of both." Toni "smoked incessantly and drank a good deal" in the latter years of her life. She died at the age of sixty-four, largely estranged from Jung. Emma died two years later, having failed to accomplish the intellectual work of her life (Stern, *Haunted Prophet,* 139–42).

53. Hannah, *Jung,* 333.

54. Maria Torok, "The Meaning of 'Penis Envy' in Women," *Differences* 4, no. 1 (spring 1992) 36.

55. A recent controversy has arisen over Jung's alleged falsification of a mental patient's case history "to advance a theory of the collective unconscious." Richard Noll, author of a book that won the Association of American Publishers' prize for the best book of the year on psychology, *The Jung Cult: Origins of a Charismatic Movement* (Princeton, N.J.: Princeton University Press, 1994), calls Jung "the century's most influential liar." If Noll's allegation is accurate, it reveals Jung's willingness to alter data in order to support his "religious" adherence to a theory (see *New York Times,* June 3, 1995).

Chapter 6: "Staying Is Nowhere"

1. Rainer Maria Rilke, introduction to *Duino Elegies* (hereafter *DE*), trans. J. B. Leishman and Stephen Spender (New York: Norton, 1939), 13.

2. Rilke's lover, Lou Andreas-Salome, brought Rilke as a guest to the Weimar Congress of the International Psychoanalytic Association, where Freud told Rilke that his daughter Anna "read Rilke's poems and could recite some of them by heart." Rilke did not have any direct contact with Jung, but Jung remarked on another occasion "how much psychology is hidden in him [Rilke]" and "that he as an empiricist and Rilke as poet or visionary had ultimately drawn from the same source, the collective unconscious" (Gerhard Wehr, *Jung: A Biography* [Boston: Shambhala, 1987], 157).

3. In his *Sonnets to Orpheus,* written concurrently with the *Duino Elegies,* Rilke described the technological world as menacing (*Sonnets to Orpheus,* trans. Richard Exner, quoted by Wolfgang Leppmann, *Rilke: A Life,* trans. Russell M. Stockman [New York: Fromm International, 1984], 356):

> Do you, Master, hear this new
> roar and vibration?
> Heralds avow
> its reputation.
>
> True hearing must die
> in this clamour and noise,
> but the machine is now
> everyone's choice.
>
> Look, the machine
> how it revenges and shakes,
> how it disfigures and breaks
>
> whom it drains of their strength;
> but we insist that it
> propel and serve us at length.

4. *Sonnets to Orpheus* 1.18: "Look, the machine: rears up and takes revenge, and brings us to crawl and cringe" (trans. Stephen Mitchell [New York: Simon and Schuster, 1985], 53).

5. Leppmann, *Rilke,* 312.

6. Ibid., 339.

7. Quoted by ibid., 42–43.

8. Was Rilke primarily concerned for the "other person's freedom," as Leppmann suggests, or did his own freedom interest him considerably more? Rilke must have received some ideas of women's emancipation from his mother, who, although fervently religious, divorced his father, an act that still shocked at the end of the nineteenth century. Also, his lifelong friend and lover, Lou Andreas-Salome, wrote an "epoch-making essay" on the emancipation of women, *Women as Human Beings.* See Leppmann, *Rilke,* 88, 291.

9. Commenting on Rilke's views on marriage, Wolfgang Leppmann makes the following gratuitous (undocumented and undocumentable) statement: "A partnership in the sense of a union of two people, if not impossible at the outset, is achieved only at the expense of one or the other partner forfeiting a portion of his or her self-realization" (Leppmann, *Rilke,* 146).

10. "Angels, (they say) are often unable to tell whether they move among living or dead. The eternal torrent whirls all the ages through either realm forever, and sounds above their voices in both" (*DE* no. 1).

11. Elizabeth Berg, *Talk before Sleep* (New York: Random House, 1994), 187.

12. Leppmann reports that, for a brief time when he was twenty, Rilke adopted the first name "Caesar" (*Rilke*, 37).

13. Leishman and Spender's translation — "being opposite, and nothing else, and always opposite" — is misleading, however. "Gegenuber sein und nicht als das und immer gegenuber" should be translated: "to be facing each other and nothing but each other and to be doing it forever" (*Duino Elegies*, trans. David Young [New York: Norton, 1978]).

14. The mother provides support and recognition for the male child; she fails, however, to insist that the child recognize *her* subjectivity and her needs. Thus he does not realize others' subjectivity or the necessity for negotiation; see Jessica Benjamen, *The Bonds of Love: Psychoanalysis, Feminism, and the Problem of Domination* (New York: Pantheon, 1988).

15. See also *Sonnets* 1.16: "Above all, don't plant me inside your heart. I would outgrow you."

16. Leppmann, *Rilke*, 179.

17. See *DE* no. 1: "Denn Bleiben ist nirgends."

18. Rilke's *Sonnets to Orpheus*, written in the same month he completed the *Duino Elegies*, also takes up the themes of pain, suffering, and death: "Don't be afraid to suffer; return that heaviness to earth's own weight; heavy are mountains, heavy the seas" (1.4).

19. Quoted by Leppmann, *Rilke*, 183.

20. *DE* no. 7: "Hiersein ist herrlich." Also, "Song is existence" ("Gesang ist Dasein") (*Sonnets* 1.3).

21. Leppmann, *Rilke*, 285.

22. Ibid., 385.

23. Michele Wallace, "Race, Gender, and Psychoanalysis in Forties Film: Lost Boundaries, Home of the Brave and the Quiet One," in *Black American Cinema*, ed. Manthia Diawara (New York: Routledge, 1993), 264.

Chapter 7: "Where the Grown People?"

1. Rainer Maria Rilke, *Duino Elegies*, trans. J. B. Leishman and Stephen Spender (New York: Norton, 1963), no. 1.

2. Tony Morrison, *Jazz* (hereafter *J*) (New York: Knopf, 1992), 11.

3. Arguably, Acton is an exception. He is the only one-dimensional character, the only character with whom the author appears to feel no sympathy, and the only one the reader cannot picture as acting out of his whole life.

4. Deborah A. McDowell, "Harlem Nocturne," *Women's Review of Books* 9, no. 9 (June 1992) 3.

5. Edna O'Brien, review of *Jazz* by Toni Morrison, *New York Times Book Review*, April 5, 1992, 30.

6. See also pp. 176 and 178 for references to the redwing blackbirds that accompanied Joe's mother.

7. Martha Nussbaum, *Love's Knowledge: Essays on Philosophy and Literature* (New York: Oxford University Press, 1990), 290.

8. *The Odyssey of Homer,* trans. E. V. Rieu (Baltimore: Penguin, 1946), bk. 5.

9. McDowell, "Harlem Nocturne," 4.

10. Quoted by Nussbaum, *Love's Knowledge,* 199.

11. Ibid., 356.

12. Martha Nussbaum, *The Therapy of Desire: Theory and Practice in Hellenistic Ethics* (Princeton, N.J.: Princeton University Press, 1994), 177.

13. Ibid., 178.

14. Ibid., 181.

15. Ibid.

16. Ibid., 185; emphasis added.

17. Ibid.

18. Toni Morrison, *Playing in the Dark: Whiteness and the Literary Imagination* (Cambridge, Mass.: Harvard University Press, 1992), 6-7.

19. Ibid., 38: "The rights of man, an organizing principle upon which the nation was founded, was inevitably yoked to Africanism. . . . The concept of freedom did not emerge in a vacuum. Nothing highlighted freedom — if it did not in fact create it — like slavery."

20. Ibid., 44.

21. Ibid., 72.

22. See also Hunter's description of the "secret of kindness from whitepeople — they had to pity a thing before they could like it" (*J* 125).

23. Morrison, *Playing in the Dark,* 53.

Chapter 8: "I Tried to Overlook Many Things"

1. *Leni Riefenstahl: A Memoir* (hereafter *LR*) (New York: St. Martin's, 1993), 148.

2. John Simon, "The Führer's Movie Maker," *New York Times Book Review,* September 26, 1993, 11.

3. Susan Sontag, "Fascinating Fascism," in *A Susan Sontag Reader* (New York: Farrar, Straus, Giroux, 1982), 319.

4. Terrance Rafferty, film review in the *New Yorker,* March 28, 1994, 108..

5. The one exception is *Tiefland,* a short film begun in 1941 and finished in 1954, after incredible struggles at every stage of the production.

6. Simon, "Führer's Movie Maker," 108.

7. Richard Corliss, "Riefenstahl's Last Triumph," *Time,* October 18, 1993, 92.

8. Brian D. Johnson, "Hitler's Director," *MacLean's,* April 18, 1994, 74.

9. Sontag, "Fascinating Fascism," 310.

10. Hans Barkhausen, "Footnote to the History of Riefenstahl's 'Olympia,' " *Film Quarterly* 28 (fall 1974) 8.

11. Corliss, "Riefenstahl's Last Triumph," 92.

12. Vincent Canby, "Riefenstahl, in a Long Close-Up," *New York Times,* October 14, 1993, C15.

13. The Goethe-Institut's policy of cosponsoring appearances of German cultural figures has to do with ensuring that there is interest in the person in the United States.

14. *Wonderful Horrible Life,* soundtrack.

15. Tom Reiss, "How the Nazis Created a Dream Factory in Hell," *New York Times,* November 6, 1994, H15.

16. Ruthe Stein, "Directed by the Third Reich," *Datebook: The San Francisco Sunday Examiner and Chronicle,* February 26, 1995, 29.

17. Ibid.

18. Sontag, "Fascinating Fascism," 314.

19. Stanley Kauffmann, "Stanley Kauffmann on Films," *New Republic,* March 14, 1994, 30.

20. Sontag, "Fascinating Fascism," 316.

21. Reiss, "Dream Factory," H16.

22. Sontag, "Fascinating Fascism," 316.

23. Ibid., 313.

24. Janet Maslin, "Just What Did Leni Riefenstahl's Lens See?" *New York Times,* March 13, 1994, H15.

25. Reiss, "Dream Factory," H15.

26. Ibid. Veit Harlan, director of *Jud Suss,* was back making German films again by 1950.

27. *Leni Riefenstahl: A Memoir,* written by Riefenstahl between the ages of eighty and eighty-five, was published in Germany as *Memorien* and in Great Britain as *The Sieve of Time: The Memoirs of Leni Riefenstahl.*

28. Yet, in *The Wonderful Horrible Life of Leni Riefenstahl,* she remarks, "Hitler did not play such an important role in my life. I made one film for him which had three parts, and out of that the press wove a legend."

29. David Culbert, "Leni Riefenstahl and the Diaries of Joseph Goebbels," *Historical Journal of Film, Radio and Television* 13, no. 1 (1993) 86.

30. The Salzburg-Maxglan Gypsies incident is documented in Henry Friedlander and Sybil Milton, eds., *Archives of the Holocaust,* vol. 19, ed. Elisabeth Klamper (New York: Garland, 1992); see Culbert, "Leni Riefenstahl," 87.

31. Culbert, "Leni Riefenstahl," 92.

32. Ibid., 178.

33. Primo Levi, *The Drowned and the Saved* (New York: Vintage, 1989), 179.

34. Maslin, "Leni Riefenstahl's Lens," H15.

35. *Cineaste,* April 1994; quoted by Maslin, "Leni Riefenstahl's Lens," H23.

36. Elizabeth Pochoda, "Hitler's Children," *Nation,* August 8/15, 1994, 153.

37. Kauffmann, "Stanley Kauffmann on Films," 31.

38. Simon, "Führer's Movie Maker," 108.

39. Rainer Maria Rilke, *Duino Elegies* (New York: Norton, 1963), no. 1.

40. Leni Riefenstahl, interview in *Cahiers du Cinéma,* quoted by Sontag, "Fascinating Fascism," 312.

Chapter 9: The Eye of the Beholder

1. A noteworthy exception is Gordon Kaufman's *In Face of Mystery* (Cambridge, Mass.: Harvard University Press, 1994).

2. Plotinus, *Enneads* (hereafter *Enn.*) 6.8.5–8, in *Plotinus, Enneads I–VI*, trans. A. H. Armstrong, 7 vols., Loeb Classical Library (Cambridge, Mass.: Harvard University Press, 1966–88).

3. The "great chain of being," described by Ernst Becker in *The Heavenly City of the Eighteenth-Century Philosophers,* is not Plotinus's universe of mirrored realities. Plotinus's universe is not connected in a chain but informed by the Great Beauty of the whole. "But if someone is able to turn around ... he will see God and himself and the All; at first he will not see as the All but then, when he has nowhere to set himself and limit himself and determine how far he himself goes, he will stop marking himself off from all being and will come to the All without going out anywhere, but remaining there where the All is set firm" (*Ennead* 6.5.7).

4. Circle imagery also occurs in *Enn.* 1.7.1; 5.1.11; 6.9.8.

5. Elizabeth Grosz, *Space, Time, and Perversion* (New York: Routledge, 1995), 25ff.; see especially chapter 2, "Feminism and the Crisis of Reason."

6. Augustine makes a similar statement about beauty as the reality of objects: asking various creatures (breezes, earth, sea, creeping things, heaven, sun, moon, stars), "What is God" elicited the answer, "He made us." Augustine reflects, "My question was in my contemplation of them, and their answer was in their beauty" (*Conf.* 10.6).

7. Later philosophers would distinguish the good and the beautiful; see, for example, Thomas Aquinas: "We enjoy the good by taking possession of the object itself; we enjoy the beautiful by the simple perception of it (*Summa Theologiae* Ia.2ae, q. 27, art. 1).

8. Thomas Pangle, *The Roots of Political Philosophy: Ten Forgotten Socratic Dialogues* (Ithaca, N.Y.: Cornell University Press, 1987), 339.

9. Ibid., 165.

10. Augustine's clearest statement of his mature social theory occurs in *De civ. dei* 19.13–15.

11. Plotinus anticipated Freud in recognizing that consciousness and subjectivity do not (necessarily) coincide. There are desires "that remain in the appetitive part and are unknown to us." These "can exert the strongest pull when we are unconscious of them.... When we have them without knowing it, we are apt, he observes 'to be what we have'" (E. R. Dodds, "Tradition and Personal Achievement in the Philosophy of Plotinus," *Journal of Roman Studies* 50 [1960] 5–6).

12. Michel Foucault, quoted in *A Foucault Reader,* ed. Paul Rabinow (New York: Pantheon, 1984), 187.

13. Grosz, *Space, Time, and Perversion,* 43.

14. Iris Murdoch, *The Sovereignty of Good* (London: Routledge and Kegan Paul, 1970), 64.

15. Martha Nussbaum, *Love's Knowledge* (New York: Oxford University Press, 1990), 356.

16. Rainer Maria Rilke, *Duino Elegies*, trans. J. B. Leishman and Stephen Spender (New York: Norton, 1939), no. 1.

17. Martha Nussbaum writes: "The experience of reading is a moral activity in its own right, a cultivation of imagination for moral activity in life, and a test for correctness of real-life judgement and response" (Nussbaum, *Love's Knowledge,* 339). Drucilla Cornell prefers the word "ethical" to refer to "the aspiration to a non-violent relationship to the Other and to otherness in its widest possible sense" ("What Is Ethical Feminism?" in *Feminist Contentions: A Philosophical Exchange* [New York: Routledge, 1995], 78).

18. Pangle, *Roots,* 165.

19. Ibid.

20. Murdoch, *Idea of the Good,* 64.

21. Isak Dinesen, "Babette's Feast," *Anecdotes of Destiny* (New York: Vintage, 1974), 60.

22. Alfred North Whitehead wrote that peace is "a broadening of feeling due to the emergence of some deep metaphysical insight, unverbalized and yet momentous in its coordination of values. Its first effect is the removal of the stress of acquisitive feeling arising from the soul's preoccupation with itself.... [I]t is primarily a trust in the efficacy of beauty, ... trust in the self-justification of beauty" (*Adventures of Ideas* [New York: New American Library, 1933], 283–84).

Index